RETHINKING THE EUROPEAN UNION

Also by Alice Landau

NEGOCIATIONS ECONOMIQUES ET RELATIONS
INTERNATIONALES: Techniques et enjeux de l'Uruguay Round

LE NEGOCIATIONS ECONOMIQUES INTERNATIONALES

Also by Richard G. Whitman

TOWARDS A 'ZONE OF STABILITY AND SECURITY' IN THE
MEDITERRANEAN? The EU and the Development of an EMEA

TOWARDS THE IGC: Perspectives on European Integration

Rethinking the European Union

Institutions, Interests and Identities

Edited by

Alice Landau
Senior Lecturer in International Relations
University of Geneva

and

Richard G. Whitman
Lecturer in International Relations and Diplomacy
University of Westminster

First published in Great Britain 1997 by
MACMILLAN PRESS LTD
Houndmills, Basingstoke, Hampshire RG21 6XS and London
Companies and representatives throughout the world

A catalogue record for this book is available from the British Library.

ISBN 0–333–66125–7

First published in the United States of America 1997 by
ST. MARTIN'S PRESS, INC.,
Scholarly and Reference Division,
175 Fifth Avenue, New York, N.Y. 10010

ISBN 0–312–16156–5

Library of Congress Cataloging-in-Publication Data
Rethinking the European Union : institutions, interests, and
identities / edited by Alice Landau and Richard G. Whitman.
p. cm.
Includes bibliographical references and index.
ISBN 0–312–16156–5 (cloth)
1. European Union. I. Landau, Alice. II. Whitman, Richard.
JN30.R48 1996
341.24'2—dc20 96–18901
CIP

This book is printed on paper suitable for recycling and made from fully managed and
sustained forest sources.

10   9   8   7   6   5   4   3   2   1
06 05 04 03 02 01 00 99 98 97

Printed and bound in Great Britain by
Antony Rowe Ltd, Chippenham, Wiltshire

Contents

Notes on the Contributors   vii

1   Introduction: The European Union in a
    Changing Context   1
    Alice Landau

Part One   **Institutions and Identities:**
                    Europe and the International

2   The New Pattern of International Relations in Europe   15
    Adrian Hyde-Price

3   The European Union in Its International
    Environment: A Systematic Analysis   36
    Antje Herrberg

4   The International Identity of the European
    Union: Instruments as Identity   54
    Richard G. Whitman

Part Two   **Institutions and Interests:**
                    Between Supranationalism and
                    Intergovernmentalism

5   The European Union at the Crossroads:
    Sovereignty and Integration   75
    Lisbeth Aggestam

6   The Capacity to Act: European National
    Governments and the European Commission   93
    Klaus Armingeon

7   Forging European Union: What Role
    for the European Parliament?   111
    Donatella M. Viola

Part Three   Interests and Identities:
                  Cleavages and Commonalities

8   European Values and National Interests   129
     Esther Barbé

9   The Cultural Semiotics of 'European Identity':
     Between National Sentiment and the
     Transnational Imperative   147
     Ulf Hedetoft

10   Conclusion   171
     Alice Landau and Richard Whitman

Bibliography   178

Index   199

Notes on the Contributors

Lisbeth Aggestam is a PhD candidate at the Department of Political Science, University of Stockholm. Her doctoral thesis involves a comparative analysis of the foreign policy roles of Britain, France and Germany in the context of the European Union. In 1995 she received a British FCO Chevening Award to study at St Antony's College, Oxford. Her previous publications have focused primarily on aspects of the European integration process, in particular on the EU's common foreign and security policy.

Klaus Armingeon teaches political science at the University of Berne, Switzerland. Previously he taught and did research at the Universities of Konstanz, Tübingen, Mannheim and Heidelberg. His research interests focus on the analysis of politics and policies in a comparative perspective – in particular with regard to the international interdependence of nation-states. He has contributed to the comparative literature on corporatism, trade unions and collective labour relations, political parties and social policies.

Esther Barbé is Professor of International Relations and Director of the Centre d'Estudis sobre la Pau i el Desarmament at the Autonomous University of Barcelona. She has published articles and books on Spanish foreign policy, European political cooperation and the common foreign and security policy, European security and Mediterranean affairs. Her recent publications include *La seguridad en la nueva Europa* (Madrid, 1995) and *Relaciones Internacionales* (Madrid, 1995).

Ulf Hedetoft is Professor of International Studies, Ålborg University. His special interests are cultural and political issues in international relations, specifically in Europe; nationalism and internationalisation; transatlantic relations; British history and identity. Recent publications include *Nation or Integration? Perspectives on Europe in the 90s* (ed.) (Ålborg, 1993); 'National identity and mentalities of war in three EC countries', *Journal of Peace Research*, Vol. 30, No. 3, 1993; 'National identities and European integration "from below": bringing people back in', *Journal of European Integration*, Vol. XVIII, No. 1, 1994; and *Signs of Nations: Studies in the Political Semiotics of Self and Other in Contemporary European Nationalism* (Aldershot, 1995).

Antje Herrberg is a Research Fellow at the European Research Unit at the University of Ålborg in Denmark. She has previously lectured at the University of Limerick, Ireland. Her research and publications focus on the role of the EU as an international actor, EU *Ostpolitik* and EU–Russian relations.

Adrian Hyde-Price lectures in politics and international relations at the University of Southampton. He was previously a Research Fellow at the Royal Institute of International Affairs, London. He has a first-class honours degree from the University College of Wales, Aberystwyth, and a PhD from the University of Kent at Canterbury. Dr Hyde-Price has published widely on European politics and international relations. His main publications include *European Security Beyond the Cold War: Four Scenarios for the Year 2010* (London, 1991) and *The International Politics of East Central Europe* (Manchester, 1996).

Alice Landau is Senior Lecturer in International Relations at the University of Geneva and Director of the Centre for Economic Diplomacy. Her research areas involve European integration as well as international economic relations. Her most recent publications include *Conceptualiser l'Union Européenne* (Geneva, 1995) and *External Dimensions and Geopolitical Determinants of European Construction* (Bordeaux, 1995). She is also author of *Les Négociations économiques internationales* (Brussels, 1990) and *The Uruguay Round: Conflict and Cooperation in the International Economic Relations* (Brussels, forthcoming).

Donatella Maria Viola, formerly R. Schuman Scholar at the Directorate General of the Secretariat of the European Parliament and Lecturer in European Studies at the University of Bristol, is EC Research Fellow at the London School of Economics and Political Science. Her current research interests are focused in the area of European social policy and European foreign policy as well as on the activities of the European Parliament. Her publications include *La diplomazia al vertice* (Reggio, Calabria, 1991) and *The EC and the Schengen Agreement* (in the *New Federalist* journal, 1992).

Richard G. Whitman is Lecturer in International Relations and Diplomacy at the University of Westminster. His recent publications include *Towards the IGC: Perspectives on European Integration* (London, 1995).

1 Introduction:
The European Union in a Changing Context
Alice Landau

Since the very beginning of its existence, the future of the European Community has been the subject of uncertainty. Now the European Community has turned into a European Union, and there is still no common European outlook on what is intended to be the outcome of the common project.

Any attempt to theorise the European Union presents a particular difficulty. The requirement to both capture the essence of the Union and the necessity of accommodating an ongoing integration process presents a double problematic. Moreover, we cannot readily turn to frameworks created to accommodate either the state or international organisations. One concept has been used to underline the increasing, though ambiguous, role of the EU, that of 'actorness' (Hill, 1993), which refers to the extent to which the EU may be considered to be a genuine actor in the international political arena. Actorness encompasses both the changing nature of the international environment in which the EU operates, and the internal dynamics of its institutional development.

INTERNAL DYNAMICS

From the internal point of view, Community building has proceeded in a epicyclical manner, which was captured only intermittently by theoretical frameworks, and with these prone to look at the process through unilinear lenses. The major school of thought, neofunctionalism, reckoned on a steady development towards federalism by the positive effect of spillover. Both the Monnet and the Schuman plans, launching the European unification process, anticipated a neofunctionalist perspective of integration defined in the 1950s. Neofunctionalism predicted that initial integrative steps in specific sectors of the economy would lead, via a 'spillover' dynamic force, to further policy coordination (Haas, 1964: 62). This trend

1

reflected Monnet's idea of *savant progressivité*: starting with the control of a strategic resource – in this case coal and steel – and gradually diffusing to related sectors of the economy (Monnet, 1976: 323). Supranationalism would achieve high-intensity integration through the requisite steps of coordination, cooperation, harmonisation and parallel national action (Taylor, 1990: 13f).[1]

Neofunctionalism was deemed to have failed in explaining the integration process from the Luxembourg compromise of the mid-1960s, through the subsequent loss of Community momentum and until the mid-1980s. More recently it has been revisited by authors to reconsider a new Community momentum. However, it has not regained widespread acceptance because of its inability to capture the contemporary *sui generis* character of the EU.

In contrast, the EU reflects a juxtaposition of *realpolitik* and neofunctionalism. The creation of the EC can be considered from within the realist perspective in the context of the postwar bipolar configuration of the international system (Waltz, 1979: 71). In this view the European unification process represents a break with a previous concern with the European balance of power, but simultaneously reflects the prevailing power relations between the actors – mainly the United States, France, Germany and Britain. The latter countries have used European unification to gain strength, and employed the institutions of the EU as arenas for exercising influence (Keohane, 1993: 15), both aggregating their interests and inducing new identities.

THE UNIQUENESS OF THE EU

Within this context, the EU cultivated a condition which is intrinsic to its existence: multilayered internal cleavages. Different opinions and national models competed as to the scope of integration the Member States should pursue. All the disputes were on the same theme: the nature of the Europe that the Six, then the Twelve, wished to construct and the nature of the relationship between the Community and the Member States. These disputes resurfaced especially when the Community was under great pressure.

Despite these cleavages, the Member States agree to cooperate even in the absence of a harmony of interests (Axelrod, 1984). One way of accounting for this cooperation is the notion of regime defined by Krasner (1983: 2) as establishing sets of implicit or explicit principles, norms, rules and decision-making procedures around which actors' expectations converge, and thereby explain why Member States engage in cooperative activities. The Member States as actors prefer a rule-based system to the uncertainties of power capabilities; they can control the behaviour of other actors, both internationally and domestically (Aggarwal, 1994: 44). Regimes give them a sense of predictability – particularly important in the context of the Cold War – in European interrelationships. Regimes provide a negotiating forum for bargaining, linking issues and enhancing states' preferences, while reducing transaction costs. Member States bargain among themselves in an effort to realise their interests; diverging interests do not necessarily have a disintegrative effect.

Member States diverge widely in their preferences, but these are not necessarily in opposition to or undermined by the European collective framework. Participation in this framework both empowers and constrains the Member State's external action, and shapes their interests. Collective choices reflect state interests, but those interests are shaped by membership in a collective framework. States' perceptions of their national interests change because of the Community framework. This feature differentiates the EU from an international regime. Community institutions are more structured than those of international regimes, and the Member States made a firm and a long-term commitment to cooperate (Wallace, 1989: 305).

A question that might be raised now is how the Member States will redefine their interests, and whether they will pursue their national interests within a cooperation framework or outside this framework. The ineffectiveness of the EU responses to the new challenges of the international environment could modify the way Member States identify the benefits and the opportunities provided by the collective framework. The divisions between Member States on the integration project have become more visible with the end of the Cold War, and the accommodation of interests may become problematic.

However, the Community is also a unique institutional setting (Pfetsch, 1995: 3), of both formal and informal integration, spreading into a region characterised by a high degree of economic and social interactions, with a complex institutional framework. That is why it is necessary to take into account the environment within which the Community operates. The profound changes to the landscape of international relations in Europe, the most recent enlargement and those to come by the year 2000 require new appraisals of the integration process.

Unlike international organisations, the EU has gained some supranational structures (Commission, European Parliament, European Court of Justice) which are combined with intergovernmental institutions (European Council, Council of Ministers). However, even in the instance of intergovernmental institutions one should not underestimate the difficulty of classifying some of these structures. For example, in the instance of the Council of Ministers the use of qualified majority voting would appear to be a manifestation of supranational tendencies.

The EU is a hybrid animal (Ginsberg, 1989) retaining both intergovernmental and supranational institutions and dimensions of decision-making. The EU can be viewed as the simultaneous building-up towards joint pooling of shared sovereignty in a consociation of governmental elites, and the building across of transnational ties (Groom, 1993: 3; Keohane and Hoffmann, 1991: 13). In this book we seek to explore how the classical opposition between intergovernmentalism and supranationalism falls short in explaining the EU. Rather than focusing on institutions, as is usually the case, we concentrate on the existing debate between intergovernmentalism and supranationalism. Indeed, it is one of a series of assumptions that we suggest need to be rethought.

The EU is more a 'cumulative pattern of accommodation in which participants refrain from unconditionally vetoing proposals and instead seek to attain agreement by means of upgrading common interests' (Rosamond, 1995: 396; Keohane and Hoffmann, 1991: 15). Furthermore, the complex network of EU institutions performs another function. The existence of structures allows the collective reinforcement of shared national norms and values; they induce a collective political identity.

This institutional complex (Van Ham 1994: 190) promotes integration and engineers a 'European identity'. In this volume Ulf Hedetoft demonstrates that the striven-for 'identity' of Europe is ultimately of a political nature – a question of states and state interaction institutionally embedded in cooperation of a unique type, an always volatile balancing point between intergovernmental and supranational modalities of integration, of framing the disputed sovereignty question in radically new ways. However, the identification of a transnational European identity is far from complete: it neglects some segments of opinion, or is even antagonistic towards others (H. Wallace, 1994: 5).

The question can be raised as to whether it is possible to conceive of a role as catalyst for a European identity by the European Parliament. In Chapter 7 Donatella Viola considers the EP which is simultaneously seeking an identity for itself and is currently composed of a plurality of countries reflecting distinct and sometime conflictual interests.

THE NEED TO RECAST THE EU

What of the contemporary existence of the Union? The international and European context within which the Union operates has undergone a profound transformation. The certainty of the bipolar Cold War international system has been replaced by an uncertainty as to the current and future configuration of this system. The question is whether the international system can now best be encapsulated as a unipolar military, multipolar economic and diplomatic system, or whether processes of globalisation require a recasting of the language to encompass a variety of new institutions, new structures and new identities. The 'global' is everywhere in the social sciences. However, very little consideration has been given to the impact of globalisation on the EU. In an attempt to rectify this lack of consideration, Klaus Armingeon examines the relationship between the Commission and the Member States in response to globalisation.

Adrian Hyde-Price demonstrates in Chapter 2 that the fall of the Berlin Wall has forced the European Union to contemplate its future. It is faced with a requestioning of old assumptions. First on the identity of the Union. What was the most important determinant of European construction: the external threat, or the cementing role of the United States? Or alternatively, was it the result of a trend toward unification which already existed independent of external pressures? The key issue is whether the collective framework, once cemented by shared values and the Cold War, can withstand increasing fragmentation and the challenges of ethno-nationalist conflicts, nuclear proliferation, large-scale migration and transnational crime. There is a need for theoretical rethinking and reconceptualisation to keep pace with the changing realities of the 1990s. The purpose of this book is to take these changing patterns as a starting point in order to rethink not only the existing methods of conceptualising the European integration process, but also the nature of the EU itself.

The EU as a model of integration had, and still has, a profound external impact, which translates into multifaceted aspects. However, this model needs to be re-explored. The European Union is a unique combination of roles and identities, and many levels can be visualised. It is not only an integration building process with economic and political facets, both directed and incarnated through the creation of institutions and structures. The EU has a presence which is more than the sum of its constituent parts. The problem is that we lack the appropriate models and concepts to capture this presence.

THE RESEARCH AGENDA ON THE EU

Walter Carlsnaes (1994b: 275) has argued that three substantive foci will continue to dominate the research agenda on the EU. The first is the development of the EU *qua* actor in the area of foreign and security policy. The second is the evolving nature and role of the state in the new Europe. The third is the role of economic relations in (and beyond) the new Europe.

The Union has long debated on the desirability of equipping itself with the means to enhance its external influence. However, the question must be raised as to whether the Union is equipping itself with the appropriate instruments. The Maastricht Treaty illustrates, with the creation of the Common Foreign and Security Policy, that the Union recognises that matters cannot remain unchanged. Still, definitive answers about the appropriate instruments remain. The EU cannot be directly blamed for what could not be anticipated. The Treaty was conceived at a time when Europe was still unchanged and divided into two stable blocs. The breakdown of the communist regimes acted as a precipitating agent of change (Keohane and Hoffmann, 1991: 27) by introducing questions of a European defence policy considered taboo since the collapse of the European Defence Community in 1954. Such changes have been enforced by the collapse of the Soviet Empire in Eastern Europe.

The 1990s are likely to become a decade of over-commitment (Rummel, 1990: 19) whereas the EU does not have the time to clarify the new questions and consolidate any new-found assertiveness. The Maastricht Treaty, far from acting as a consensus builder about the future role of the EU *vis-à-vis* the rest of the world, has brought unresolved questions and underlying tensions into the open (Carlsnaes, 1994: 275). The President of the Bundesbank, Hans Tietmayer, pointed out in September 1995 that 'despite the Maastricht Treaty, much is still unclear at present' (*International Herald Tribune*, 16 September 1995). Indeed it is not clear whether the EU will be best captured as a manifestation of intergovernmentalism or supranationalism. Perhaps the only certainty is an acceptance of an ongoing and uncertain process of transformation and a continuing juxtaposition of supranational and intergovernmental elements. It is this fusion that requires new ways of conceptualising what is happening within the EU.

Lisbeth Aggestam and Richard Whitman each consider the appropriateness of retaining clear-cut distinctions between intergovernmentalism and supranationalism in the study of the EU. Lisbeth Aggestam argues that sovereignty and supranationalism is not a zero-sum game. Transfers of authority to the European level do not automatically erode the Member State's power. Though it is obvious that supranationalism has an impact upon the sovereignty of states this is not a uniform process. Richard Whitman argues that the objective that the European Union sets itself to assert its identity on the international scene requires consideration of the instruments available to give effect to this aspiration. In contrast, the existing literature on the European Community tends to maintain the distinction between the Community's external competencies as governed by the founding Treaties in contrast to the Common Foreign and Security Policy conducted among the Member States on an intergovernmental processes.

In summary, it is recognised that it is difficult to explain this multi-dimensional entity by reference to a single theory. No single theoretical framework captures the complexity, the internal dynamics, the richness of the network and the external personality of the EU. Each theory captures some of these aspects, but none its entirety. There is a need to combine different approaches that would harness international relations, political science and the emerging discipline of European studies.

INSTITUTIONS, INTERESTS AND IDENTITIES

This volume has as its organising principle three concepts: institutions, interests and identities. However, each author uses these concepts in different ways, though they are conceived as tools which allow them to rethink the EU.

Institutions are conceived in the widest possible sense as fulfilling the functions of ordering, governing and administering. Therefore, what are considered as institutions in this text are not merely bodies which are performing constitutionally defined functions. They are both points of convergence and arenas of conflict, within which interests and identities become formulated. If we consider the EU as an example of an institution, it becomes apparent that the EU is not only a supranational body, or the sum of national institutions, but rather is a more subtle blend of convergence and difference. The EU has not become a single political community, but rather has emerged as a form of governance, interwoven with the Member States. If we consider the Commission, the European Parliament and the Council as constituent components of this political community, the same contradictory processes become apparent. They are fora within which a variety of interests and identities are expressed. They are instrumental to the European construction.

Identities can be understood in terms of points of reference. The points of reference are those which act to illustrate both differences and similarities. Identities encompass a set of loyalties that, rather than being exclusive, can coexist. Institutions are both the repository and the expression of identities and interests. Institutions can have multiple identities, both expressing local and national interests, and also formulating common interests. Institutions also provide familiarity and identity in periods of turbulence, and can act as poles of stability. Paradoxically, in a state of uncertainty and instability that is the current European context, institutions – far from unequivocally providing identification or leadership – are suffering from indecisiveness and hesitancy.

Institutions and identities can be considered as ways of propelling interests. Likewise institutions and identities can be created as means of furthering interests. In the context of the European Union, there is both the internal process and the international process of formulating and articulating interests and policies. For example, from an internal perspective the Commission as a promoter and mediator has succeeded in upgrading common interests, while in some vital areas there has been a startling setback of the whole enterprise, with Member States failing to find common interests. If we consider that there has been the formulation of interests with respect to the world beyond the European Union, it has to be noted that this is not a single interest, but a complex set of interacting and overlapping national interests.

THE EU IN ITS ENVIRONMENT

There was also no common conception of what Europe's role should be in world affairs (Miall, 1993: 54). As long as the Cold War provided a safe-harbour status quo, the Community could nestle and develop comfortably alongside Soviet–American antagonism. It kept a number of awkward questions off the European agenda: most notably defence, dominated by the USA and managed within NATO. Successive transatlantic crises were resolved by the West European acceptance that its role was primarily devoted to the economic field. The EC played an increasingly active role in the core of economic diplomacy in the 1970s and 1980s characterised as a 'civilian power' (Duchêne, 1972). In the strategic area, the United States retained the power to lead and to negotiate bilaterally with the Soviet Union.

The institutional and legal frameworks, through which the Union conducts its foreign policy, are an additional complicating factor in seeking to conceptualise the international role of the EU. Some of these activities are fully within the Community's competence, understood as those matters covered by the founding Treaties, while foreign and security policy is ruled through intergovernmental arrangements. The EU remains formally a civilian power, lacking any direct military capability, although some instruments are now at its disposal. These, to mention only the Western European Union (WEU), still need to find their proper place within the web of existing institutions, between independence and dependence on NATO.

In the last instance, the EU cannot resort to military coercion to command obedience. It is not able to conduct an unchallenged foreign policy because it lacks the crucial attribute of supranationality in this area. It has an identity, though an incomplete one, mostly felt in economic diplomacy, as a powerful entity in trade negotiations, a donor and coordinator of aid alongside the World Bank or the International Monetary Fund. Even in this uncontested competence of the EU, Member States' interests are challenging those of the Community.[2] Therefore, it is imperative to construct new tools to facilitate the understanding of an increasingly complex set of interactions between the Community institutions and the Member States.

The EU has one more issue on its agenda, that is to enmesh the Eastern and Central European countries in its web of social and economic interactions and robust institutional framework. It might affect the deepening process, but the enlargement is about to bring a beneficial self-reappraisal. The current enlargement is of a radically different nature from previous ones, which sculptured some of the instruments of the integration process. The East European candidates will complicate economically and politically the whole integration process. It is not a question of adjustment. The new members could exert a pressure on the Common Foreign and Security Policy (CFSP), looking for security if Russia continues to object to their entry into NATO. They would bring their foreign policy concerns, mainly their relations with Russia, into the European Union (Michalski and Wallace, 1992: 21). So far, debates on the eastwards enlargement, rather than providing incentives to convergent ideas, have provoked divisions between Member States. However, if this challenge is completed, it may well contribute to enhancing the way the EU perceives its own identity and its European role.

Antje Herrberg argues that to these two levels of analysis, one which refers to the inside, one to the outside, it is desirable to add a third dimension which is capable of encompassing the European Union as a synergy of these two accounts. She advocates the system theory because it captures a system of relationships which characterise the EU.

The question of globalisation cannot be eluded when rethinking the EU. The capabilities of national governments have declined due to globalisation. The question is whether such a loss of efficiency can be compensated by a shift of national competencies to the European Commission. Klaus Armingeon argues that the EU is exposed to and suffers from global challenges almost to the same extent as national states. The nation state's inability to act due to globalisation is a problem that cannot be solved by the European Commission. Moreover, he provides an empirical analysis revealing that the capacity to act of nation states has not substantially diminished since the most recent wave of globalisation.

The EU is not only a question of institutions, of identities; it is also much more – a political presence. It relates to the wider international context. On one side, global regimes serve to legitimise and support the general development of the EU, for example the World Trade Organisation, which relates to its core principles of free market and trade (Andersen and Eliassen, 1993: 12). On the other side, the international environment asserts the actor-like capability of the EU, and this might contribute to the exacerbation of the tension between national sovereignty and the process of integration.

The 1970s and 1980s were characterised by the EC inching towards self-reliance and struggling for assertiveness. The process of assertiveness culminated in the 1980s and 1990s with the doubling of the EC membership, the Single European Act and the Single Market. The EU is a European structure, a pole of political stability and an economic promoter; by virtue of those attributes it attracts the states from its periphery. It can fulfil its required role only if the Member States maintain the same commitment to the institutional framework that they have established and intensify their efforts to integrate. However, the changes in 1989 also deeply affected this process. The EU was required to perform a more comprehensive role, not merely in the economic field as conveyor of financial flows to Eastern Europe but as a provider of security. Once again, it is impossible to isolate the EU from the environment. The EU has a more visible role, because of a process of distancing between the EU and the United States.

The thrust of this volume is to explore these facets of institutions, interests and identities. The guiding ethos of this book is that the EU should be captured through different lenses, theoretical, political and cultural. It is difficult to explain the multidimensional aspects of the EU, its complexity, and one has to investigate through different levels of analysis. Far from being divergent, they are complementary. We are helped by the diversity of the contributors of this volume, all of them representing different backgrounds and adopting different approaches to the study of the EU. It is only through such pluridisciplinary visions that we may be better able to apprehend the new realities of this hybrid animal called the EU.

NOTES

1. This typology fits for regional schemes, because what matters is the capacity and the will of member countries to abandon sovereignty in increasing

domains of competence. At the lower level, governments are involved in a process of intensive consultations, though they retain powers and responsibility. *Cooperation* entails a limited involvement of states in a joint enterprise. *Harmonisation* reflects the ability to identify and exploit existing compatibilities between states, though it does not mean adopting common positions. *Association* concentrates on functional arrangements with the same avoidance of associating questions of political commitment. *Parallel national action* refers to the co-ordination of member countries' legislation with the help of common institutions and arrangements. The final form of adjustment is *supranationalism* by which governments allow an international institution to manage an area of common interest.

2. Member States are contesting the Commission's exclusive right to negotiate agricultural and labour standards in the World Trade Organisation.

Part One
Institutions and Identities: Europe and the International

2 The New Pattern of International Relations in Europe

Adrian Hyde-Price

It is now widely recognised that the collapse of communist autocracy and the end of the Cold War marks a major watershed in modern European history. In a widely quoted article Francis Fukuyama declared that it signified no less than 'the end of history' (1989). More recently, Eric Hobsbawm (1994) has argued that it marks the end of the 'short twentieth century'. Whatever one may make of these specific claims, there is now little doubt that the *annus mirabilis* of 1989 constitutes a historical watershed comparable in scope and intensity with the French Revolution and the outbreak of the Great War. European politics, society and culture have irrevocably changed – most spectacularly in Central and Eastern Europe – and a new phase in the continent's history has begun.

The dramatic changes in European politics and society have been accompanied by even more dramatic shifts in the pattern of European international relations. A new topology of power relations is emerging in the continent as new states appear and long-established relationships across Europe adjust to the end of the bipolar divide. Not only have the structures of European power relationships been altered, the dynamics of European international relations have also changed. This is reflected in the radically new security agenda in Europe: whereas in the dark days of the Cold War Europeans were concerned first and foremost with the threat of continental wide warfare between two nuclear-armed alliances, the security agenda is now dominated by a series of diffuse 'risks' and 'challenges', such as ethno-nationalist conflict, nuclear proliferation, large-scale migration and transnational crime.

At the centre of the evolving structure of international relations in Europe today is the European Union. The EU is not only an increasingly pervasive force in the daily lives of the citizens of its Member States, it is also the focal point of the foreign policies of most East European states, and an increasingly influential presence in the global economy. Some would suggest that the successful evolution of the European Union from its origins in the European Coal and Steel Community of the 1950s has profoundly altered not just the nature of European international relations, but also the identity of Europe itself. Such far-reaching claims are debatable, but what does seem certain is that the very nature and shape of Europe in the twenty-first century will be intimately bound up with the future development of the EU.

While few would dispute the historical significance of the collapse of the bipolar divide in Europe, there is very little agreement on what these changes mean and their implications for European international relations. Assessing their significance and implications has been made even more difficult by the almost manic depressive mood swings which have occurred over recent years. The inauguration of the Solidarity government in Poland, the breaching of the Berlin Wall and the 'Velvet Revolution' in Czechoslovakia were greeted with a wave of unrestrained joy and jubilation. These feelings of exhilaration were hardly dented by the violence that accompanied the 'Christmas Revolution' in Romania. Gorbachev's talk of a 'common European house' seemed to be becoming reality. President Bush proclaimed the imminence of a Europe 'whole and free', and in November 1990, the Conference on Security and Co-operation in Europe (CSCE) summit of Heads of State and Government adopted the grandly named 'Charter of Paris for a New Europe'.

This mood of naive optimism quickly evaporated in the face of both growing ethno-nationalist conflict in Eastern Europe and the Balkans, and doubts about the European integration process. The post-communist search for societal solidarity in Central and Eastern Europe revived long-suppressed nationalist identities, with bloody consequences in the Balkans and in Russia's 'near abroad'. Within Western Europe, hopes that the post-Maastricht European Union would provide a stable and cohesive core for a new Europe of concentric circles – a vision held particularly strongly in Paris and Bonn – faded in the face of growing popular doubts about the scope and direction of the integration process. To cap it all, the European economy slid inexorably into recession – in part due to the financial strains of German unification.

Consequently there is little consensus on how European international relations have changed and what the shape of the new Europe will be. The purpose of this chapter is to explore the changing nature of international relations in Europe. This is no easy task, and this essay should therefore be seen as a contribution to the debate, rather than an attempt to provide a definitive answer to such a complex question. It begins by considering the nature of the Westphalian states' system and its evolution in the nineteenth and early twentieth centuries. It then assesses the impact of the Cold War on Europe and the emergence in Western Europe of a 'pluralistic security community'. Finally, it seeks to evaluate the consequences of the demise of the bipolar divide for this security community, and considers the changing dynamics of international relations in Europe. It concludes by assessing the arguments of those who suggest that the collapse of the Cold War has provided a catalyst for the disintegration of the Westphalian states system itself.

THE WESTPHALIAN STATES SYSTEM

The 1648 Treaty of Westphalia is traditionally regarded as constituting the founding moment of the modern states system. This treaty not only ended the Thirty Years War (a brutal conflict which brought appalling human suffering and material devastation to vast swathes of central Europe), it also created a new diplomatic order based on the sovereignty of legally equal states. States had, of course, existed prior to Westphalia, but they did so in a very different legal, diplomatic and political context than that created in 1648.

In medieval Christendom, which was finally and irrevocably destroyed by the carnage of the Thirty Years War, power relations were organised not vertically into separate states with clearly defined geographical borders, but rather horizontally across the whole of Christendom on a functional basis. In this medieval system, the Latin Church exercised a universal spiritual role which impacted on the exercise of power by the secular authorities; lay authority was primarily in the hands of kings, princes and nobles; townspeople and merchants were largely autonomous; and the Holy Roman Empire provided an overarching political structure across much of central Europe. Medieval Christendom was therefore characterised by a complex multidimensional structure with an overlapping and interlocking system of lay and religious authorities. It was a international system which proved 'exceptionally turbulent, dynamic and enterprising' (Bull and Watson, 1984: 13), but one in which violence and the breakdown of social order were an ever-present threat.

This medieval order was eroded from within by a series of social, economic and cultural developments. The Renaissance turned men's minds to classical models of statehood (given that much of the political philosophy of Graeco-Roman civilisation had been concerned with the *polis*, the self-governing city-state); the Reformation broke the authority of the universal church; and the wars of religion of the sixteenth and seventeenth centuries led many Protestants and humanists to develop arguments in favour of state sovereignty independent from any external authority. From the four-teenth century to the mid-seventeenth century, therefore, a growing number of Europeans saw their main political task as building sovereign states capable of providing domestic stability and security from external threats. This led to a rejection of feudal obligations and the claims to universal authority by both the Catholic Church and the Holy Roman Empire. As Adam Watson has written, beginning in Italy and spreading throughout the area of medieval Christendom, 'the complex horizontal structure of feudal society crystallised into a vertical pattern of territorial states, each with increasing authority inside defined geographical borders' (Bull and Watson 1984: 15). By the mid-seventeenth century, the hegemonic authority of both the Pope and the Holy Roman Emperor had collapsed. The emergence of a new international system based on formally sovereign states was given legal expression in the 1648 Treaty of Westphalia.

'The Treaty of Westphalia', Kalevi Holsti has written, 'organised Europe on the basis of particularism. It represented a new diplomatic arrangement – an order created by states, for states – and replaced most of the legal vestiges of hierarchy, at the pinnacle of which were the Pope and the Holy Roman Emperor.' Westphalia led to 'the creation of a pan-European diplomatic system based on the new principles of sovereignty and legal equality', and 'paved the way for a system of states to replace a hierarchical system under the leadership of the Pope and the Habsburg family complex that linked the Holy Roman and Spanish Empires' (Holsti, 1991: 25–6). The Treaty of Westphalia was undoubtedly one of the most important events demarcating the medieval from the modern period in European history, but as Lynn Miller notes: 'Like all such historical benchmarks, Westphalia is in some respects more a convenient reference point than the source of a fully formed new normative system' (Miller, 1994: 20).

FROM THE 'EUROPE OF VERSAILLES' TO THE 'EUROPE OF YALTA'

The key feature of the Westphalian states system was the existence of legally sovereign states functioning without a higher source of legitimate political authority. In this anarchic international system, states struggled to preserve their sovereignty and ensure their security in the face of both internal and external threats. Given the absence of an overarching source of authority (such as the Universal Church and the Holy Roman Empire), states needed to devise other means to regulate their conflicts and maintain the stability of the international system. Hedley Bull has suggested that they did so by creating five 'institutions': diplomacy, the balance of power, international law, war and the management role of the Great Powers. He argues that the modern international system contains not just elements of struggle and competition between states, but also elements of cooperation and regulated intercourse. He therefore speaks of the emergence of a 'society of states' (Bull, 1977: 13). In the eighteenth and nineteenth centuries, Europe's society of states was regulated by a mixture of diplomacy and periodic wars. A guiding principle – enshrined in the 1815 Congress of Vienna – was the balance of power: this belief, that no one state should dominate the European continent, was the premise upon which the Concert of Europe (between the Great Powers) operated.

This European balance of power was irredeemably shaken by the rise of a unified Germany (Deportes 1979: 116). The creation – through 'Blood and Iron' – of a Prussian-dominated *Kleindeutschland* produced a major challenge to the European balance of power. Thus was born the contemporary 'German Problem': the problem, in other words, of how to integrate – or at least contain – the prodigious economic strength and military potential of a unified German state, situated at the very heart of the European continent. It was the failure to resolve this conundrum that led to the two world wars of the twentieth century. The existence of a unified Germany has thus been a crucial factor determining the nature and dynamics of European international relations.

'What is wrong with Germany', A.J.P. Taylor once wrote, 'is that there is too much of it' (1967: 21). At the same time, Germany's enormously productive economy and vibrant society has been of such concern to its neighbours because of its central geographical location – its *Mittellage*. Indeed, David Calleo has argued that 'The German problem does not somehow emanate from some special German "character"', but from its geography:

>...Unlike Britain, Russia, or the United States, the Germans lacked the space to work out their abundant vitality. Moreover, because of geography, Germany's vitality was an immediate threat to the rest of Europe. Modern Germany was born encircled. Under the circumstances, whatever the lesson of the wars between Germany and its neighbours, it cannot be found merely by analysing the faults of the German. (1978: 206)

One final aspect of the 'German Problem' in the past has been the political character of the German state. Realist theorists of international relations tend to discount domestic factors when analysing state behaviour:

this is patently absurd in the case of Germany. The Germany that Bismarck created, and upon which Hitler constructed the National Socialist state, was characterised by a propensity towards authoritarianism, militarism, intolerance and economic protectionism.[1] The domestic political complexion of the German state is thus a crucial factor determining the nature of international relations in Europe.

The burgeoning strength of the Wilhelmine Reich led to the destabilisation of the European balance of power. This in turn precipitated the Great War of 1914–18 – a war which marked a decisive watershed in modern European history. The war also led to a major reshaping of the map of Europe, as four multinational empires (the Habsburg, Ottoman, Russian and German) came crashing down. The peacemakers who gathered in Paris in 1919 wanted to create a new international system based on new principles and institutions. The key note was struck by President Woodrow Wilson in his famous Fourteen Points speech to the American Congress. His radical aim was to forge a 'peace without victory', combining order with justice (Holsti, 1991: 177).

This belief in the right of nations to self-determination was the guiding principle of the 1919 Treaty of Versailles. A 'Europe of Versailles' was thus created based on the principle of national self-determination, which was manifested in the creation of a number of new territorial states on the ruins of once-mighty multinational empires.

Despite the best intentions of the peacemakers of 1919, this 'Europe of Versailles' was to prove inherently unstable. The territorial settlement of 1919 generated new grievances and nationalist irredentia; the mechanisms for conflict resolution created by the League of Nations were ineffective; economic recession undermined weak democratic institutions in Central and Eastern Europe; and a number of Europe's traditional Great Powers (notably Germany, Russia and Italy) were implacably hostile to the new international order. It is therefore not surprising that the fragile peace of Versailles was to collapse into renewed continent-wide violence.

The Second World War once again led to a profound reshaping of Europe. Although there was no formal peace settlement, the foundations for a new postwar order were laid at a series of summit meetings between the wartime allies. The most famous – or perhaps infamous – of these was the Yalta summit of 4–11 February 1945. This summit has subsequently acquired a political symbolism it does not really deserve. In popular mythology, it is now seen as a grand exercise in Great Power geopolitical engineering.[2] This is not historically justified.[3] Nonetheless, the 'Europe of Yalta' does provide a well-used form of political shorthand to describe the postwar European order.

The 'Europe of Yalta' was distinguished by five unique characteristics: the decisive role of the superpowers in European affairs; the creation of two military-political alliance systems (NATO/EEC on the one hand and the Warsaw Pact/CMEA on the other); the division of Germany; nuclear deterrence; and the existence of a small group of neutral and non-aligned countries (Hyde-Price, 1991: 47–9). This structure of power relations was to define European international relations for four decades. It was an arrangement which brought stability and order to Europe, but at a cost of much injustice – primarily in the Soviet bloc, but also in the West – as well as the ever-present threat of nuclear armageddon. However, the existence of this Cold War security system was also to provide the context for a process of profound and far-reaching transformation in European international relations – the emergence in Western Europe and the wider transatlantic area of a 'pluralistic security community'.

POSTWAR WESTERN EUROPE

As we have seen, twice this century, Europe has torn itself apart in brutal wars between its leading nation-states. The Great War of 1914–18 was a particularly traumatic experience, and led many Europeans to search for new ways of managing their international relations. However, the peace settlement that followed the 'war to end all wars' unfortunately sowed the seeds of resentment that were to lead to the Second World War. This war was to prove even more bloody and destructive than the Great War. The horrors of the 1939–45 war stimulated a new generation of statesmen to attempt to fashion a durable and just peace settlement without repeating the mistakes of Versailles. The year 1945 therefore provided both the occasion and the opportunity for attempting to reshape the politics of the continent in ways which would make future wars between its diverse peoples both politically unthinkable and economically impossible.

Unfortunately, aspirations for a continent at peace with itself and the rest of the world were thwarted by the onset of the Cold War. By 1949, Europe had split into two distinct political, economic and military groupings, each viewing the other with undisguised hostility and suspicion. Yet this bipolar division also had the unintentional effect of stimulating the sort of cooperation and integration advocated by proponents of a 'United States of Europe'. In Western Europe, the perception of a powerful external threat provided a major stimulus towards political, economic and military cooperation.

In 1949, The North Atlantic Treaty Organisation (NATO) was created (parallel efforts to create a European Defence Community with an integrated army also took place, although this ultimately failed due to opposition in the French National Assembly). The NATO Alliance was subsequently to develop into the bedrock of Western European security, with an integrated military command structure and a sophisticated system of political consultation and intergovernmental decision-making. A little while later, efforts to create an institutional framework for political and economic integration in Europe bore fruit when, in April 1951, the European Coal and Steel Community (ECSC) was created. The purpose of this organisation was to provide a supranational framework for integrating the coal and steel industries of the major West European economies – in particular, those of the French and West Germans. Yet, as Jean Monnet remarked when the Treaty was signed, 'This isn't just coal and steel. It is the beginning of a process – a dynamic process to build a great market for all the people of Europe' (Reinicke 1993: 11).

At the same time, the founders of the ECSC harboured an even more ambitious long-term aim. They hoped that by meshing together what were the leading economic sectors of the time, war between member states would become structurally impossible. This aspiration was articulated in the preamble of the ECSC Treaty: the ECSC, it declared, would create 'a broader and deeper community among peoples long divided by bloody conflicts', and would 'lay the foundation of a destiny henceforth shared'. The 1957 Treaty of Rome (which created the European Economic Community) also had this long-term goal in mind: as the signatories declared, they were 'determined to lay the foundations of an ever closer union among the peoples of Europe', and called upon 'the other peoples of Europe who share their ideal to join in their efforts'. At the heart of this integration process in postwar Western Europe was the political, cultural and social process of Franco-German reconciliation – a development which has proved of major consequence for the stability and security of Europe.[4]

By the late 1950s and early 1960s, Western Europe had not only recovered from its wartime devastation and experienced a process of sustained economic growth, it had also achieved significant advances in political, economic and military integration. This integration had two dimensions to it, formal and informal (W. Wallace, 1990: 54).

In postwar Western Europe, formal and informal processes of integration have become very much intertwined. The European Community attempted to forge a 'common market' through the creation of common rules and regulations, which in turn helped shape patterns of interaction and norms of behaviour. At the same time, informal processes of integration were driven by impersonal economic, social and technological forces.

The result of these postwar developments in Western Europe has been to create a region characterised by a high degree of economic and social interaction, with a dense institutional structure. At the same time, the nature of Western European societies have changed, with the development of social market economies, pluralist civil societies and democratic polities. Throughout Western Europe, a broad consensus has emerged around shared values and principles, particularly as regards human rights, liberal democracy and basic social welfare provisions.

Together, these developments have had a profound impact on the nature of international relations in the region. Up to the middle of the twentieth century, European states were locked into a complex and shifting balance of power arrangement. These states jealously guarded their sovereignty, and engaged in power politics based on *realpolitik* calculations. Within these *realpolitik* calculations, military assets constituted the key element in the assessment of relative power relationships.

This whole pattern of international relations in Western Europe was radically changed by postwar social, political, economic and institutional developments. As Karl Deutsch (Deutsch et al., 1957) recognised early, a 'pluralistic security community' has emerged embracing the North Americans and the West Europeans. Within this pluralistic security community, the threat and use of force plays no part in inter-state relations. War is no longer a rational instrument of policy in relations between states in the transatlantic community.[5] In Hedley Bull's (1977) terms, an 'international society' has developed within the transatlantic states system, in which cooperation and 'sociability' between states has largely superseded traditional *realpolitik* instincts.

A profound transformation in the essential nature of European international relations has thus taken place in the postwar period. This has led to a far-reaching change in the structural dynamics of the Westphalian states' system. An 'international society' has emerged embracing the mature industrial pluralist democracies of the transatlantic community. Within this international society, relations are conducted on the basis of international law within a complex institutional ensemble. The states within this community share common normative values, associated primarily with human rights, liberal democracy and market economics (Hanson, 1993: 28–41). Most significantly, relations between them are no longer conducted against the background of a threat to resort to force. This is the most startling and most positive change: after centuries of internecine warfare, the peoples of Western and Central Europe now enjoy peaceful inter-state relations. Kant's dream of a 'Pacific Union' has become a reality (Kant, 1992). This is of tremendous significance, for as Professor Chris Brown (1993) has suggested, 'if physical violence is no longer a serious option then in practice sovereignty has been seriously weakened, whatever the legal position. In the absence of an effective right to resort to force, sovereignty is, it seems, a very amorphous notion.'

THE TRANSATLANTIC 'PLURALIST SECURITY COMMUNITY'

The emergence of a transatlantic security community in the postwar period is a development of such profound and far-reaching significance that it demands careful analysis. The first question to be asked is what developments have contributed to its emergence. Here, five factors are of significance:

(1) *Informal integration*. The thickening of networks of economic and social exchange, the emergence of a common market, the spread of complex interdependence and the impact of globalisation on the region have all produced the economic and social preconditions for peaceful cooperation. We will return to this theme later in this chapter.

(2) *Formal integration*. The creation of structures of institutionalised negotiation, compromise and cooperation help facilitate and channel the processes of informal integration. The most important institution in this respect is the European Union, although the Council of Europe is also important, as are NATO and the WEU in the security sphere. The existence of robust multilateral organisations such as the EU and NATO also provide an indispensable framework for integrating Germany into the European states' system. The EU in particular provides a historic solution to the age-old 'German Problem' in that it provides an institutional mechanism for harnessing Germany's immense creativity and enterprise to broader European concerns. Through Western Europe's institutional ensemble, therefore, Thomas Mann's dream of a 'European Germany' rather than a 'German Europe' has become a reality.

(3) *Stable liberal democracies and social market economies*. There is a growing consensus in the academic and policy-making community that democracies do not fight wars with each other. The spread and consolidation of democracy in the transatlantic area is thus a factor of major import in the emergence of a pluralistic security community. At the same time, the consolidation of democratic polities is only possible in the absence of major social cleavages. In this respect, the creation of social market

economies has been particularly beneficial for the health of liberal democracies in Western Europe.

(4) *An external threat.* Cooperation within any group is greatly facilitated if that group shares a common perception of a significant external threat. In the Cold War years, the existence of a perceived Soviet threat provided a major impulse to cooperation between states within the transatlantic community. It forced West European states to develop novel forms of partnership and cooperation, and provided the impetus for integrating the *Bundesrepublik* into both NATO and the EEC.

(5) *The US pacifier.* In postwar Western Europe, the USA has played the role of a benign hegemon. It provided Marshall Aid to the Europeans on the understanding that they buried traditional animosities and cooperated together. As the Dutch scholar Ernst H. van der Beugel (van Ham, 1994: 191) observed, from 'the moment of the launching of the Marshall Plan, it became apparent that European integration was a major objective of American foreign policy... It pursued this aim primarily within the framework of its stand against communist aggression.' Since then, the USA has often been able to play both a mediating role and to provide leadership in a way that would be impossible for any of the West European Great Powers. For this reason, the US has been dubbed by Joseph Joffe (1984) 'Europe's American Pacifier'.

FORWARD TO THE PAST? THE TRANSATLANTIC SECURITY COMMUNITY IN THE POST-COLD WAR ERA

The end of the Cold War raises an intriguing set of questions about the nature and durability of the transatlantic security community. The central question is whether this security community, which has so fundamentally changed the nature of foreign and security policies in the area, will survive the end of bipolar confrontation. Which of the above five factors are decisive in the formation of the security community? Was it the product of the Cold War, with a clear external threat and the consequent need for a leading role for the USA in Western European affairs, or was it the result of underlying secular forces associated with globalisation and the spread of complex interdependence? Will the transatlantic security community prove strong enough to survive the disintegration of the Soviet Union, the end of bipolarity, the declining US role in Europe and the growing instability of Central and Eastern Europe? These are more than intellectually challenging questions: the answers to them will affect the future stability and security of the European continent.

As the mood of naive optimism which accompanied the ending of the Cold War has dispersed, some commentators have painted a dark and deeply pessimistic picture of Europe's future. Europe's future, they suggest, will resemble all too closely its past. The stability and order that bipolarity brought will give way to multipolar instability. Multilateral cooperation will be torn apart by centrifugal pressures. European security alliances will fragment along regional lines. Europe will loose its 'American pacifier'. Germany will reject its postwar *Westbindung* and proceed to impose its hegemony on *Mitteleuropa*. The dream of an 'ever closer union' will give way to a *Europe des Patries*. In short, European international relations will return to their nineteenth- and early twentieth-century patterns, characterised by shifting multipolar alliances, balance of power considerations and *realpolitik* calculations by competing sovereign states.

One exponent of these gloomy perspectives is John Gray. He has argued that the end of the Cold War promises not only to unravel 'the central institutions of the post-war settlement, such as NATO', but also to spell the end for 'the liberal universalism of the Western settlement of 1919' (Gray, 1993: 48; Hyde-Price, 1991: Part III).

This pessimistic scenario has been expounded with even greater intellectual coherence in the writings of John Mearsheimer (1990). Mearsheimer is a neo-realist, and consequently rejects the view that international organisations and institutions can fundamentally alter the behaviour of states. In an oft-quoted article written in 1990, he argued that Europe was heading for a new period of instability and conflict. His argument is based on the assumption that the decisive element determining state behaviour is the absence of a central authority in the anarchic state system. This means that no state can be constrained other than by countervailing power, which is normally of a military or economic nature.[6] Mearsheimer postulates that the decline of bipolarity and the emergence of a more multipolar international system will increase uncertainty and instability, leading states to pursue traditional power politics based on military capabilities as well as political will and economic interests. For Mearsheimer, the existence of a common market does not modify what he regards as the natural propensity of states to act in accordance with the principles of *realpolitik*. His Hobbesian view of the world leads him to the conclusion that conflicts within the European Union and NATO will intensify, and that the institutional complex in the transatlantic area and the existence of a common market will not restrain the foreign and security policies of sovereign states acting in conditions of international anarchy.

GLOBALISATION, INTERNATIONAL ORGANISATIONS AND
DEMOCRACY

The pessimistic scenarios of Gray and Mearsheimer are presented in a
cogent and intellectually rigorous way. The brutal starkness and simplicity
of their central thesis – that Europe's past is also its future – has a seduc-
tive appeal for those overcome by the current mood of Euro-pessimism.
Their bleak visions may well have provided a sobering antidote to the
naive optimism which accompanied the demise of the Cold War. But both
Gray and Mearsheimer and writers of their ilk underestimate the
significance of the postwar transformation of European international
relations.

To begin with, they overlook the impact of complex interdependence
and globalisation on Western Europe. By the 1970s, it was widely recognised that Western Europe had been deeply affected by thickening webs of
economic and social interdependence. Since then, a new wave of economic and technological changes – associated primarily with transport and
communications – have occurred, signifying an intensification in the more
long-term process of modernisation.[7] This is creating an increasingly glob-
alised international economy, society and polity. The impact of globalisation has been particularly marked on Western Europe, given the relative
smallness of its states, its geographical compactness and the intensity of its
interactions.[8]

Globalisation is changing the nature of international relations in a
number of significant and potentially far-reaching ways. First, it is deepening the interconnections and transactions between actors across continents,
and between different issue-areas. Second, it has stimulated the proliferation of international actors. There are now a growing number of important
international exchanges above and below the level of the traditional
nation-state, including transgovernmental linkages, transnational
exchanges, intergovernmental regimes and supranational organisations.[9]
This has created an increasingly multilayered international system, in
which different societies and communities around the world are connected
by multiple channels (i.e. interstate, transgovernmental, transnational).
Third, globalisation has generated a much more dialectical interaction
between domestic and international policy. This is an inevitable consequence of the proliferation of new actors, above and below the level of the
state. Joseph Frankel (1988: 219–20) has observed that 'The linkage
between domestic and international affairs has grown greatly in both
directions. On the one hand, rapidly growing domestic needs and demands
have become increasingly dependent upon international politics; on the

other, international politics has become increasingly affected by domestic conflicts.'

The contemporary Western European state is thus enmeshed within an extensive network of global interconnections, deeply permeated by transnational forces and increasingly unable to fulfil its core domestic functions without recourse to international cooperation. This has led some commentators to speak of the 'crisis of the territorial nation-state' (Cox, 1993: 263).

The second mistake of the latter-day Cassandras like Gray and Mearsheimer is that they exaggerate the fragility of Europe's multilateral organisations, particularly the European Union. The problems associated with the ratification of the Maastricht Treaty do not necessarily presage the unravelling of the integration process. Deepening integration in the Community has always proceeded in waves, and has tended to slow down in times of recession (W. Wallace, 1990: Chapter 5). But there can be little doubt that deeper integration corresponds to both the underlying development of the European economy and the political requirements of post-Cold War Europe. Certainly, there are voices on the margins of European politics advocating the dissolution of the EU, but they do not represent mainstream political or economic forces. A Europe of tomorrow without the EU is thus as unimaginable as a USA without federal institutions.

The existence of multilateral institutions such as the EU is important for European international relations because, although they may not be able to command Member States to pursue particular policies, they can and do encourage them to pursue their national interests through cooperation with other states. Participation in international institutions can thus help change states' perceptions of their national interest. When states find international institutions broadly helpful and constructive, they generally refrain from unilaterally adopting disruptive policies (Stein, 1990: 52).

Thus the existence and operation of international institutions helps to shape the expectations and behaviour of the participants, thereby encouraging the emergence of habits and constituencies that will support a cooperative international regime (Snyder, 1990: 30).

The third mistake of contemporary Euro-pessimists is to underestimate the cultural, social and political changes that have taken place in Western Europe since 1945. Rising living standards, the creation of an increasingly literate and skilled population, more complex patterns of social stratification, the emergence of vibrant civil societies, the consolidation of constitutional governments, the spread of democratic values – these changes have created stable and prosperous liberal democracies. This has had a major impact on international relations in Western Europe. It has been particularly significant in Germany because it has neutralised another aspect of the historical 'German Problem'.

These developments have consolidated Western Europe's pluralistic security community and have helped removed the threat of war from intrastate relations in the region. In a recent article questioning the widely held proposition that democracies do not fight each other, Raymond Cohen (1994: 220–21) nonetheless concludes that this claim 'does contain, incontestably, a historical core of truth. Since 1945 the North Atlantic/Western European states have enjoyed an uninterrupted period of peaceful relations.' This he ascribes to two key factors: democratisation and economic interdependence. He also suggests that the emergence of this transatlantic 'Pacific Union' has been facilitated by 'ancient ties of civilisation and culture'; diplomatic *linguae francae* (French and English); a common Christianity; governing elites with much in common; 'a strong sense of shared identity enshrined in communal organisations and legislation'; and a shared normative commitment to 'outlawing war as a legitimate instrument of statecraft within the community' along with 'mechanisms for the peaceful resolution of international conflict'.

Thus the belief that the end of the Cold War heralds a return to past patterns of international relations in Europe – with rivalrous states pursuing their national interests in a shifting balance of power system – overlooks the impact that globalisation, multilateral institutions and democracy have had in Western Europe in the postwar period. The end of the Cold War has undoubtedly generated new elements of turmoil and instability, particularly in the Balkans and the fringes of the former Soviet Union. It has also introduced a note of uncertainty and self-doubt into Western European politics. But underlying social, economic, political and cultural trends continue to favour the further consolidation and expansion of the transatlantic security community. The task facing the present generation of Europeans is how to extend this security community steadily eastwards in order to lay of the foundations of the Germans call a *Europäische Friedensordnung* (a 'European peace order').

INTEGRATING EASTERN EUROPE INTO THE TRANSATLANTIC SECURITY COMMUNITY

The pattern of international relations in contemporary Europe exhibits sharp discontinuities between distinct regional zones (Hyde-Price, 1993). In the West, there is a 'pluralistic security community' in which war, and the threat of war, no longer play a part in interstate relations. In the East, where there are fewer institutional structures, weaker webs of economic interdependence and relatively immature political democracies, international relations correspond more closely to traditional balance of power arrangements based on *realpolitik* calculations. At the same time, a new 'Concert of Europe' between the Great Powers has emerged, reminiscent in some respects of the age of Metternich (Zelikow, 1992). New mechanisms for conflict prevention and crisis management within the recently institutionalised Organisation for Security and Co-operation in Europe (OSCE) framework also provide the embryonic structures for a system of pan-European collective security, similar in some ways to the League of Nations. Finally, the OSCE has facilitated the emergence of common European norms, focused around concepts of human rights and market economics.

If post-Cold War Europe is to avoid instability and conflict, then the pluralistic security community of Western Europe must be consolidated and extended into post-communist Central and Eastern Europe. This is indeed the long-term project facing the new Europe. Only on this basis will the contemporary Concert of Europe survive and the OSCE be able to develop into an effective institution for conflict prevention and crisis management. However, achieving this will be no easy task.

Extending the influence of the transatlantic security community eastwards has a number of dimensions:

(1) *Informal integration.* The integration of the economies of Central and Eastern Europe into the European Economic Space and ultimately into the markets of the European Union involves issues of market access; privatisation and de-monopolisation of former command economies; substantial foreign investment; and financial and monetary convergence. Informal integration will develop as the economies of the region are transformed and opened up to the forces of globalisation, technological change and deepening economic exchanges.

(2) *Formal integration.* It is now widely recognised that the 'new Europe' will be built up on the basis of a series of overlapping and interlocking institutions (Hyde-Price, 1993: 249). Europe's new institutional 'architecture' will therefore be multilevelled and functionally differentiated. Within this complex institutional ensemble a central role will be played by the European Union. The EU is already under pressure to open itself up to new members from the East, and it is likely that by the early twenty-first century the Union will have doubled in size. This formal integration is important because by providing a clear legal and institutional framework, informal integration processes can be greatly facilitated.

(3) *Security guarantees*. Foreign investment in, and trade deals with, the countries of Central and Eastern Europe will suffer if major doubts about the stability and security of the region linger. The countries of Eastern Europe are seeking either firm security guarantees from NATO and the WEU or membership in these alliances. NATO has proved reticent in meeting these requests from its former Warsaw Pact enemies, but has sought to strengthen security relationships in the continent by creating the North Atlantic Cooperation Council and, more recently, the 'Partnerships for Peace' programme.

(4) *Democratisation*. Given the tendency of liberal democracies not to wage wars on other liberal democracies, strengthening democratic institutions and attitudes is of vital importance for European security. Common values and principles are also an important feature of a security community, as Deutsch himself stressed.

INSTITUTIONAL STRUCTURES AND INTERNATIONAL RELATIONS IN EUROPE

When seeking to understand the new, post-Cold War dynamic of international relations in Europe, two key factors stand out. The first and most important factor affecting the behaviour of states is not simply the existence of common markets (i.e. a common economic space marked by extensive economic exchanges and a high degree of interdependence). Rather, it is the existence of both complex interdependence and robust international institutions.

Complex interdependence, which has had such a far-reaching impact on European international relations, provides an economic basis for closer international cooperation by forging structural bonds between countries and nations. However, it does not automatically produce peaceful relations and mutual cooperation between former rivals in the international system. Indeed, it can produce conflict, as states struggle to escape the vulnerability that interdependence creates.

If complex interdependence is to facilitate a process of closer interstate cooperation and 'peaceful competition' (in the literal sense of the term), then it has to be institutionalised. This involves the development of institutional frameworks for bi- and multilateral forms of diplomacy, which can draw up mutually acceptable rules, regulations and codes of behaviour. International institutions can facilitate agreements among governments (along with other international and transnational actors such as firms) because such institutions provide a framework for orderly multilateral negotiations and encourage linkages among issues. Bargaining and log-rolling will become commonplace, and states will acquire a vested interest in maintaining these institutions. Since states participate within these institutions over a long period of time, governments have fewer incentives to cheat. Within these institutions, reputations of reliability can be established and common interests among states may therefore be realised more easily.

Thus one goal of the emerging new European security system should be to enmesh the countries of Central and Eastern Europe in an institutionalised network of deepening interdependencies. By institutionalising interdependence, it may be possible to ameliorate nationalist conflicts and create a new cooperative security regime in Europe. This in turn will contribute to the progressive extension of the transatlantic security community, producing what Francis Fukuyama finds so boring about the end of the Cold War – namely, the progressive 'common marketisation of the international relations' (Fukuyama, 1989).

The second key factor referred to above is as follows. Although the institutionalisation of interdependence provides the best hope of extending the transatlantic security community eastwards, it must be recognised that creating new institutions or extending existing ones is often easier said than done. International institutions are notoriously more difficult to build than to maintain.

As we have already seen, some have argued that postwar western institutions have largely been erected with the assistance of the USA, which, in its role as a benign hegemon, has not only provided the impetus to cooperate, but has also helped the formulation of regime rules and guarded against breaches of these rules (Keohane, 1984). One writer has suggested that 'the more symmetrical the distribution of power, the harder it is to establish institutional arrangements initially but the more effective they are once formed' (Young, 1992: 186). Robert Keohane has also suggested that institutions will be more easily created in 'dense policy spaces', since *ad hoc* arrangements in such areas are likely to interfere with one another unless they are based upon a common set of rules and principles (Keohane, 1984: 79). This means that developing new institutional structures should prove easier in Europe than in a continent like Africa where existing institutions are relatively scarce and weak.

Extending the scope and membership of existing institutions can also prove problematic. NATO, for example, has so far resisted giving firm security guarantees or the promise of membership to any of its suitors from the east. This is because it fears creating new political and military divisions in Europe; it does not want to generate new security dilemmas by granting membership on a selective basis; and because of concerns that an expanded membership would undermine the Alliance's cohesion. NATO has therefore concentrated on developing new links with the new democracies of Central and Eastern Europe, and talks generally about 'projecting stability and security' into the region. The European Union, on the other hand, is likely to open up to new members from the east – although not immediately. However, expanding the EU raises a series of complex problems. First, expansion could well lead to institutional paralysis in the absence of 'deepening' (i.e. institutional reform and more effective decision-making procedures), but such deepening is politically contentious in a number of EU countries (not least the UK). Second, expansion to the east would involve considerable financial cost for existing EU members. Third, new and relatively poor members from the east would be in direct competition with the EU's existing 'poor' members from around the Mediterranean – namely Spain, Portugal and Greece. Finally, new members from Central and Eastern Europe could bring their ethno-national conflicts into the EU, causing the same sorts of problems as the Gnaeco-Turkish relationship has done for NATO and for the EU's relations with Turkey.

THE DEMISE OF THE WESTPHALIAN STATES SYSTEM?

Earlier in this chapter we considered how the nature of international relations in Western Europe has changed in the postwar period given the emergence of a 'pluralistic security community'. In conclusion, we need to address the issue of whether the nature of the European states system – the origins of which can to traced back to the 1648 Treaty of Westphalia – has itself changed in significant respects.

There is little dissension from the view that the end of the Cold War signifies the end of the Europe of Yalta (characterised by bipolarity and East–West conflict). More controversially, some have gone further and suggested that it is not only the Europe of Yalta that has passed away. As Pierre Hassner notes, the 'order of Versailles (the borders and states that emerged from the Ottoman and the Austro-Hungarian empires)' is also being challenged by the processes of political fragmentation and decomposition in Europe. At the same time, as Hassner (1993: 53) notes, the 'order of Westphalia – the idea of a system based on territoriality and the sovereignty of states – is also being called into question.'

The durability of the Westphalian states' system has been questioned because of a series of secular trends in global politics. Globalisation and political fragmentation have been eroding the effectiveness, sovereignty and legitimacy of the nation-state. In Western Europe, the traditional powers of the nation-state have seeped upwards to the European Union; downwards to local and regional levels of government, and outwards as industrial production, finance and service industries have become increasingly transnational in organisation. This has led some to pose the question: what will replace the order of Yalta, Versailles and Westphalia? In other words, what sort of international system is likely to develop in Europe in the twenty-first century as a result of globalisation and political change?

Clearly, no definitive answer to this question can be given. But I would suggest that the post-Cold War system in Europe is likely to be increasingly complex, multidimensional and multilayered. It will tend to be characterised by a variety of actors, authorities, loyalties and identities. Indeed, it may well resemble the model of 'A New Medievalism' outlined by Hedley Bull which he described as 'a system of overlapping authority and multiple loyalty' (1977: 254–5). Such a system might prove less orderly than the states system of Westphalia. Nonetheless, it does seem to accord with current trends in Europe. If such a neo-mediaeval system does indeed emerge in Europe in the twenty-first century, it will force us to rethink many of the fundamental concepts and values upon which our societies are based, including the nature of democracy, human rights and security.[10] It will also force us to think anew about how we can achieve both order and justice in the European international system.

NOTES

1. For a provocative study of these issues, see Blackbourn and Eley (1984).
2. 'To find the main reason for today's threat of war, we must go back to the year 1945, to Yalta. It was there that a helpless Europe was divided; it was there that agreements were reached for military zones of occupation that would become spheres of interest as well. Yalta gave birth to a system of international relations based upon a state of rivalry and equilibrium between the Soviet Union and the United States. Whether the three old gentlemen who met there knew it or not, the idea of the Iron Curtain was born at Yalta', (Konrad, 1984: 1).
3. 'Contrary to Yalta's later reputation, an agreement to partition Europe was not reached there. It was rather the deplorable lack of any clear consensus on this and other matters that explains the summit's notoriety' (Masty, 1988: 17).

4. For a discussion of these and related aspects of European integration process, see Jopp et al. (1991).

5. For an interesting perspective on this see Coker (1992).

6. This 'neo-realist' view of international relations is associated primarily with Kenneth Waltz (1979); see also Keohane (1986).

7. Antony Giddens (1990: 520) has argued that globalisation 'should be understood as the reordering of time and distance in our lives. Our lives, in other words, are increasingly influenced by activities and events happening well away from the social context in which we carry on our day-to-day activities.'

8. Antony McGrew (1992: 320) has argued: 'Processes of globalization vary considerably with respect to their global reach and the extent to which they penetrate different regions of the globe. Thus some regions are more deeply implicated in global processes than others and some are more deeply integrated into the global order than others. Even within nation-states some communities are enmeshed in global networks whilst others lie completely outside them. And this unevenness is replicated across different issue areas; for instance, the same nation may well be highly integrated into one set of global activities but be hardly implicated at all in others. Coming to terms with the unevenness of globalization is an essential ingredient of a more critical appreciation of its dynamics and consequences.'

9. Joseph Nye and Robert Keohane (1972) define 'transnational interactions' as 'the movement of tangible or intangible items across state boundaries when at least one actor is not an agent of a government or an intergovernmental organisation'.

10. For a discussion of the impact of globalisation on democracy see Held and McGrew (1993), and for a recent discussion of the changing nature of security see Waever et al. (1993).

3 The European Union in Its International Environment:

A Systematic Analysis

Antje Herrberg

THE EU IN THE INTERNATIONAL ENVIRONMENT: EUROPEAN FOREIGN POLICY

The European Union and its foreign policy dimensions have generally been treated in *sui generis* terms, which increases the complexity of analysis in comparison to national foreign policy (Moravcsik, 1993). It is clear that coming to terms with the interaction of 15 not entirely converging policy agendas and one overarching institution is by no means an easy task. In the literature on the topic of the European Union in the international environment, as Richard Whitman observes in Chapter 4, no common ground has emerged. It appears that individual contributions in the literature seem to form parts of a mosaic with no clear pattern or consensus apparent.

In addition, the indecisiveness of the European Union in acting and reacting to international events has lead policy makers and academics to search for differing solutions and conclusions.[1] European Political Cooperation (EPC), the process by which the Member States of the European Community sought to cooperate in the area of foreign policy, has been largely analysed as a purely voluntary affair within the institutional context of the European Union. This has undergone a change with the European Common Foreign and Security Policy (CFSP) under the pressures generated by the end of the Cold War that were noted by Adrian Hyde-Price. Collaboration is becoming the imperative of European action, while it still represents a problematic mix of old and newly arising internal and external challenges. In the literature on this topic we can survey a form of pessimism that overshadowed the debate when the European Union failed to respond adequately to the Gulf or the Yugoslav crisis (Salmon, 1992; Wiberg, 1993). This is clearly reflected in the theory-informed approaches which have sought answers to the question as to whether the European Union is, or will be, capable of assuming an actor-like capability (Hill, 1993).

This chapter, in discussing European Foreign Policy (EFP), stresses the necessity of considering elements both inside and outside the European Union. In this light, attention needs to be paid to the increasing actions and interactions of the European Union with the world beyond. If we want to embark on such an analysis the realisation is that EFP cannot be studied in a vacuum and the role of the Member States needs to be integral to such an approach. The assumption here is that European policy towards third actors is a reality and to comprehend this reality this chapter will construct a system of relationships between known variables.

In offering such an approach, it should be clear that this attempt does not offer a new theory of international relations, nor does it aim to find a key to unlock the complexity of the dynamics of the European Union. The aspiration is to clarify some crucial methodological considerations and questions which may guide future theory formation. It is the operation of the European Union in a multilevel context encompassing the international environment, the European Commission and its constituent Member States which presents an analytical challenge which needs to be approached in a methodical manner.

The reality of EFP presents us with a range of issues. Firstly there is the lack of insight that might be offered from comparative approaches as the Union has been largely studied through a *sui generis* approach. Secondly, the European Union actually interacts with the international system alongside the representations of its own constituent Member States. As a consequence, the conceptualisation of the European Union involves the consideration of multilevelled and multidimensional interactions. In this chapter the stress is not upon the content of EFP, but rather upon its process, and thereby emphasises the importance of thinking in methodological terms about the European Union operating in an international context.

This chapter is broken down into two parts; the first section will iterate the problems that arise in the study of the European Union within the international environment; the second part outlines a systematic approach for the study of EFP and assesses its validity. The systematic approach offered places an identified set of variables in a causal relationship as the basis for further research into the interests of the Union and the variety of challenges that it faces. In this discussion the issues of identity and interest receive special consideration.

THE EUROPEAN UNION WITHIN THE INTERNATIONAL
ENVIRONMENT

A majority of studies which have analysed the 'new Europe' and its external challenge, appear to have a predominantly empirical orientation with
little interest in theory-informed analysis (Jorgensen, 1993). It is clear that
in the study of this new Europe, old problems continue to persist in the
study of international relations. It appears that the approaches to the study
of the European Union in the international environment are shaped by
three principle criteria. The first refers to the organisation of the international environment itself: In what type of international environment or
structures is the EU acting? Do we see the EU operating within a multipolar, unipolar or bipolar international structure? Are we analysing the EU
within a context of hierarchy, anarchy or the complex interdependence to
be found in structural realism (Pijpers, 1990)?

Second, how can one analyse the capabilities which it receives, in part,
from its constituent units (the Member States and the Commission) and
how does this influence the international environment? If by analysing the
EU as a dependent variable, how can one analyse the powers which it
receives, in part, from its constituent powers (the Member States and the
Commission) and how this power relates to the international environment?
Third, who owns and exercises power in the international system? Does
the state remain the significant unit of analysis or have other actors
emerged (Brown, 1992)? In general each of these questions have generated considerable theoretical reflection. In particular some authors have
attempted to comprehend these criteria in application to the study of the
EU as an international actor (Jorgensen, 1993; Smith, 1994).

These problems have their relevance in European foreign policy analysis. However, it appears that each focus upon a single problem leaves out
an essential dimension of the argument. Foreign policy analysis of the
European Union is carried out either at the expense of the individual
Member State, the collective or the international environment. When the
outside is the viewpoint, that is in asking how the European Union is
affected by the international environment, structure is taken as the ontological primitive.[2] When asking, on the other hand, how the European
Union's performance in the international environment is shaped by its
Member States, the structure, the international system is left out and the
ontological viewpoint focuses upon the agent, the Member States. The
combination of both agent and structure ontological viewpoints is generally seen as incompatible (Carlsnaes, 1994). However, both of these
approaches miss out on the rise of the international state and its relation-

ship with existing political authorities and the autonomous dynamic of the institutions that arise. While accepting it might not be possible to blend these ontological viewpoints, there is, nevertheless, scope for viewing them as causally interlinked.

Hollis and Smith stipulate that there are 'two plausible stories to tell, one from the outside about the human part of the natural world, and the other from inside, a separate social realm. One seeks to explain, the other to understand...(and) combining the two stories is not as easy as it at first seems' (Hollis and Smith, 1990: 6–7). In addition, Goldmann (1994) argues that in the interpretation of an intricate story, such as one that involves the European Union, one should make use of all possible creative concepts in the application of theoretical considerations. Others however, are convinced that there is no way to combine these 'explaining' and 'understanding' accounts (Carlsnaes, 1994a).

It appears that combining understanding and explanation of the European Union in the international environment presents difficulties. At first sight it appears that two discrete levels of analysis need to be consulted, one which refers to the outside, and another which refers to the inside. The aim of establishing a third level of analysis which is capable of encompassing the European Union as a synergy of these two accounts could be viewed as both a desirable but a difficult option.

In line with Hollis and Smith (1990), 'understanding' here is seen as a concept that needs to be understood from within, exploring the meaning of why the European Union does exist and what the CFSP entails for the Member States. The question is essentially who, and what, makes up the institutional structure of the European Union in its foreign policy development. 'Explanation', on the other hand, seeks for its purpose to abstract the complexities of the internal (the European Union and its Member States) and external behaviour (the European Union and other international actors). These concepts are employed in this chapter because we want to interpret both the actions deriving from the place of the European Union within the international environment and how the actions of the EU impact upon this environment. Here we question how the international environment affects the European Union's foreign policy. What is missing from these two interpretations is what European foreign policy represents.

While accepting the above arguments as relevant to the analysis of European foreign policy there is a requirement for a third level of analysis that connects the 'within' and the 'outside'. This is because the cooperation in European foreign policy is taking place within the European Union which, as an institution which possesses both supranational and intergovernmental characteristics, will promulgate foreign policy to the outside world. In doing so, these levels are not thrown into one construct; rather they will be viewed as operating in a causal relationship. Modelling these relationships will help us in thinking about complex interactions occurring at either level of analysis. One can model the process of EFP formation in three levels of analysis. These three levels provide a useful framework to encapsulate a differentiation of units which will subsequently be applied in a systematic framework.

The Micro Level

The micro level helps to understand the European Union from a bottom-up approach. This level refers to the individual Member State of the European Union. The state level acts as a legitimiser for the society from which it derives and is the organising structure in formulating demands to the supranational bargaining level, the European Union. In order to maintain its status quo, a state, in transferring its authority toward the European level, will try to keep the support of its own civil society. The state might regard the institution of the European Union as a tool to further its national interests, because it may reduce the transaction costs of achieving certain goals on a unilateral basis. On the other hand, the collaboration required within the European Union can also be perceived as an impediment to the nation-state, for example when demands articulated by one state are not in accord with the aspirations of its own society or with the societies of the other states which take part in this collaborative exercise. It is in this instance that the role of national identity and European identity are of relevance. The activation of national identity versus European identity, which became a prime issue in politicising the ratification of the Maastricht Treaty, is an indication of this complex process.

In European foreign policy, the support of civil society is conditional upon how specific the expectations are of a third actor in the international system. Collaboration at the supranational level is facilitated if states transfer pragmatic interests relating to broad values which do not impinge on the sense of national identity. Therefore it can be reasoned that the political elite of a state will always try to bring forward demands that are, in essence, pragmatic and utilitarian, thereby preserving legitimacy derived from civil society. Other state actors will support such a supranational institution when it reduces the transaction costs of achieving their interests.

States have sometimes generated a 'Eurocompatible' adaptation of their own structure to facilitate the transfer of interest to the European Union level. Instances of this include the change of the Member States' legal systems to facilitate the processing of directives or the creation of special 'Euro' lobbies (Klöti, 1991).[3]

The Meso Level

The meso level refers to the European Union as an institutional actor, which is seen to have its own distinct set of dynamics. The interaction dynamic occurs when demands and interests channelled by the states interact with EU institutions which display a separate 'corporate' identity. Because states tend to assume a political identity associated with pragmatic demands, cultural identity is largely left out of this calculus. A democratic reform of the European Union which brings the citizen closer to the policy processes of the European Union might well change this phenomenon. The discussion in the latter part of this chapter will go into greater detail as to how decision-makers bargain on the basis of a common denominator in EFP and why they might agree to cooperate on specific issues with other states that are not on the policy agenda. The lack of action in EFP is often derived from the incompatibility of the two sets of identities on this level.

The Macro Level

In the area of EFP, the role of the 'international', the macro level, is decisive. Identity formation within the meso level in the European foreign policy level is essentially reflexive. If actors and institutions recognise and perceive the European presence as significant enough as to respond to it, then EFP can be said to have its own identity. The macro level of analysis encompasses the stability and the instability of the international system and refers equally to its norms. This is an important factor if we consider the expectations third actors invest in the European Union, and how adaptive it is towards changes in the international system. The international system 'selects' the EU to be a significant actor if it fulfils certain norms. A possibility is that the European Union does not fulfil the norms of the international environment and the expectations of third actors. In this case the international environment will select those institutions and Member States which fit into the established norms more effectively. In sum, the task is to strike a balance between a parsimonious approach that simply analyses the phenomenon in question, while simultaneously not falling into the trap of an over-simplification.

MODELLING THE EUROPEAN UNION AS A SYSTEM

The European Union's presence is a complex one. Hence there is a benefit in describing this phenomenon in simple terms with a view to mirroring reality where the researcher has the option of interlinking empirical references. A model can be seen as a metaphor. Therefore, by seeing the European Union as a conceptual system, we are able to use metaphors which could well also perform the function of a more developed theory (Nagel, 1961; McClelland, 1970; Reichenbach, 1949).

In employing a model for the European Union, there is an implicit quest for predictive power. While this should not mean that we have to think only and exclusively about forecasting the future, it should be equally possible that we can predict phenomena that have occurred in the past. Models employed should be simple and should be viewed as tools that have analytical capabilities to facilitate the treatment of causal relationships in a valid and thorough manner. The increased complexity of the post-Cold War 'order' requires a more thorough understanding of the conditions which give rise to systems, what shapes their 'identity', what their dynamic characteristics are and what new, important, independent variables arise.

In considering the complex interactions that occur both within and outside EFP, it is desirable to construct a model that is parsimonious enough to accommodate the forces present but which focuses on the most important issues in relation to the issue we are dealing with. The contention here is that the presence of the European Union should be seen as a two-level game (Kelstrup, 1992). Therefore, as we are dealing with complex triangular interactions, we require a methodology that will help us to recognise complex interactions so we can make an attempt to fill the gap between understanding and explanation.

Just as we are using the model as a metaphor, the term *system* is employed equally so.[4] It is now the task to construct a system of concepts and relationships of how we can solve this problem. But here again, the system that one aims to model depends on the specific hypotheses that one poses in relation to phenomena. Reality consists of a number of multiple systems which are equally determined by differing criteria. The particular system that one constructs to consider one question might well include or overlap with other systems. Just as we can construct a system of EFP, we equally could establish a system examining cultural identity or an institution, say the European Parliament.

The focus upon systems theory in the literature of international relations in the past twenty years has been upon Waltz's approach towards system theory, which has been thoroughly discussed (Dougherty and Pfaltzgraff 1971; Jervis, 1978; Ruggie, 1982; 1989; Brown, 1992). Mirroring the reality of the Cold War, theories of the international system were simple, parsimonious and static (Snyder and Jervis, 1993).

The fact that systems theory appears not to be *en vogue* is due to two principal reasons. First, it represents the realist school of thought constructed at the height of the Cold War, an approach whose utility is disputed. The second mainly concerns the criticism of Waltz's *Theory of International Politics* (1979), which asserts that structural features explain little unless actors' perceptions of meaning are taken into account (Wendt, 1992). The logic of the conventional systemic theory is to take structure, whether international or domestic, as a determinant of state and interstate interaction. The relationship of the state to its society is largely omitted. Waltz's model implies that structure determines behaviour in terms of mental processes of rational calculation, where people act on behalf of their definition of the situation most closely resembling reality as assessed by outside observers. This action is expected to give sufficient explanatory power to structural theory.

The high degree of abstraction present in (international) systems theory arguably offers little of utility to policy-makers. Taken as a theory, this is probably so. However, the system model, used to relate complex phenomena in a more lucid manner, allows the positing of new hypotheses concerning the European Union as a foreign policy-making system.

The general systems approach provides a linkage between the inside (input) to the outside (output). Therefore, systems are categorised by designating a whole set of functions by virtue of their interconnectedness (Rapoport, 1964; Boulding, 1956a; Easton, 1965; Friedrich, 1963; Kuhn, 1962; Mesarovic, 1962; Haas, 1969). Utilising this definition one may first recognise the integrating powers on the micro level, the corporate identity on the meso level, and the recognition of the interconnectedness of the whole as a system. Consequently, we can use such a device to evaluate European foreign policy where such a system can be readily distinguished from the environment from where it receives stimuli. Understood as a purely analytical device, variables can be defined that shape the system.

EFP as a system refers to the national interests of the individual member states (which are termed units) concerning a specific issue area under which the EFP is expected to produce action. Variables include: the assertion of national identity and its pressure at the state level; the level of integration already present in the policy issue; the perception and relationship of states with regard to the specific issue; the degree of identity or independence at the institutional level; the reaction of third states towards EFP and participants in EFP; and, notably, the pressures and constraints of the international system.

The system as a dynamic device acquires a memory over time. That is, if the system operates smoothly and effectively in some issue areas there is a strong likelihood that it will do so in the future.[5] This built-in memory device gives it a consciousness. This consciousness is dependent on the interaction of the different elements of interests, identity and identity of interests.

The European Union, as an open system, is embedded in an equally open international system, which is shaped by a multitude of systems and units (such as the Member States or sub-state actors) and is also coupled in varying conditional ways, at each time depending on the arrangements of its parts (Snyder and Jervis, 1993: 4). It is argued by James Rosenau that the international system can be divided into distinct levels of analysis: 'To distinguish between systems and subsystems is to provide a methodology for unravelling complexity. By their very nature, complex systems encompass both wholes and parts. We can begin to understand them only if we employ a method that allows us to move our analytical eyes back and forth between systems and subsystems and thus between collectivities, their subgroups, and the individuals that comprise them' (Rosenau, 1990: 41).

Hence, if we consider the international environment, the European foreign policy system is a subsystem which is embedded in a complex, overlapping and concurrent international system. The EFP system receives inputs both from its individual units and the international system. These units represent states in a position to be 'heard' by the (sub)system, the European Union. In European foreign policy, Member States of the European Union formulate their interests through inputs consisting of specific demands which are backed up by support structures. Support may consist of quantitative (material support) or qualitative structures (iterated bargaining in other issues). How these demands are converted into outputs will be discussed more specifically below (see Figure 3.2 later).

The simple diagram in Figure 3.1, portrays the European Union as an open system which receives inputs from and formulates outputs to the environment. While the 15 member states of the European Union form an integral part of the system, they are at the same time in close interaction with their societies and the international system as well. The system hence has multiple feedback loops.

Four important features of this system should be noted. The first refers to *organisation*. The world polity or its subsystems could be easily perceived as a disorganised whole where the number of variables are indefinitely large and behaviour is erratic and unknown. The contention here is that one could conceive of the European Union as an organised

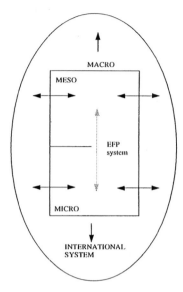

Figure 3.1   The European Union as a (foreign policy) subsystem of
the international system

(sub)system. In doing so, we have a purpose in seeking patterns that are
fundamental to the understanding we have of the European Union.

The second feature is the dynamics of *interaction*. The European Union
as an interactive (sub)system displays both supranational and intergovernmental dynamics. It is for this reason that the dynamic of the European
foreign policy (sub)system revolves around an identity of interests rather
than one single identifiable identity. As pointed out before, the European
Union in the meso level consists of two sets of identities: the corporate
identity of the Commission, and the interests of the states which come to
bargain for specific measures. These identities are detached *per se* from
the classic definition of European identity since they exclude the European
interest in the representation of purely pragmatic interests by the state
level, and also because the corporate identity of the European Union
shows little democratic relevance to the nation-state. When the definitions
of identity meet, a closed EFP system may come into existence. The
specific issue of European identity is discussed in greater detail by Ulf
Hedetoft in Chapter 9 of this volume.

Thirdly, it is important to consider the *cohesiveness* of the system. With a
strong sense of an all-encompassing European identity, the more cohesive,

i.e. the tighter, the system is the more effectively it can react to the international system. On the other hand, in the formulation of demands by the individual Member States towards a European foreign policy response, there are common notions of political identity, as for example in the belief in democracy and in the protection of human rights that EFP attempts to promote in other parts of the world. The EFP will remain pragmatic and its development is thereby triggered and strengthened by external stimulus.

The cohesiveness will also affect the stability of a system: the tighter the subsystems are interlinked in their specific interests, the greater the impact of significant actions of one component (or actor) on other components, and the greater the chance for a system change. The degree of tightness and interlinkage depends, in other words, on how successfully the European Union defines its aims and how these act as a specific guide to policy promoting a clear identity to the outside. The prerequisite is the existence of an identity of interests which may be general enough to achieve support with an articulated body of values related to the political identity (see also Haas, 1969: 101). Only in this way can the states still act as legitimisor of their national and civic values. Accordingly, the international identity of the European Union clearly differs from European identity at large.

Paradoxically we can expect that the creation of a supranational European identity, as evident in an ever closer (if unlikely) interlinkage of an identity of interests, is a destabilising factor for European foreign policy. That is, if one state acts in contradiction of the identity of interests, the greater is the impact on the identity of interests and the greater the likelihood of a system breakdown. The contradictory action of one state in bringing about a system breakdown may have the result that the other states will have to offer an account of this failure to their own civil societies. Further, the failure to act will cause the international system to resort to bilateral relations with individual member states. It is evident that a decision taken by the EFP (sub)system can be binding only to the extent that it is supported by its Member States.

Hence, it is not surprising that European foreign policy has to this date remained a soft agreement: no specific measures have been taken and cannot be taken to bind actors into a specific decision-making system. In fact, the present arrangement of *ad hoc* practice conducted on a set of interests, evolving into an identity of interests when promulgated to the international system, exists because an all-encompassing identity formation has not been possible.

Fourth and lastly we can derive from the above that the European (sub)system increasingly *decentralises* when decisions taken by one subsystem or component are not followed by the system as a whole. This might have counter-effects within the system and could have a direct relevance on the effectiveness of the presence of the European Union presented to the outside world (Herrberg, 1994). However, in the international system the predisposition of most international relations is to view tightly coupled systems as both destabilising and dangerous (Jervis and Snyder, 1991). A systems goal is stability. This stability is challenged, depending on the level of analysis, by the virtues and the aspirations of the individual and the organising structures of the (sub)system and the international system.

It has been established that the foundation of the international system is the principle of sovereignty (Wendt, 1994). Member States in the European Union, who aimed to protect their sovereignty in the Cold War era by establishing the European Economic Community, now share their sovereignty in institutions. While this is so, states may seek to cooperate initially to find a broad solution to a common problem. When specific issues arise, the state, will only cooperate in so far as its political identity does not undermine its legitimacy to its society. If specific issues penetrate and go beyond the political identity, states will opt to take that route in order to assure their legitimacy. In other words, the state will not engage with specific issue areas on the meso level which have a likelihood of impacting upon sensitive issues for the nation. Summing up, we can establish from the above that organisation, dynamics, cohesiveness and stability are all proceeding in a specific manner in a causal direction, linking the three levels of analysis.

Figure 3.2 exemplifies that each level of analysis, either the bottom-up or the top-down, can separately explain the European Union in its international environment. It is important to realise that EFP can follow from either level, where it is required to act in accordance with the rules of the (sub)system (micro and macro) and the international system (macro) (Kotarbinski, 1966: 247).

The subsystem's variable, consisting of both the micro and meso levels, clearly works with three sets of dynamics: first, when the Member States come to represent interests individually; second, in the way in which they evaluate the expectation of others; and third, how the institutionalised level develops norms on the basis of these expectations. These interactions will consequently feed into the policy *filter* which processes two sets of identities, namely those of the identity of interests in cooperation, and the corporate identity of the Commission, converting them into one recognisable identity in an issue area directed to an actor not part of the system in which they operate. It is only then that the filter produces what can be labelled a European foreign policy.

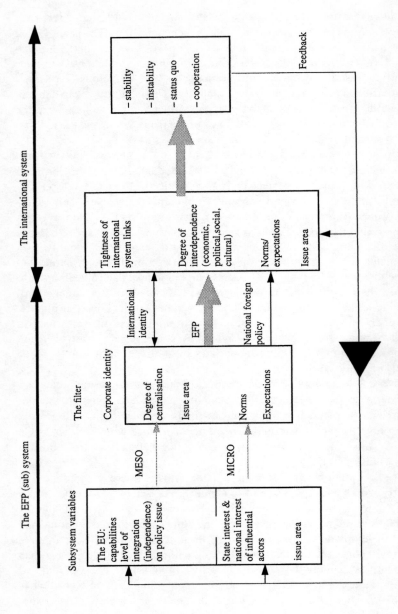

Figure 3.2 The European Foreign Policy System

The extent to which these sets of identities converge is decisive for policy formulation. European foreign policy has been most successful in steering economic diplomacy. Here its political goals are broad enough to preserve the identity of interests to such an extent that it converges with the corporate identity of the Commission, which now largely steers and implements economic diplomacy. An example of this activity includes the highly successful TACIS (Technical Assistance for the CIS) and PHARE (Poland and Hungary Assistance for Economic Restructuring Programme) programmes geared towards the newly established democracies of the Eastern and Central European states and the newly independent states of the Commonwealth of Independent States. In the formulation of an interim cooperation agreement between Russia and the European Union, the international identity came to the surface, when various economic aid initiatives were stalled because the intervention in Chechnya by Russian forces was opposed by both the Commission and the European Parliament (*Agence Europe*, 8 September 1995).

Each of the analytical units distinguished has a set of identities; while they are not mutually exclusive, they interact in a certain dynamic in the European foreign policy (sub)system. In the filter, the interaction of states and the institution might also activate interests to expand its organisational tasks when in the process of channelling interests to further a common output. However, while the filter channels *ad hoc* common demands made by its units, this does not mean that all of the units involved seek to realise identical values through it.

Within the norms of the EFP, interaction revolves around three principal patterns.

(1) Interaction is based on accommodation on the basis of the minimum denominator. Member States act strategically in pursuing their interests. Sometimes these interests have a high political salience in the national administration, thereby requiring the support of the civil society of the nation-states. Interests which have this political saliency are inflexible, and the establishment of an identity of interests which could by filtered by the Commission to produce outputs is hardly possible. States choose this route only because they are otherwise constrained in the choice of means to achieve these interests. These interests are often so specific to one nation-state that they are incompatible with other interests. Any cooperation on this one specific interest formulated by one state would incur reduced gains for another actor. As such, the filter serves only as a communication tool, but rarely filters common outputs into the international system. In this case, the interaction proceeds not from the foreign policy-making

(sub)system to the international system, but back to the micro level. While, therefore, there is no 'common action' on these issues, the meso level has nevertheless processed the interest, where other state actors will be informed and have given their input and position before an action was taken. What could occur, however, is that states, while not sharing the specific interest of the state which has put forward a demand, might agree to cooperate. In pragmatic empathy to the other state, they will recognise the need to collaborate, while making a compromise of their individual sovereignty. In their support these states will expect a return in negotiations with partners on other issues. Or in other words, concessions do not go beyond what the least cooperative bargaining partner wishes to concede.

(2) Another way of interacting concerns the splitting of the difference method (of which the Prisoner's Dilemma is an example), whereby issues are resolved between the final bargaining positions. In this method, co-operation entails equal gains to each of the Member States – this way an identity of interests evolves. In this way, the corporate identity of the Commission plays an important role because it assumes the role of a mediator. Within this dynamic, demands absorb and are converted into outputs. The corporate identity should be flexible enough to adapt to the identity of interests. Rules and norms within the EFP system, present in the conversion from interests, need to be accepted and all partners in the negotiation process are seen to upgrade the common interests of all parties. This is how the EFP system evolves an identity from within.

(3) If the international system equally recognises the output, the EFP will acquire an international identity. If the sets of identities do not clash – and this is the third scenario – the EFP system can be said to have a supranational character and an identity. This way of decision-making would allow the creation of a CFSP embodied in spirit in the Treaty on European Union (TEU). It has, at times, proceeded in a declaratory fashion and pursued economic diplomacy which had an effect in that some actors recognised the European Union as a clearly definable identity. Generally, however, Member States have produced separate outputs parallel to those of the Commission.

What are the outcomes of such outputs? As can be seen in Figure 3.2, any system has a feedback loop, which, after producing outputs to the international system, will convert to inputs at the micro level and the meso level. These inputs feed again into the system as a form of memory. If the feedback is negative, i.e. the international system refuses to recognise EFP, or the output has resulted in negative, unexpected results, the support structures will be withdrawn by the states as a way to support their legitimacy to their citizenry.

One outcome of a positive feedback concerns the stability which is expected under the cooperative behaviour achieved. This stability is achieved with the establishment of both informal and formal rules, norms or codes of conduct in which states have promulgated their interests. If the international system gives an expected response to the output produced, common expectations about the appropriate behaviour of the participating states may deepen these norms (Wendt, 1994). This accounts also for a positive feedback arising from the international system when the Member States will give an expected response to the output produced. If this occurs, states are more likely to continue their cooperation on the meso level because the pragmatic behaviour of states in formulating an identity of interest does not impinge on the societal levels.

In the case of a negative feedback one could expect instability or the likelihood of change in the meso level. This occurs when outputs receive no feedback at all, because they are not being recognised by any actors in the international system. An additional case could be if, in addition to outputs produced at the meso level, the micro unit (one Member State) produces an output on a unilateral basis which is contrary to the meso output. If, contrary to the expectations of the states, some outputs also have an impact on the cultural identity, or harm the interests of societal actors, these societal actors will try to undermine the legitimacy of the state which will then retreat from formulating its interests on the meso level.

If cooperation is achieved at both the micro and the meso levels, the pattern of interaction remains at a status quo; there is no initiative and no capacity for an upgrading of interests or for strengthening the collaboration between the micro and meso levels. Because an issue area might not be of the same interest to all of the Member States involved, the meso output will be a watered-down version of an output from a micro unit. While states and the institutions will continue to interact with each other on the meso level as a way to communicate common interests, these are unilaterally generated with a view to the present and future expectations of other actors. An institutional inefficiency, or a lack of quantitative support structures, will promote such a behaviour. The upgrading of the institutional competence of the European Union is one solution to this problem.

What has been reiterated throughout this chapter is that in European foreign policy there is a clear and causal interrelationship between these levels. This model, therefore, allows us to establish the impact of the international system on the units and the subsystem. At the same time it allows us to establish the linkages with important variables that are at work in the process of cooperation at either level of analysis. It is within the EFP filter that the conversion of interests and identities takes place.

However, the model poses one problem: one could easily be trapped in a circle of analysis, because feedback processes are occurring at all times feeding inputs into the micro and the meso levels. In the context of this model, this argument also suggests that we have to continue to ask about the concept of identity in terms of interests. As we have seen, the definition of European identity does not imply that its meaning is necessarily fixed (see also: de Vree, 1972: 80; Presley, 1960: 216).

The crunch question is, of course, the issue of the enlargement of the European Union, and whether this presents a case for arguing that a subsystem should, or could, have an optimal size. It is clear, however, that the newly democratised countries of Central and Eastern Europe which might join the circle will broaden the spectrum of political identity. Whether this could upgrade the efficiency of a European foreign policy mechanism remains to be seen. Another imminent issue is that the institutional side of the meso level needs to be considerably strengthened so as to overcome any breakdowns in communication among the states concerned. The institutional mechanisms which could accommodate a more specific output procedure have been and will be the focus of heated debates throughout Europe.[6]

Hence while the preceding account has advocated a systematic methodology, each of the steps and considerations have not been fleshed out to their full potential. However, in rethinking the European Union attention should not be paid only to the theoretical debates as such, but also to the methodological implications of the New Europe. Hence this sketch should be seen as part of a more encompassing project, one in which all researchers and students who are concerned with the new roles of European foreign policy are invited to contribute.

NOTES

1.   This is clearly reflected in the first report of the group of experts for the CFSP: *Die Voraussetzungen für eine glaubwürdige GASP im Jahr 2000.* Brussels, 19 December 1994.

2.   'Ontological' is the status and structure of the reality that was discussed, and refers to the subject to be investigated and our relation to it. A 'primi-

tive concept' is the basis of explanation in the sense that everything else is derived from this. From this, all other concepts are formed.

3.   Due to the untransparent decision-making processes of the European institutions, but an increasing awareness of the importance of the decisions taken, lobbies have established themselves in Brussels, for example large trade associations or single-issue lobbies such as those promoting Third World aid or human rights.

4.   That is as a 'dormant metaphor' rather than a 'dead metaphor'. While the former are quasi literal terms that help to conceive the topic through a different vehicle, to help in the process of problem-solving, the latter depicts its misuse. Here, metaphors have become so familiar, and so habitual, that we are not aware of their metaphorical nature and use them as literal terms (Mesjasz, 1993).

5.   For example, this became apparent when the Commission was entrusted with the task of coordinating international assistance efforts to Poland and Hungary at the 1989 meeting of the Western Economic Summit in Paris. The Commission succeeded in coordinating operations now known as those of the G-24. It should be added that the PHARE programme, for example, is financed by the Community budget with the Member States having a consultative role.

6.   The first paper that ignited this debate in view of the 1996 Intergovernmental Conference was that produced by the CDU/CSU parliamentary group of the German Parliament, co-authored by Mr Schuable and Mr Lamers and entitled *Reflections on European Policy*. It contains several suggestions for how the CFSP or external action could be strengthened (Agence Europe Documents, 7 September 1994).

4 The International Identity of the European Union:
Instruments as Identity
Richard G. Whitman

To Europe, a new acronym was born on 1 November 1993: the EU. The alacrity with which the new appellation of European Union has been taken up mocks the arduous process of the ratification of the Maastricht Treaty. The establishment of the European Union (EU) was not the herald of a transmogrification of the European Community; the elements contained within the Treaty have long been a part of the discourse on the future direction of the Community. The indeterminacy as to what constitutes the final project for this entity have been apparent since the signing of the Treaty of Rome and remain unresolved under the Treaty on European Union (TEU). The goal articulated in the respective Treaties remains the same 'ever closer union'.

The establishment of the European Union in the afterglow of the Cold War, and speculation as to the form and content of the post-Cold War international system marks a confluence in which the question of the significant actors in international relations is urgent. The uncertainty as to the final form in which the Union will be manifest, and the context within which it is now operating, lends itself to divergent patterns in the study of the significance of the international role of the Union.

One possible response to this state of flux is a preference for empirical over theoretical applied study (Keohane and Hoffmann, 1990: 276). The safe harbour of case study offers a tranquil resting place – away from the shifting currents of theory (that have recently been whipped up into a raging storm by postmodern and post-structuralist discourses). Studies of the international role of the Union that have given explicit consideration to theory have been marked by a promiscuity in the use of methodology, epistemology and ontology.

There has been a convention within the literature on the European Community of maintaining the distinction between the Community's external competencies as governed by the founding Treaties in contrast to

European Political Cooperation (now superseded by the Common Foreign and Security Policy) conducted among the Fifteen on an intergovernmental basis. The studies that have given separate attention to both these processes have undoubtedly greatly enhanced and deepened our understanding of the Union (Fielding, 1991; Nuttall, 1992).

In the instance of the external competencies of the European Community, arrangements are regulated by the Treaty of Paris, the two Treaties of Rome and their successive amendments. The Treaties demarcate areas of external competence for the Communities, expanding as the common policies of the Community expand, and to which Member States subscribe as signatories of the Treaties. In these areas of competence powers are formally granted by the Member States to be exercised on their behalf by the institutions and instruments of the Community as laid down in the Treaties.

The other dimension of the international activities of the Union are those that are usually designated as intergovernmental. The separation is on the grounds that this aspect of external relations stands outside the Treaty-based relationship of the institutions. European Political Cooperation (EPC) has been designated in these intergovernmental terms by successive commentators upon the process.

The successor to EPC, initiated by the Treaty on European Union, is the Common Foreign and Security Policy (CFSP), introduced by Title V, Article J of the Treaty. The CFSP represents a rite-of-passage for the Union, in Lodge's words, with 'the breaking of the security taboo' (Lodge, 1993: 227). The Treaty designates two methods through which the Union can pursue the objectives of the CFSP. The first, building upon EPC by 'systematic co-operation between Member States in the conduct of policy' and secondly, going beyond EPC by the designation of 'joint action' areas.

The spirit of this chapter is that separate consideration of these two processes, both empirically and conceptually, can be at the cost of neglecting study of the factors that are common to both sets of policies and can lead to a failure in exploring conceptual frameworks that may accommodate both sets of processes.[1]

There is an additional benefit in conceiving external relations and CFSP together. With the ratification of the Maastricht Treaty and the establishment of a three-pillar structure of the European Union there is now a single institutional framework that warrants study in totality. In the structure adopted to give expression to the European Union there is a departure from the manner in which the Community has organised itself previously. The three pillars are not accorded the same standing in the Treaty on

European Union. The Communities pillar retains its primacy (TEU, Article A).

The subsumption of both facets of the policy that are explicitly directed towards the outside of the Union, accompanied by the commitment to a single institutional structure, gives us an identifiable entity worthy of attention. Furthermore, the objective that the European Union sets itself, 'to assert its identity on the international scene' (TEU, Title I, Article B), requires us to give consideration to the instruments available to give effect to this aspiration. This chapter intends to highlight those instruments available to the Union for this purpose.

The first theme explored here is that of the attempts to characterise the Community against notions of what constitute international actors and the use of these measurements as attempts to gauge its performance by reference to the literature of international relations. The plea is then made for the clarification of the instruments the Union has at its disposal. It is only when these have been clarified can an assessment be made about the ability of the Union to realise its objectives.

The notion of international identity is not intended as a synonym for 'foreign policy' or 'external relations' which, as has been mentioned above, have had currency in the literature on the European Community. The use of the term external relations has been applied to identify purely EC Treaty-based competencies (Redmond, 1992). More broadly the term has been used as an attempt to broaden foreign policy to unify both the political and economic facets of relations (Clarke, M., 1992).

The chapter contends that although there is disagreement among scholars about the content and context of foreign policy, there is broad agreement within the wider literature that foreign policy is a function of the nation-state, i.e. nation-states and foreign policies are synonymous and this makes its application to the EU problematic.

The intention is not to posit a theory to explain or predict the formulation of the international identity of the European Union. Rather the intention is to refine and to make explicit the assumptions that will inform later empirical work. The second assumption of the chapter is that the international identity of the European Union can be conceptualised in a systematic manner. The assertion here is that there is a requirement to go beyond an administrative perspective, a focus upon the formal structure of policy-making (Clarke, M., 1992: 76–94). There is a requirement to attempt to identify a variety of sources or influences that both characterise, and influence, the international identity as it currently stands. These sources of influence are not all formal parts of the policy-making and implementation process, but can be viewed as having an impact upon the formulation of the international identity.

THEORISING THE INTERNATIONAL IDENTITY

It was asserted in the introduction that the focus for this study is the international identity of the European Union, the intention for this approach being to both inform, and to be informed by, the literature of the field of international relations (IR). This requires a brief consideration of the application of international relations theories to the European Community and now the European Union.[2]

The assertion is that the literature upon the international significance of the European Union (EU) can be considered in two dimensions. Firstly, that the EU has been considered within the literature of IR against existing preconceived concepts of what constitute the significant actors for an understanding of international relations. Secondly, there has been the construction of some new conceptual categorisations to fit the case of the EU and an attempt to measure the actor capability of the EU (Nørgaard, Pedersen and Petersen, 1993: ch.11). Both of these dimensions within the literature have given consideration to whether the EU is significant in the international arena.

In any account that makes reference to the literature of IR, the current status of the field prevents the emergence of any one conception within which to consider the EU. In the second account, the construction of some new conceptual categorisation to fit the international identity of the EU, two points are to be made. Firstly, such an approach should not need to imply that the nation state has been subsumed by a new EU entity. The treatment of relations between the EU and the constituent states of the European Union does not constitute a zero-sum game. Secondly, the designation of what constitute the criteria of actor capability for the EU can be to the cost of making clear the assumptions about the environment or structure within which this actor is located.

INTERNATIONAL RELATIONS THEORY AND THE EUROPEAN UNION

International relations denotes the transgression of national boundaries, with the substance of these transgressions encompassing a variety of phenomena. The potential scope and range covered by international relations would appear to put it beyond the mastery of a single field of study and suggest that any attempt to master its entirety would, of necessity, be interdisciplinary.

Two important assumptions about international relations underpin this study and immediately suggest the problematical nature of the application of international relations theory to the EU. Firstly, IR remains overwhelmingly dominated by literature and foreign-policy concerns generated from within the United States (Dyer and Mangasarian, 1989). Despite its advocation, a 'Eurodiscipline' of IR has yet to be realised, as Apunen (1993: 17) has noted: 'The existing mainstream of IR is unequivocally an Anglo-American tradition...' The question as to whether a putative Eurodiscipline should satisfy itself with the digestion or modification of this tradition, or to engage in wholesale contestation of the tradition, remains open.

Secondly, there is an acceptance of the premise that it is no longer possible to consider that the literature on theories of international relations can be conveyed through three competing perspectives or paradigms dubbed variously as 'realism', 'pluralism' and 'structuralism' (Viotti and Kauppi, 1993; Little and Smith, 1991; Olson and Groom 1991). Such threefold divisions are now highly contested and do violence to the complexities of the literature. The 'post-positivist' revolution in the literature of international relations, manifested in the emergence of critical theory, postmodern, feminist and historical-sociological guises, has created a new complexity in the theoretical literature of international relations (Smith, 1994). Although this has yet to make a sustained impact upon the study of the international role of the European Union there is an emergent body of theoretical literature substantive enough to be surveyed (Carlsnaes and Smith, 1994). Furthermore, the introduction of considerations of meta-theory have introduced a concern with ontology and epistemology that was not previously apparent in the literature and is exemplified by the work of Antje Herrberg contained in the previous chapter.

The notion of competing paradigms was not only confined to being a familiar device for organising and disseminating theories of international relations. It has also impacted upon the study of the international role of the EC/EU. The stress within each perspective upon different actors, processes and outcomes has been significant for raising different criteria as to whether the EU is to be considered significant in international terms.

The question that prevailed was whether there was sufficient explanatory redundancy within each (or any) of these three perspectives to help account for the international role of the EU, and whether it was considered to be significant in international terms. The importance of the work conducted through these three accounts was that it opened up a debate as to what was the appropriate framework within which to consider the international significance of the EC/EU. Furthermore, it is in the incommensurability of the three perspectives or paradigms that space for a debate on the EC/EU as an international actor was created. An alternative perspective, to be pursued after the accounts of each of these three perspectives, is whether the EU is *sui generis* in the context of international relations and requires the construction of a distinctive conceptual framework.

REALISM

Realist writers have given direct consideration to the EU, in the context of a denial of its role in international relations. This is best encapsulated by Hedley Bull's statement in 1982: '"Europe" is not an actor in international affairs, and does not seem likely to become one; the Europe with which I am concerned is the Europe of state governments' (Bull, 1982).

The thrust of Bull's thesis is that Western Europe cannot consider itself to be a 'power' in the international system unless it creates a defence identity free from reliance upon the military resources of the United States. However, even if there was the creation of a 'supranational' defence identity in Western Europe, this is viewed as a source of weakness in defence policy rather than of strength; the nation-states of Western Europe are viewed as irreplaceable receptacles of loyalty and units for making war are thereby the real sources of power.

Realism has found adherents who have sought to use the theory to account for developments within EPC (Pijpers, 1990, 1991). A denial that the EU constitutes a consequential actor in the international system, on the basis of a lack of means to project aggregated power (defined in strictly military terms), illustrates a recurrent criticism of realism's lack of consideration of economic issues – especially where there is an apparent disaggregation between economic and military power. The poverty of viewing power in terms of relative capabilities is that questions of 'transformative capacity' are side-stepped (Giddens, 1985).

The recurrent criticisms of realism were heightened in the 1970s with the sustained critique by pluralist perspectives, stressing realism's inability to incorporate transnational and transgovernmental actors in analysis of the international system. Pluralists were contending that there could also be forces transforming the essence of the international system away from the balance-of-power formulation of the realists. Realists were deemed unable to comprehend or accommodate the growing complexity and increasing interdependence of the global economy. The realist response was twofold: firstly, to refine a systemic account of international relations – as exemplified by the work of Waltz (1979); and secondly, attempts were made to modify realism to accommodate international economic issues. 'Neorealism' was part of a 'general lament/nostalgia' for a perceived decline in the status of the United States from a position as an economic 'hegemon' in the international system (Snidal, 1987: 580). Advocates of 'hegemonic stability theory' equated US dominance with international stability (Krasner, 1983; Keohane, 1984). A relationship was offered between hegemonic stability and the development of international 'regimes'. In an international system characterised by a hegemonic structure, international regimes will develop and their rules, norms, principles and decision-making procedures will be relatively precise and obeyed. In the event of a decline of the hegemon, a resultant decline in the regimes can be expected.

Regime theory has now been subsumed, alongside the study of international organisations and conventions, into the perspective dubbed variously neoliberal institutionalism, new institutionalism or rational institutionalism (Keohane, 1989). Adherents of the perspective attest that the literature has 'demonstrated that co-operation is possible even on realist premises' (Keck, 1993: 35). The greater claim is also made that it represents a synthesis of realism and pluralism at the systemic level of analysis.

The EU has attracted attention as an example of an international regime and more recently as the most significant test of theoretical virility in the ongoing interparadigm between neorealists and neoliberals (Baldwin, 1993). Hoffmann in the early 1980s, drawing upon the work of Krasner, stated that regimes are most likely to be established in areas where joint action is anticipated to produce better results than uncoordinated individual actions and that the EU was an example of this form of cooperation (Hoffmann, 1982).

The EU, designated as a regime in this formulation, has not served to anticipate a 'European super-state', but rather to preserve, regenerate and adapt its constituent nation-states. More recently, with the new insight offered by neoliberal institutionalism, Keohane and Hoffmann have turned their attention to the EU and retained the analytical primacy of the nation-state. The EU is viewed as an experiment in the pooling of sovereignty rather than the repository of its transference (Keohane and Hoffmann, 1990).

The notion has also been advanced that the EU was intermediate between a regime and a federation (Wallace, 1983). However, this conflates the two very different frames of reference within which both notions operate. Federalism implies here the ability to characterise the decision-making processes of the EU as analogous to those of a federation and this is a theme that Lisbeth Aggestam takes up in Chapter 5. In the federalist account the expectation is for the formulation of the EU as a single actor in international relations with powers to conduct foreign affairs solely ascribed to one level of the state.

In the regime theory explanation, the location and role of the state is not a matter of semantics, but rather is central to the theoretical rationale. There is no obstacle to considering whether the EU constitutes a 'federation', but this is ontologically incomparative to regime theory in the consideration of foreign policy. In Wallace's (1983: 406–7) terms a federation is marked by the presence of a central authority constituted by the members disposing to: 'an association of states, which has formed for certain common purposes, but in which the member states retain a large measure of their original independence'. This is pertinent in that it raised the question of the EU as the most appropriate level of analysis. The concept was applied to the EPC process in Bulmer's advocation of a two-tier analysis (Bulmer, 1991). In this account explanation for processes and outcomes is sought at the level of the Member State.

The question as to whether the EU was actually the basis for the regeneration rather than for the suppression of the nation-state in Western Europe has been well rehearsed by economic historians (Milward, 1987, 1993). The realist theory of international relations gained credibility, as a perspective from which to account for the EU during the 1970s, as integration theories waned in the face of intergovernmentalism and eurosclerosis (Kirchener, 1992: Ch. 2) .

PLURALISM

The mid-1970s were witness to a sustained challenge to the tenets of realism within IR – the overbearing concern with states, maintaining a separation between domestic and international politics and the primary importance of issues of power and peace.

Two related themes gained prominence in the literature. One theme was, 'transnationalism': the assertion that there are actors *in addition* to states that play a central role in international affairs. The term transnational organisation has been limited in some quarters to non-governmental organisations (Keohane and Nye, 1974), international organisations being viewed as important by facilitating the formation of transgovernmental formulations among national governmental officials that may conflict with national interests.

Another theme of the pluralist literature – 'interdependence' – challenged the realist distinction between the domestic and the international on the grounds that 'the domestic power of the state can be sustained only through international economic co-operation and political accommodation' (Hanreider, 1978: 1276).

Pluralist insights were considered fruitful in application to the EU, with regard to the dilution of the distinction between domestic and international politics (Webb, 1983). Significantly it is within this intellectual climate, marked by a concern with the variety of international actors, that there was the birth of the concept that has been endured in the debate on the international role of the Community: civilian power Europe. We will return to the concept below.

In consideration of whether the EU has a foreign policy the problematic distinction of maintaining a separation between high and low politics has remained within the literature (Morgan, 1973). Likewise, interdependence has recently resurfaced under the guise of globalisation. The question as to how far interdependence actually changed the reality of the power structure of the international system was raised in an effective form by Strange (1988).

The Pluralist perspective appears to offer a variety of avenues within which the EU can be explored and acts as a useful counterweight to the rigidity of categorisation promulgated by realists. The pluralist perspective offers consideration of collaboration as a counterweight to realism's conflictual view of international relations. The cost is a loss of parsimony and a heavy degree of voluntarism. At a minimum, interdependence and transnationalism are merely empirical phenomena, not explanations of the way that units act (Clarke, M., 1992: 4–5). In the context of defining the EU in international relations, a means of accommodating difference is gained over the realist conception of a unified actor, but at the cost of not exploring potential similarities.

The pluralist perspective also downplays two important areas with respect to the EU. Firstly, there is the extent to which conflict and the perceptions of national interest held by the Member States are required aspects of a full understanding of the EU. Secondly, maintaining a distinction between high/low politics is still perceived as an important concern by the Member States themselves as the three-pillar structure of the European Union initiated by the Maastricht Treaty illustrates.

STRUCTURALISM

Structuralist perspectives have been a less popular means of conceptualising international relations.[3] The 'structuralist' approach, in its economic guises, maintains the state, conceived in economic terms, as central to its analysis, but in the sense of its role as representing economic interests.[4] However, the centrality of the state is conditional upon the state servicing the interests of a dominant class. The relationship between states in the system is conceived in terms of the structure of a capitalist world-economy.

An illustration of work falling within the structuralist perspective is the world systems approach of Wallerstein (1974). In Wallerstein's view, the relationship between states is cast according to a threefold categorisation. 'Core states' maintain economic dominance over 'peripheral states' by determining both the conditions and content of the latters' economies. An intermediate category of semiperiphery states are important to maintain the stability of the world system. Semiperiphery states aspire to membership of the core, but also engage in exploitation of the periphery, thereby precluding the possibility of a polarised world system. The structure between the core and periphery is additionally maintained by the support from elites within the periphery states who benefit from the relationship.

The world systems perspective of structuralism has been applied in relation to an examination of the EU (George, 1991). The assertion is that the EU has engaged in an attempt to displace the US from the primary core status within the capitalist system. The proposition is that in order to facilitate this goal, the EU has engaged in a variety of activities, for example by attempting to create favourable conditions for inward investment, promoting the development of European multinationals, creating a new monetary regime with the EMS and constructing the single market. As a result of these measures:

> There emerged an economic zone centred on West Germany and extending beyond the EC to embrace the EFTA states, and also to incorporate in a more dependent status the ACP states associated under the Lomé convention. Beyond this, the logical further extension of this economic zone was into Eastern Europe, a traditional partner for the Germans; and into the Middle East, where the concentration of capital in the hands of oil-producing states after 1973 was added to their possession of the oil itself as an important incentive for the West Europeans to forge closer links. (George, 1991: 60–1)

World systems theory signifies the use of analysis in which the international identity and the foreign policy of the Union are accounted for using a holistic structural account.

The three perspectives, realism, pluralism and structuralism, within the discipline of IR remain influential in ordering and promulgating the theoretical literature of the discipline. Each offers three separate views of the EU within three differing notions of what constitutes international relations. If we turn to the specific question of what constitutes foreign policy we are confronted by a similar problematic. The acknowledgement that there is a difficulty in defining foreign policy is well rehearsed in the literature (Clarke and White, 1989). This is to be expected in a realm in which there is no consensus on the manner in which study should proceed. In place of agreement on a definitive *foreign policy* there is the recurrence of keynote concepts that set the parameters of debate.

As Smith has noted '...all perspectives on the subject of international relations contain statements about foreign policy' (Smith, S., 1988). In the literature of IR, the *state* and *foreign policy* are coterminous; all perspectives within IR have a conception of the *state* and of a resultant foreign policy. Where the differences emerge is around the conceptualisation of the *state* and its centrality to an understanding of international relations, and, in consequence, there are differing accounts of foreign policy.

In the realist perspective, the focus upon the state as a unitary actor assumes foreign policy to be the exercise of rational choice in the pursuit of national interest expressed in terms of power. The pluralist challenge to the tenability of the notion of the state as both a unitary and a rational actor reformulates perceptions of foreign policy. The state is viewed as an amalgam of individuals, bureaucracies and interest groups engaged in political and organisational processes that belies the aggregated notion of foreign policy conveyed by the realist account. Likewise, the issues on the foreign policy agenda are expanded and complicated by processes of inter-dependence and transnationalism. In the structuralist perspective, an understanding of the state in international relations is subordinate to an understanding of a global structure of political and economic interests. Foreign policy is to be viewed as one possible conduit of relationships of dominance and dependency that transcend state-centred analysis.

The problems we face in seeking to study the international identity of the European are profound. The absence of a general theory of foreign policy with which to adjudicate as to whether the European Union is in possession of a foreign policy or to assess whether and how the EU is an actor of international significance hampers accumulative research. The alternative, the retreat to case study, does not permit a shirking of theoretical assumptions underpinning such work.

THE EU AND NEW CONCEPTUAL CATEGORISATIONS

A debate on how to categorise the EU as an internationally significant actor was conducted from the early 1970s by attempting to construct a new conceptual category (Laursen, 1991). The debate focused around the issue of whether the EU was a 'civilian power' or a putative 'superpower'. A focus upon the EU as the manifestation of an integration processes emerged much earlier and such will not occupy us here.[5]

François Duchêne's notion of a civilian power Europe has resonated through the debate on the international identity of the EU (Tsakaloyannis, 1989). Duchêne's advance of civilian power Europe is most striking for the unsystematic manner in which it is advanced. The contention was that maintaining a nuclear and superpower stalemate in Europe would devalue military power and give scope to 'civilian forms of influence and action':

> Europe would be the first major area of the Old World where the age-old processes of war and indirect violence could be translated into something more in tune with the twentieth-century citizen's notion of civilised politics. In such a context, Western Europe could in a sense be one of the world's civilian centres of power.   (Duchêne, 1972)

Duchêne's conception of a civilian power Europe rested upon the inconceivability of a nuclear armed European federation and banishment of war from Western Europe:

> The European Community's interest as a civilian group of countries long on economic power and relatively short on armed force is as far as possible to *domesticate* relations between states, including those of its own members and those with states outside its frontiers. This means trying to bring to international problems the sense of common responsibility and structures of contractual politics which have been in the past associated exclusively with 'home' and not foreign, that is *alien*, affairs.
> (Duchêne, 1973: 19–20.)

The changed European context post-Cold War and the tentative exploration of questions of defence within and around the EU framework would appear to render the civilian power hypothesis obsolete. However, it offers contemporary insights. Firstly, the wider European context within which the Union operates is crucial for understanding its own significance. Secondly, the Union's pursuit of a distinctive diplomacy would appear to be imbued with the notion of 'civilianising' relations by creating forms of institutionalised association, partnership and cooperation. In short, there is the impact of a set of normative values on the international identity projected by the European Union.

A contemporary view of the EU with that held by Duchêne was Johan Galtung's (1973) assertion that the European Community was a superpower in the making. The EC was characterised as a *Pax Bruxellana*, an attempt to create a eurocentric world with its centre in Europe and a uni-centric Europe with its centre in the Western half of the continent. The power of the emerging superpower is categorised as twofold: the resource power and the structural power. The resource power of the Union is relative to that of the other superpowers then in existence. Structural power is considered to be the international structures which the EU is promoting that will serve as instruments of structural power.

Without accepting the premise of Galtung's argument – that the EU is a neo-imperial entity – it is possible to utilise two elements to explore the international significance of the Union. The Cold War context in which these latter approaches were articulated is no longer in existence and the relevance of the notion of superpower, as then conventionally understood, is no longer useful. However, a comparison of the resource power at the disposal of the EU would be one measure through which to explore the relative international significance of the Union.

Gunnar Sjöstedt (1977) adopted a distinctive tack upon the question of how to give consideration to whether the EU is an international actor. Instead of attempting to align the EU with an existing international actor category, Sjöstedt constructs criteria of actor capability as a means of assessing whether or not the EU can be assessed as possessing actor capability. The properties that are identified as necessary for actor capability are sevenfold: a community of interests; a decision-making system; a system for crisis management; a system for the management of independence; a system of implementation; external communication channels and external representation; community resources and mobilisation system. However, the objection to the use of this framework is that it posits the prerequistes for actor capability without addressing the significant sources of influence that assist in giving an account of why the actor conforms to particular behaviour. In short it ignores the environment within which the actor operates and through which it seeks to implement its policies.

TOWARDS AN ALTERNATIVE?

Sjöstedt's specific attention to the requirements of accounting for actor capability returns us to the emergent concern with second-order theorising on the European Union. Metatheorising has recently entered the debate on the international significance of the European Union (Jorgensen, 1993).

Jorgensen has articulated the metatheoretical incommensurability of existent approaches to the study of EU external relations (understood as both treaty-based and intergovernmental competencies). Theoretical approaches to the study of the Union have been categorised as to their location within a metatheoretical matrix of ontology and epistemology.

Jorgensen has assigned theories as to whether they are agency interpretive, agency objectivistic, structural interpretive or structural objectivistic perspectives. Jorgensen makes clear that the choice of the level of analysis has far-reaching consequences for any subsequent steps that are taken in the research process of the EU's external relations. The article is extremely insightful but the implications of considering the EU as a unit of analysis are not fully explored.

Without engaging in a direct debate on epistemology and ontology the starting point for an alternative is proposed here in which the European Union remains the unit of analysis. The starting point, in contrast to Sjöstedt, is to propose a set of existent phenomena for which explanation is being sought. Furthermore, the focus is upon one of the facets that Sjöstedt identifies: a system of implementation. Therefore, this chapter is a plea to clarify the capabilities of the Union by the identification of the instruments that the Union has utilised as the first stage in beginning an exploration of actor capability. Therefore, it is not an attempt to close the capability–expectations gap identified by Hill (1993) but rather to seek a greater clarification of the capabilities of the Union as a prelude to conceptualisation of Europe's international role.

The 'system of implementation' identified as necessary for actor capability above can be characterised as a set of instruments that are available to the European Union These instruments are not formally identified by the Union as its 'system of implementation' but provide a typology by which we might establish a framework to consider the extent to which the EU is fulfilling its aspiration to assert its international identity. In short, the exercise here is pre-theoretical.

It is possible to identify five sets of instruments available to the Union that provide manifestations of the international identity: informational, procedural, declaratory, transference and overt.[6]

(1) The area of *informational instrument* concerns the promulgation of overviews of the rationale of the Union's relationship with the world outside. The informational form of the identity would designate the areas in which the Community has formally expressed a rationale for policy either in strategic or in specific terms. Examples of the strategic rationale might include articles of the founding treaties (Article 110), the declaration of the Rhodes Summit on the Europe of 1992 or the Luxembourg Report on the establishment of European Political Cooperation and now

Title V of the Treaty on European Union establishing the Common
Foreign and Security Policy.

Specific rationales are intended to designate the intention to establish or
to reorientate policy in a particular area. Examples of specific rationales
include the declaration on the situation in the Middle East in November
1973 or, more recently, the Council of Ministers' directive in January
1990 authorising approval for association agreements with Central and
Eastern European countries. Some of these latter rationales are given procedural expression, as in the instance of the Lomé Convention or the relationship with the Association of South East Asian Nations (ASEAN).

(2) The *procedural instrument* dimension of the Union refers to the
standing institutionalised relations that are established, for example either
in regionalised form as noted above, or constituted on a bilateral basis
such as with the United States.

(3) The *transference instrument* denotes the financial and technical
assistance relationships that the Community has created outside the
Community, e.g. the Tacis programme or the European Development
Fund. The transference dimension can also denote negative transference –
the use of sanctions.

(4) In the *declaratory* sphere, the well documented communiqués of the
EPC process illustrate the substantial use that the Union and its Member
States make of this dimension.[7]

(5) The *overt instrument* refers to the physical presence of the
Community and its representatives outside the Community. This can be
either on a permanent basis, for example the establishment of the external
delegations of the Commission, or more transitory – visits of the troika or
the bicephalic troika or the dispatch of monitors, for example, to the
Russian elections.

The question is then raised as to what framework within which to consider the decision to have recourse to these instruments. A tentative suggestion is offered here drawn from a theme within the literature of
international relations. The process of the implementation of the international identity of the EU could be treated as a system analogous to the
treatment of foreign policy elsewhere within the literature (Kegley and
Wittkopf, 1991). Furthermore, this takes up the suggestion offered by
Antje Herrberg in the previous chapter that a variety of EU phenomena
may be amenable to systems thinking.

The treatment of the instruments of the international identity of the EU
in this manner requires qualification. The use of a systems approach is not
an attempt to assert that the EU can be classified taxonomically with
nation-states. Neither is the use of a systems approach part of any project

to construct a general theory of foreign policy. The contention of this approach is that by using a systems framework, as suggested by its application to the study of foreign policy, insights may be offered to construct a framework to assess the instruments of the international identity of the European Union.

If we are to adopt a system as the organising framework for our study there is a requirement for the sources of influence upon the international identity and their respective relationships to be stated in a more explicit form. The application of systems thinking and systems analysis has been widespread across both the sciences and the social sciences (Boulding, 1956a, 1956b). Systems thinking makes conscious use of the particular concept of wholeness captured in the word 'system' to order thinking. (Emery, 1981). More specifically, in the field of international relations systems approaches have proved attractive in the search for a general theory of international relations at either an individualistic level (Rosenau, 1971) or at a holistic level of analysis (Kaplan, 1957).

The application of the idea of systems, as developed in Easton's work (heralded as a revolution of political science), was to the political system of a state. Easton (1953, 1965) took the political system as indistinguishable from the state, and interactions were taken as the unit of analysis as opposed to political structures. The framework offered by Easton was intended to serve as the basis for a general theory of political science. Utilising a systems approach does not require a commitment to such congruency, or sharing epistemology with theorists who have adopted the systems metaphor.

With respect to external sources of influence upon the implementation of the instruments of international identity of the European Union, we have to be clear about the boundary we are creating. Clearly, we are not distinguishing in terms of a domestic and an international environment. Rather, we are interested in those elements that are outside the system that constructs and represents the international identity but which are of substantial importance for accounting for the international identity of the EU.

Firstly, we could designate the milieu: the geographical, economic and technological status that coincide with the Fifteen and both give the Union significance and inform the areas of concern for the Union. Secondly, there are the changes in the structure of the international system which have been of particular significance to the Union both within Europe and beyond. Thirdly, it is necessary to make clear the network of relationships that the Union has created for itself and which defines its international environment.

Richard G. Whitman

The second of the sources of influence that have been examined are
those that have been designated as legal sources. This denotes both the
formal system of rules under which the international identity operates and
the differing legal instruments through which relations can be conducted.
This requires the designation of the requisite articles within the Treaties
and the formal system of rules that have governed European Political
Cooperation and now the Common Foreign and Security Policy.

The third source of influence is the decision-making structure. A focus
upon this structure requires an emphasis upon how the decision-making
structures for both the external relations and EPC/CFSP have been progressively drawn together.

The fourth source of influence is the Member States. The Member
States could be considered as aggregated entities viewed as important in
several areas. Opening up the motivations of the Member States opens up
another unit of analysis: firstly, the specific areas of foreign policy interest
that their membership have placed upon the Community agenda and the
consequence of each enlargement upon the international identity; secondly, areas of concern that have been retained by the Member States as
unsuitable for Community consideration; thirdly, attitudes towards intergovernmentalism or integration and the impact upon the international
identity. Consideration can also be given to the European Parliament as
having a distinctive role beyond its formal competencies, and to the fact
that it has contributed a dimension to the instruments available as part of
the international identity of the Union (Bieber, 1990).

It is important to bear in mind that the sources of influence identified
above are specified by their functions in the construction and representation of the instruments of the international identity and not by their formal
political or constitutional authority. The assertion of this study is that the
specification of a set of sources that both impact upon, and articulate, the
international identity represents a systematic treatment of the Union that is
not prevalent in the literature.

Two formidable problems face this systems approach and are beyond
the focus of this chapter: firstly, how to introduce a sense of dynamism
into the account, secondly, how to account for change, over time, in the
structure of the system. In the latter instance the recent uptake of interest
in integration theory remains to be explored further.

In short, the proposal is for an exploration of the international identity
given expression as the instruments that are available to the Union. The
policies pursued by the Union through the instruments of international
identity represent recourse to common instruments. The proposal is for a
framework intended to identify the international identity of the Union as

distinctive from yet composed, in part, of attributes of the Member States. The assertion is that, although the Member States inform, and are informed by, the international identity of the Union, it is possible to retain a conceptual and analytical distinctiveness.

To recount, the goal the Union has set itself, to paraphrase the words of the Treaty, is the assertion of its identity on the international scene. The goal of this chapter is to begin consideration of how manifestations of this aspiration might be identified.

NOTES

1. A notable attempt to consider and codify both of these policies within a common framework was Ginsberg's work on joint actions (Ginsberg, 1989).
2. It is to be noted that reference will be made to the EU throughout although, of course, those scholars who were commenting prior to November 1993 will have been focusing upon the entity then entitled the EC.
3. Only about 10 per cent of the English language literature surveyed was considered in a survey to represent the structuralist perspective (Alker and Biersteker, 1984).
4. I fully acknowledge that there are also political-structural perspectives, most notably the work of Modelski (1978).
5. Ginsberg (1989) has utilised Schmitter's concept of externalisation for application to the EU. The question as to the logic of integration and its external implications I have left open.
6. These forms of the international identity have been drawn, with modification, from M. Clarke (1989).
7. *European Political Cooperation Documentation Bulletin* (Luxembourg, Office for Official Publications of the European Communities, various editions).

Part Two
Institutions and Interests: Between Supranationalism and Intergovernmentalism

5 The European Union at the Crossroads:
Sovereignty and Integration
Lisbeth Aggestam

The unique evolution of the European Union (EU) has posed a quandary to EU analysts since its inception. Its institutions and legal capacity have confounded traditional distinctions made between sovereign states and international organisations. The EU is a highly developed and multifunctional regional organisation committed to promoting 'an ever-increasing union' among its peoples, without necessarily forcing the withering away of the sovereign Member States.

There has been much debate and controversy whether membership of the European Union is posing a threat to state sovereignty. The European integration process has promoted a gradual transference of authority and power to the EU institutions, raising questions about the relevance of sovereignty. At the same time, it could be argued that state sovereignty expresses an important political reality as a fundamental principle in the international system of states.[1] This tension between sovereignty and integration is central in this chapter to understanding the political processes in the European Union.

The Union is markedly different from a purely intergovernmental organisation, in which Member States refuse to accept any formal limitation on the national veto. The EU institutions, on the other hand, have extensive competencies to make and revise policy, not least after the significant changes that the Single European Act (SEA) and the Treaty on European Union (TEU) consigned to the EU institutions. These new dimensions of policy-making and institutional transformation will be explored in this chapter.

The Maastricht Treaty contains far-reaching goals and intentions that raise questions about the future direction and purpose of the European Union. Moreover, the EU extended its membership in January 1995 and the queue for membership continues to grow. Enlargement(s) will have a great impact on the character, identity and cohesion of the EU. Considering that each enlargement will affect political coalition-building and the effectiveness of EU institutions, one may ask whether the Union will be able to continue to deepen the level of integration when new economic and political interests are added to the already heterogeneous EU.

SOVEREIGNTY AND THE PROCESS OF INTEGRATION

Integration may be seen as qualitative changes in the context of decision-making and as a positive goal to be achieved for more cooperative inter-state relations (Sullivan, 1976: 248). Integration can also be described as a centralisation of power and a gradual transference of authority and power from one level to another (Saeter, 1993: 88). From one perspective, this transference of authority to the European level may be interpreted as eroding what normally is associated with sovereignty, that is, the exclusivity and supremacy of the state. However, a 'zero-sum' perspective of the European integration process does not take us very far.

'Integration' is a multidimensional phenomenon and that is why there is a problem of conceptualisation and precise definition (Dougherty and Pfaltzgraff, 1981: 453; Ginsberg, 1989: 31). Part of the problem is that some scholars regard integration as a condition, while others see it as a process or a combination of the two. The distinction between 'formal' and 'informal' integration that Wallace (1990: 54) suggests is worth keeping in mind, as well as the fact that integration may connote interconnected but distinct aspects, such as economic, social and political integration.

The point of departure in this chapter is that the unequalled European integration process does not necessarily mould the founding of a formal sovereign union. Yet, one has to recognise that there exists a delicate institutional balance between state sovereignty and the process of integration. That Member States have had their freedom of decision and action constrained by an international organisation is not entirely original, but the institutionalised and legitimised way in which this occurs in the EU is rather different and new. To some extent, the EU institutions bypass the Member States' authority by dealing directly with the citizens and by acquiring some functions traditionally exercised by the state. It may therefore be appropriate to talk of the evolution of a supranational authority. Yet, the degree of transfer of functions from national to EU institutions is settled within an intergovernmental bargaining process (Moravcsik, 1991). In the ensuing sections of this chapter, intergovernmentalism and supranationalism will be examined, which may reveal the extent to which there exists a sensitivity to the transference of sovereign powers to the European level.

INDEPENDENCE AND INTERDEPENDENCE

'Independence' is frequently associated with the central aspects of sovereignty, referring both to political and legal aspects (Held, 1993: 216).[2] However, it may be useful to think of state sovereignty in terms of the constitutional (legal) aspects of statehood, while interpreting national independence as a state's freedom of action, even if the two ideas are closely interlinked and may be difficult to keep separate (Goldmann, 1994: 9). Thus, independence will primarily be analysed from the perspective of a state's autonomy in relation to the dynamics of international society, particularly in the context of the European integration process.

In the latter part of this century, many states have experienced restrictions on their autonomy, due to the evolving patterns of interdependence and the 'internationalisation' of issue-areas. This is the result of the rapid advancements in technology, communications and industrial and financial integration. 'Informal' integration of this kind has tended to undermine national boundaries and powers (Wallace, 1986: 367–9). This presents a basic dilemma to many European states of how to cope with interdependence, while at the same time securing some degree of autonomy. Governments of increasingly interdependent states have partly lost the control and authority over what occurs within their countries, as this 'globalisation' overleaps geographical and political boundaries. As Ingvar Carlsson, the Swedish Prime Minister, stated bluntly: 'While politicians have a "formal right to decision-making" in the national context, they face an increasing powerlessness.'[3]

Moreover, the domestic and foreign policies have become more complex and intermixed. This is exemplified in the overlap between international and domestic politics, where several domestic policy sectors include an international dimension (Holsti, 1983: 66; Karvonen and Sundelius, 1990: 22). Hence, governments find it more difficult to centrally control and coordinate policy in a coherent manner and to maintain an identifiable domestic–international distinction. Yet, as Hanrieder (1978: 1276) points out, this is also a consequence of the expanding state involvement in most aspects of social and economic life.[4]

Recognising the many ways that interdependence dictates international life, some states have chosen to exercise their sovereign authority by yielding parts of their decision-making prerogatives to an international body. In order both to regain and to exercise greater control over things that affect people's lives, states have become less inhibited in creating supranational institutions and making decisions at this level. As Rosenau (1981: 205) notes, this demonstrates the curious combination that '[t]here

Lisbeth Aggestam

is considerable evidence that the nation-state is maintaining its independence and authority even as global interdependence mounts and supranational entities acquire added authority.'

At the same time, one has to acknowledge that participation in an
international institution may well result in the state feeling less free to take
a line contrary to that which is being promoted by the majority of its
members. Even if the possession of a national veto is available, it does not
necessarily mean that it can be used without adverse political repercus-
sions. However, membership in an international institution generally
involves not just giving, but also receiving. On many questions, states will
have more influence and a better chance of achieving an approximation of
their goals in the collective pursuit of 'joint-maximisation' (Stein, 1983:
139–40). On this basis, it may be concluded that political independence (in
the sense of being able to pursue national interests) is enhanced in some
areas as well as diminished in others. The goals and interests may remain
national while the means become international, expressing what
Goldmann (1994: 11) calls 'the paradox of nationalistic internationalism'.

This perception is particularly evident between the highly interdependent EU Member States, where the majority of the members have accepted
that the withholding of national policy instruments may prove to be coun-
terproductive in some cases. Instead, the EU tends to be viewed as a forum
where access and influence over decisions have real effect, by increasing
the collective influence of its members. Hence, the benefits of participation
have increasingly been perceived as outweighing the reluctance to give up
sovereign prerogatives (Wessels, 1991: 136). The argument is that governments can achieve more of their national objectives through common
rather than unilateral action. This is also reinforced by the fact that the
Member States in the EU are viewed by many third countries as a coherent
force in international relations. This is explored by Richard Whitman and
Antje Herrberg in this volume. The EU speaks, for example, on behalf of
its members in the GATT negotiations and at the Organisation for Security
and Cooperation in Europe (OSCE). The implication of this is twofold.
From one perspective, it constrains national freedom to manoeuvre. From
another, it offers opportunities for individual members to mobilise EU
resources in support of national policy objectives.

However, a strong element of conditionality is still attached to
European integration. There exists a trade-off between the loss of autonomy and the attainment of influence. This requires a careful balancing of
costs and benefits by individual member governments. In addition, they
must consider how the domestic publics in the individual EU countries
perceive costs and benefits flowing from the Union. Yet, the trade-off

between the gains in influence and the costs involved in circumscribing a state's autonomy is not clear-cut or easily perceived. As has been witnessed in the post-Maastricht debate, there is not necessarily a congruence of opinion between the political elites and the general public in this regard.

INTEGRATION THROUGH INTERGOVERNMENTALISM

Divergent views have been expressed about how the European Union ought to be organised and how the integration process between the members should proceed. The supranational and intergovernmental positions are probably the most influential and contrasting in this debate. Supranational arguments are mainly (but not exclusively) put forward by federalists, who argue that some kind of federal structure is required to handle the increasing interdependence and to make the EU a more effective actor. Proponents of intergovernmentalism, on the other hand, contend that the problems arising from interdependence can be managed on an inter-state basis (George, 1992: 52). In this view, the nation-states are in a continuous process of sensitive adjustment, both to each other and to developments at the global level. However, the Member States never envisage relinquishing fundamental powers to a supranational authority. The conclusion is that governments refuse advancement of integration beyond a certain threshold, which could profoundly undermine their effective control of national decision-making.

Moravcsik (1991: 46) points to three principles that 'intergovernmental institutionalism' is based on: intergovernmentalism, lowest common denominator bargaining, and strict limits on future transfers of sovereignty. Intergovernmentalism may be characterised as a framework in which member governments gather to consider policy on the basis of unanimity, rather than on majority vote. This means that the view of a minority will be respected and that the pace of integration can only proceed as far as the most reticent Member State will permit. According to Moravcsik (1991: 47), this common denominator is crucial to establish among the three large EU Member States, especially in discussions on sovereignty-related reforms. The consent of smaller states can be 'bought off with side-payments'.

This focus on national interests and states as the principal actors has sometimes been depicted as a 'Gaullist' approach (Ifestos, 1987: 118). Sovereignty tends to be regarded as a basic element of statehood and governmental status, while it could be argued that proponents of supranationalism adopt a more 'functional view' of sovereignty (Webb, 1983: 12).

At the core of intergovernmental analysis lie the problematic notions of 'high and low politics'. It is argued that governments are able to determine those policy areas where the assertion of national control is considered critical to national sovereignty and independence, and those policy areas where they could contemplate relinquishing parts of their authority to international institutions (Hoffmann, 1982; Morgan, 1973). This distinction made by some 'realist' scholars is sometimes related to the differentiation between 'foreign policy' and 'external relations'. Foreign policy is associated with national independence, involving such matters as security and sovereignty, which are regarded as intrinsic elements of statehood and governmental status. They could therefore not be considered negotiable by governments (Webb, 1983: 12). In contrast, external relations containing economic and technical domains refer to 'low politics' with a lesser salience in the minds of the public in terms of associations with sovereignty and nationalistic attachments (Ifestos, 1987: 78). As mentioned above, this distinction can be problematic in the sense that different issues call for divergent patterns of policy-making. An issue characterised as 'high politics' may be divided into several issues receptive to different processes of policy-making, while for example more technical issues may become areas of 'high politics' (Judge, Earnshaw and Cowan, 1994: 42).

The development of the EU into an international actor does, however, create a tension between the inclination to national independence and the process of integration (Sjöstedt, 1977). Yet, as I pointed out in the previous section, many policy issues are no longer purely national concerns. Moreover, it has become increasingly difficult for an EU member to follow policies that are consistently out of line with those of the other member states. Nevertheless, the contention is also true that 'each government views the EC through the lens of its own policy preferences' and that 'EC politics is the continuation of domestic policies by other means' (Moravcsik, 1991: 47).

The main postulate of an intergovernmental approach to the EU is that national governments have successfully retained power, despite the evolving integration process (Bulmer, 1983: 355; Moravcsik, 1991: 47). Governments have avoided an 'open-ended authority' to central institutions of a supranational kind, which might infringe on their sovereignty. Instead, the importance of the governments is institutionalised in the European Council and the Council of Ministers, where the habit of consensus-seeking tends to be the norm (despite the possibility of majority voting as stated in the SEA and TEU). The adoption of unanimous positions in the Council greatly limits the possibility of the European Parliament achieving a policy impact by utilising divisions among the

Member States (Judge, Earnshaw and Lowan, 1994: 42). This is some-times interpreted as intergovernmentalism predominating over suprana-tionalism, or as national interests proving stronger than a 'Union-wide' interest. While it is certainly true that agreement on reforming the Union (the so-called Intergovernmental Conference) is characterised by inter-governmental bargaining, the European Union as a whole has moved down the road to forming some kind of a supranational authority. The question is – what does this denote? This is what we will explore in the section below.

SUPRANATIONAL INTEGRATION AND COOPERATIVE FEDERALISM

In contrast to the intergovernmental approach, proponents of supra-nationalism generally view sovereignty as an anachronism in an interde-pendent world, since it no longer corresponds to the capacity to exercise full control or effective freedom of choice (Webb, 1983: 12). Supra-nationalism consists of a number of interrelated elements, of which major-ity voting in an international institution is one of the most noteworthy. Viewed from this perspective, it is not an express power or right as such, but rather a political quality accorded to an institution. However, it is important to underline that supranationalism is, to a great extent, a matter of approach and interpretation.

For Haas, the notion of 'supranationality' denotes 'a cumulative pattern of accommodation in which the participants refrain from unconditionally vetoing proposals and instead seek to attain agreement by means of com-promises upgrading common interests' (Keohane and Hoffmann, 1991: 15). This is a more modified view compared to the one Haas (1964: 16) proclaimed in his earlier neofunctionalist work, in which he stressed the shifts of loyalties and political activities towards new institutions with jurisdiction and authority over the nation-states. Nevertheless, Haas still describes European integration as 'the existence of governmental authori-ties closer to the archetype of federation than any past international organ-ization, but not yet identical with it' (Keohane and Hoffmann, 1991: 15).

Federalism is a relatively conscious legal-political strategy as to how integration can best be promoted. The essence of the integrative process is the evolution of new supranational structures, which limit the power of the Member States. This strategy does not merely imply a centralisa-tion of power, but rather a distribution of powers and responsibilities to several political levels, in order to accommodate both diversity and unity (Hay, 1966: 92). Yet, the shortcoming of this view of integration is that it does not help us in explaining how integrative forces and processes arise and proceed. It only provides a strategy for the final stage of integration.

The term 'cooperative federalism' may be a more suitable description, with its emphasis on the mixture of both federalism and intergovernmentalism. As Wessels (1991: 149) notes, '[t]he central features of this process lead neither to a federation in the traditional notion nor an extensive use of intergovernmentalism.' Rather, it points to the complexity of the Union as a hybrid system containing both intergovernmental and supranational dimensions of decision-making.

To clarify the concept of supranationalism, I think it is important to keep two features of supranationality separate, even if they are closely interrelated in praxis. First of all, we may talk of supranational decision-making referring to majority or weighted majority vote. This was, for example, evident in the Single European Act, which reinforced supranational decision-making by providing for qualified majority voting on issues relating to the completion of the internal market. Secondly, we may refer to supranational institutions, relating to the degree that international institutions enjoy independence from the Member States. The EU Commission and the Court of Justice are often characterised as supranational. The principle of direct effect and the supremacy of EU law over national law makes national courts no longer sovereign in areas within the competencies of the Treaties, and national parliaments no longer sovereign in passing new legislation in those areas.

Hence, supranationalism raises questions both about qualitative changes in the context of decision-making and about the power and authority of international institutions. This, in turn, may lead us to contemplate the way in which such developments have weakened the authority of states and their capacity to survive in their traditional form. It is obvious that supranationalism affects the sovereignty of the state, especially in the exclusive competence of a government within its territorial frontiers. The traditional claim that sovereignty entails a consent to all legal obligations requires that cooperation operates on the basis of the unanimity rule (James, 1986: 187). Where a state is bound in law by the decision of an international institution, majority rule would clearly infringe the principle that states must remain in control of the extent of their legal duties. Notwithstanding this, international practice clearly shows that states asserting themselves to be sovereign have at times agreed to be bound by the majority of an international institution, as the absolute adherence to the unanimity rule would make cooperation more difficult.

In summary, it is worth keeping in mind that although the concept of supranationalism refers to a process of integration, from an intergovernmental to a more 'federalising' process, we are not talking of a federation as such. If the process finally led to this 'end-product', the concept of supranationalism would lose its meaning. That would imply that the members had decided to give up their status as sovereign states in favour of a sovereign European Union. Instead, the European Union of today may be described as a forum in which the Member States are 'pooling' their sovereignty (Williams, 1990: 302). Implicitly, this is an abdication of exclusive sovereignty in a limited field, where the EU exercises the collective sovereignty of the Member States through a decision-making process of qualified majority rule. As mentioned earlier in this chapter, a zero-sum perspective between the existence of sovereign Member States and the European Union may be less constructive when analysing the integration process. The EU is a flexible, disaggregated series of patterns, arrangements and institutions that express a collective, yet pluralistic, identity. There is no single or uniform policy process. The patterns of policy-making and the roles of member governments and EU institutions vary considerably from sector to sector, depending on the extent of EU involvement, the type of instruments used, and the continuing importance of national policies.

'A UNION OF STATES WITHOUT UNITY OF GOVERNMENT'

Brewin has expressed the idea that while the European Community clearly is not a sovereign state, it is, however, better conceptualised as 'a union of states' rather than as an international organisation (Brewin, 1987: 1). The idea of 'European Union' is the subject of a large number of diverging interpretations. However, Brewin's description is well depicted, especially since the Treaty on European Union (TEU) came into force. This strengthened EU institutions, yet it by no means approximates a realistic image of a modern sovereign state.

Unlike conventional international organisations, the European Union is a political structure set up by the Member States, whose objective is to go beyond merely inter-state arrangements typical of institutional activity at the international level, to stronger and more effective institutions. The EU bears a supranational character, in that its central institutions can act on behalf of the Union. For example, the EU enjoys international legal personality with a capacity to participate in the international legal community by having rights and duties attributed to it by international

law (Hay, 1966: 18). In this process, the role of the Treaties is of para-
mount importance, with their provisions on specific areas of policy and
their allocation of institutional responsibilities. This distinguishes the
EU from other international organisations, by providing the promoters of
common policies with constitutional authority and mechanisms for com-
pliance. Yet, as will be demonstrated below, it remains 'a union without
unity of government'.

THE INSTITUTIONAL INDEPENDENCE OF THE COMMISSION

The Commission is the executive body of the Union and often described
along with the Court of Justice as the most supranational element in the
EU system. It is made up of individuals who must, according to the
Treaties, act independently 'in the general interest of the Communities'
(Ludlow, 1991: 98). This pledge of allegiance to the European Union,
as opposed to national interests, implies an important supranational
role, in that each Commissioner may appeal to public opinion or
important social groups throughout the Union. Yet, despite the insis-
tence on the independence of the Commission, it may be worth remem-
bering that the Commissioners themselves are appointed by their own
national governments and they are therefore dependent on them if they
seek reappointment.

However, the characterisation as an 'executive' must not obscure the
fact that EU policy and direction mostly originate with this institution. In
fact, the Commission tends to favour policy formulation as opposed to
policy execution (Ludlow, 1991: 107). That is why the Commission often
has been seen as an important vehicle in the European integration process.
The 'strategic goal-setting' and policy drafting frequently emanates from
this institution. The 'political leadership', especially under the
Commission President Delors, has played an important part in keeping up
the integration momentum (Ludlow, 1991: 98). In addition, the
Commission is the one which prepares the budget, though it is decided by
qualified majority voting in the Council. This role is quite unlike that of
the central body of any other international organisation in spirit and in
content. That is why the political prominence of the Commission attracts a
whole range of interest groups who are eager to influence the shape of the
Commission's initial proposals. It should, however, be noted that the
Commission normally consults national representatives at every stage of
formulating its policy proposals, as the 'shadow of a possible veto' in the
Council of Ministers eventually decides the fate of the proposals.

Nevertheless, the right of initiative, and being the guardian of the Treaties, implies a powerful position in influencing the bargaining positions of the Member States. This function of 'political management' also entails the supervision of the implementation of EU policies. In the case of non-compliance, the Commission can intervene with the Member States to demand conformity with their obligations by recourse to the Court of Justice.[5] In pursuing this aim, the Commission is aware of the need to anticipate the responses of governments and that is why it does not take any rash action in taking governments to the Court without exhausting all other avenues to a settlement first.

Responsibility for implementation may also be delegated to the Member States due to political considerations and the Commission's own lack of resources (Ludlow, 1991: 105). At the end of the day, one often finds that both the Member States and the Commission are cooperating in the implementation of EU policy. Thus, the working method of the Commission is characterised by seeking consensus and consultation with the Council, the European Parliament and the Member States in order to increase the effectiveness and support for EU policy.

THE COUNCIL OF MINISTERS: A COMMON EXERCISE OF SOVEREIGNTY

The Council of Ministers, transformed into the Council of the European Union by the Maastricht Treaty,[6] can be characterised as the EU's actual legislature and focal point for decision-making. The Council consists of one national representative from each member government. However, it may be more appropriate to talk about Councils, considering that different ministers are involved depending on the type of issue and subject under discussion. The ministers meet every month, dealing with many different areas like, for example, agriculture, transport, education and the environment. Apart from the Agricultural Council, the most politically significant is probably the Council of Foreign Ministers.

The Council of Ministers is able to make laws which apply directly within all the Member States. The enacting of legislation is, however, quite unlike the legislative process in national parliaments. Contrary to the practice of national parliaments, the legislative functions take place behind closed doors and the European Parliament has only a minor influence on holding the Council members accountable. Furthermore, the constant formal and informal gatherings within the Council require preparatory meetings of officials. These include working groups and subcommittees, creating a pattern of transgovernmental exchanges of information and informal alliances of subgroups within different national governments. The administrative substructure, COREPER (Committee of the Permanent Representatives), is particular important in preparing and even completing the Council's work. This therefore further erodes the traditional boundary between domestic politics and foreign policy, and between bargaining inside a state's government and with other governments. Moreover, the Council normally bases its decision on what the Commission has initiated and prepared. The two institutions are therefore interrelated and work closely with one another.

If the Commission is the institution representing the general European interest, the Council of Ministers is assuredly the one in which the particular interests of each Member State are brought forward and that is why its role tends to be a contradictory one. Comprising the representatives of the Member States, it is a body that articulates and concerns itself with national interests, yet this was not what was intended when it was first established. Unanimous voting and the spirit of seeking consensus are still widely prevalent, especially on new policies (despite an increase in majority voting since the SEA and TEU). This reflects to some extent the perpetuation of intergovernmental bargaining with the consequence that the basic objectives of these legislative acts tend to be watered down in order to reach a common denominator. This is quite contrary to the supranational spirit in the original Treaty of Rome, with its aspirations to base decision-making on common interests and majority voting procedures. For some traditional federalists, the Council has therefore been seen to represent a major obstacle to progress towards a truly federal system (Wessels, 1991: 138).

An effective group, such as the Council of Ministers, offers the prospects of substantially increasing the collective influence of its members. On the one hand, this constrains a Member State's freedom of decision and action. On the other, it presents opportunities for individual members to put collective weight behind some of their approximate national objectives, which otherwise might have less of an impact. In this sense, EU policies may be viewed as an attempt to manage rising interdependence. As Wessels (1991: 137) pertinently notes: 'In the tension between the need for investment in common or co-ordinated policies and the strong preference to keep ultimate sovereignty, the Council is the major control mechanism through which states give up autonomy for well-guaranteed access and influence.'

This practice brings the EU system close to what we described above as 'cooperative federalism'. In this sense, we may well talk of the Council as 'a body at the supranational level' (Wessels 1991: 137).[7] This delegation of real powers to the Council of Ministers and its complex decision-making is markedly different from the more intergovernmental coordination of foreign policies.

The appearance of sovereignty having been pooled or ceded to the Council creates the impression that the centre has an independent external identity, necessary for maximising the overall interests of the constituent members. Therefore, when we talk of 'a common exercise of sovereignty', we may want to qualify it by referring to reconciliation of national interests among the Member States and an identification of common interests that exists across their boundaries. The procedures in the Council are novel and the EU legal system is indeed unique, and may justifiably be called supranational. Still, it is essentially an expression of the state's adjustment to changing conditions. The Council exists and serves the Member States at their discretion. The characteristics of the EU require a re-evaluation of the concept of sovereignty and recognition that sovereign powers can be transferred in parts. The process on which the members are engaged is not explicitly designed to supplant the Member States, but rather to complement them. It adds extra levels of government to cover areas that the national governments cannot handle alone, i.e. working out common solutions to common problems. Hence, the functions and effectiveness of the EU institutions are largely dependent upon the political will of its members.

THE EUROPEAN COUNCIL: THE COMMON ROOF OF THE EU PILLARS

The European Council can be described as the supreme organ or the 'common roof' of the three pillars in the European Union (Michalski and Wallace, 1992: 18). It is an outgrowth from European Political Cooperation (EPC), which contributed to regularise the summits of Heads of State and Government. In 1974, it was officially labelled the European Council, making it the seat of strategic decision-making for the European Community. However, in formal and legal terms it was not incorporated in the Treaties. Apart from promoting EPC, the European Council has worked as a source of political guidance for the whole Union and provided a vital link between the institutions of the EU and EPC.

The European Council is a 'hybrid' institution. Its decisions on their own have no legal force and it is explicitly intergovernmental. Hence, the European Council draws its legitimacy solely from summit communiqués, while it is left to other EU institutions to take the appropriate legislative and executive measures (Ifestos, 1987: 186–7).

The European Council symbolises the fact that the Heads of State and Government have arrogated to themselves the pace and direction of the integration process. It is perceived as the forum where the Member States ultimately guard their vital national interests. They set the general targets for action and arbitrate on contentious issues. Major and difficult issues which have failed to reach agreement can only be resolved at the summit. It is mainly Heads of State and Government who have the authority and the political clout not only to impose unwelcome decisions, but to reconcile them with political forces and pressure groups back in their home countries. That is why vital decisions regarding the future of the Union are normally settled in this forum. Thus, the European Council has indirectly a major impact on EU decision-making, and the process has therefore become more overtly politicised. The problems at stake have become politically more sensitive with the evolving integration, which has resulted in a more active public debate over EU issues.

From another perspective, the European Council can be interpreted as a response to the widening networks of foreign relations, in that the Member States seek a better intergovernmental cohesion to ensure that coherent policy signals will be picked up by the outside world. It is an exercise in coalition-building to increase the member governments' influence on international affairs (Bulmer, 1985: 92–4).

Overall responsibility for decisions in the Union is hard to tie down, though ultimate responsibility lies presumably with the European Council. The Heads of State and Government are individually held responsible in their national parliaments and by their electorates. And there is a reason for choosing this arrangement: the Presidents and Prime Ministers of the sovereign Member States constitute the ultimate legitimacy for the supranational integration process.

FROM COLLECTIVE TO COMMON FOREIGN POLICY-MAKING

The significance of European Political Cooperation (EPC) has increased since it was first established in 1970 as a loose intergovernmental framework. Its subsequent development has led towards a more complex institutional mechanism for concertation of the Member States' foreign policies. Although the framework of EPC and the subsequent CFSP often has been described as the most 'traditional' inter-state activity in the Union, it does constitute a genuinely new approach of cooperative collective diplomacy in an increasingly complex world. The list of EPC declarations shows that the Member States have succeeded in reaching common positions on numerous occasions, thereby creating a package of foreign policy standpoints, despite historically disparate interests and views. The Member States have committed themselves towards a better mutual understanding of international problems, through regular exchanges of information and consultations (the consultation reflex). This includes a commitment to consult other members before adopting national positions on foreign policy issues of general interest. When a common position is formed, it should constitute the central reference point for national policy (Lodge, 1989: 231).

However, EPC has operated and acted irregularly, which can make the task of analysing its actor behaviour difficult. The decentralised and intergovernmental character of EPC and the absence of an institutional centre has meant that it has been rather difficult to project cohesion and a united voice at critical times. EPC has mainly been a forum for consultation and selective common declarations, rather than an encompassing political process. That is why it has not succeed in producing consistently harmonised foreign policies. This is partly due to the fact that political power and control are not centralised but dispersed among its members. This allows room for a wide range of interpretations and permits the participants a great deal of freedom of action. Yet, one should not underestimate the fact that the habit of working together creates its own dynamic, which engages the national officials involved in a process of 'problem-solving' and confidence-building.

The consolidation and linkage of the EC and EPC in the preamble of the Single European Act (SEA) established EPC under a treaty form but did not fundamentally alter its character. The SEA confirms the distinctive juridical base of the EC and EPC systems, which to some extent signifies the Member States' continuing ambivalence over the relationship between the EC and EPC.

The political and strategic consequences of the events that have taken place since 1989 had a distinct impact on the Treaty on European Union, which established a Common Foreign and Security Policy (CFSP) as the 'second pillar' of the Union (Title V). This means that the CFSP has become more closely connected with the overall integration process, both conceptually and in practical terms. However, the purpose and direction of the CFSP are surrounded by some confusion and disagreement. The TEU (Article JI, paragraph 2) contains a long list of objectives, yet these tend to be vague in that it is not clear precisely how these objectives will be attained.

In some ways, the CFSP is not dramatically different from EPC. It remains an intergovernmental framework characterised by a vertical hierarchical structure with national representatives as the ultimate decision-makers, and a horizontal structure with intensive interbureaucratic contacts. The role of the 'Presidency' is particularly important in preparing and implementing decisions and in acting as a spokesperson for the Member States. The Commission is fully associated with the proceedings, but it does not play the same vital role as in the EU Council of Ministers. Instead, the Commission performs the function of a coordinating organ between the EU (based on the revised Treaty of Rome) and the CFSP. In some cases, the implementation of CFSP goals may require the use of EU instruments (for example, trade and aid measures). The European Parliament has no legal jurisdiction over CFSP activities and plays therefore a more limited role.

The unanimity rule is retained and thereby the right to block a decision. However, when 'joint action' has been decided it will be binding and the details of implementing it may be settled with a qualified majority vote. Still, the CFSP is not part of the EU system based on the Treaty of Rome and is therefore not subject to the same decision-making procedures, nor subject to judicial review by the European Court of Justice (Nicoll and Salmon, 1994: 207). Consequently, the commitments remain 'political' rather than 'legal', if only in the sense that there is no way of enforcing them. This symbolises the fact that the participating governments have been somewhat reluctant to relinquish important foreign policy instruments to a supranational authority.

What is new about the CFSP is that the Member States are more aware of the limitations of 'declaration politics' as pursued in EPC. The lack of a defence dimension circumscribes the capacity to intervene effectively in an international crisis. Both in the Single Act and in the Maastricht Treaty, the Member States expressed their determination and willingness to co-operate on security, albeit in the latter treaty the explicit statement of a defence dimension was added. The changing threat perception on the European continent has been followed by a reconsideration of the future role of the EU and brought security and defence onto its agenda.

However, the idea of expanding the scope of the EU to issues of military security is sensitive. After all, entering into the security and defence realm is not uncontroversial, considering that the Union for a long time conceived of itself as a 'civilian power' lacking military might and ambitions (Lodge, 1994). The diversity of national inhibitions about the full acceptance of collective European defence responsibilities has made the Western European Union (WEU) the most convenient forum for discussion and cooperation on military issues. The Maastricht Treaty does not contain provisions for a common defence policy, but the intention to make the WEU 'an integral part of the development of the European Union' is stated. This linkage can be viewed as a compromise between a more supranational policy and an overt dependence on NATO. In the discussion of defence, there is a division among the Member States on the priority they wish to give to NATO and the linked discussion of the role of the WEU. The resilience of NATO and the sheer cost of self-reliance in the defence field have so far limited the extension to cover military questions.

The attempt of the Union to frame a wider and more coherent political role has made it more visible in the international system. Yet, the uncertainty about the means and objectives of the CFSP leads to the conclusion that we cannot speak of a common foreign policy *per se*. There continues to be an ambivalence among the Member States as to the balance between the costs to their national sovereignty and the benefits they derive from pursuing a common or harmonised stance in international affairs. That is why the notion of a 'European interest' is controversial, as it implies the subordination of the members' interests in a largely abstract common regional interest.

CONCLUDING REMARKS

Analysing the European Union is an intriguing task considering that it is without precedent and parallel. It consists of a group of states which are working closely together on a wide range of issues and without doubt a new kind of arrangement has been established. The relative institutional independence that the Commission, the Council of Ministers and the Court of Justice enjoy does not find a counterpart in other international organisations.

However, the process on which the members are engaged is not explicitly designed to supplant the Member States, but rather to complement them by adding extra levels of government to cover areas which the national governments cannot handle alone. It is a 'problem-solving' approach, in that they are attempting to work out common solutions to common problems. Yet, a strong element of conditionality is still attached to the momentum of integration. There is an interplay between the reluctance to become dependent upon other countries and the rewards of participation.

The complex decision-making and the superiority of EU law can certainly be viewed as part of the process of 'federalising' the Union.

Lisbeth Aggestam

Nevertheless, the EU cannot be described as a fully fledged federation. There are several reasons for this, among which the lack of a coherent common foreign and defence policy is one. Furthermore, the Union has not proved convincing in moving much beyond the primarily negative stage of integration (the removal of barriers) to a positive one that would promote a European identity and interest. The principal problem is that it is not easy to set out coherent goals and clear definitions of interest, given the pluralism resulting from the Member States.

It seems like a fair conclusion to say that the Member States of the European Union are stuck between sovereignty and integration. Most of them recognise the necessity of closer integration and collaboration on many issues, but are unable or unwilling to mobilise the imagination or the coalition of political forces needed to establish a central political authority of the Union. Where the Member States finally strike the balance between sovereignty and integration will be a challenge for them in the future.

NOTES

1. The idea of state sovereignty can be viewed as a critical concept separating states from other units in the international system. This 'external' aspect of sovereignty is an organisation principle for the basis of the international system of states: see James (1986).
2. Held makes a distinction between *de jure* and *de facto* supreme power which is constructive to keep in mind when we talk about sovereignty. The first refers to the legal aspects of sovereignty, while the latter accounts for the factual determinants of the exercise of supreme power. See also I. Clark (1989).
3. *Dagens Nyheter* (26 October 1994).
4. See also Milward (1992).
5. The judicial function exercised by the Court of Justice has steadily redefined and extended the area of Community competence. It has asserted itself (along with the Commission) as the guardian of the interests of the Union against 'disobedient' Member States.
6. The earlier title is, however, still very much in use and is therefore employed in this chapter.
7. In contrast to Keohane and Hoffmann (1991) Wessels characterises the Council as a supranational rather than an inter-state body.

6 The Capacity to Act:

European National Governments and the European Commission

Klaus Armingeon

My theme is the capacity to act of governments in democratic political systems. Governmental capabilities face two challenges according to recent analyses. The first, the socioeconomic and political integration of OECD countries, entails a loss of autonomy and efficacy in domestic policy-making. 'The times have passed by in which national economies could be steered by national economic policy' (Scharpf, 1994a: 60). Michael Zürn holds that 'the national state has lost its efficacy in the domains of security, culture, communication and welfare' (Zürn, n.d.: 233–7). Another author argues that 'the nation-state has become an unnatural, even dysfunctional, unit for organising human activity and managing economic endeavour in a borderless world' (Ohmae, 1994: 78). The second challenge varies between countries and concerns the dominant modes of political decision-making. In some countries most decisions are taken in the course of bargaining, leading to grand coalitions and compromise; in other countries the dominant mode is majority decision-making within a competitive party system (cf. Lehmbruch, 1976: 12). In those countries where bargaining rather than majority decision prevails, decision quality is not necessarily worse, but the system of decision-making is cumbersome and there is some danger that it may be easily paralysed by conflicts which arise in the bargaining process (Scharpf, 1992: 25). Particularly in times of rapid social and economic change – and this applies to the last two decades – this inertia and susceptibility to bargaining breakdown might have fatal consequences for crisis management and policy reform. Until recently the hypothesis of the inferiority of bargaining systems – compared to majoritarian ('Westminister') systems – was widely supported in political science and, in particular, there was a shared conviction that bargaining systems were less efficient and efficacious in reaction to difficult policy-making challenges (Lijphart, 1994; Abromeit, 1992).

A solution to these two problems might be the shift of regulative competencies to a supranational level of decision-making (cf. Scharpf, 1991:

622). For obvious reasons in Europe this means the European Union. But because the centre of decision-making is the Council of Ministers and the European Council (Rometsch and Wessels, 1994), which are organised on an intergovernmental basis, the European Union resembles nations with interlocking systems of politics in that it is prone to blockage and inertia (Scharpf, 1994b). Since the European Parliament cannot play the same role as a national parliament, the European Commission as a supranational organisation endowed with considerable competencies seems to be the institution most able to regain the policy-making capability which nation-states have lost. This is supported by developments since the end of the 1970s which have led to the increasing influence of the Commission in the European Union (George, 1992: 9–16; Ludlow, 1991; Rometsch and Wessels, 1994). As an efficacious supranational institution, it could become the government of the European Union (cf. Weidenfeld, 1994: 34).

In this chapter I discuss whether the capabilities of national governments have actually declined due to globalisation (leading to economic interdependence) and – in some countries – joint decision-making leading to interlocking politics. I will also analyse whether such a loss of efficacy can be compensated by a shift of national competencies to the European Commission. I argue that all these hypotheses are valid only to a very modest extent. The European Commission is a system of joint decision-making at least as much as the Council. In addition, the European Union is exposed to and suffers from global challenges almost to the same extent as nation-states. In this regard the nation-state's inability to act due to globalisation and joint decision-making is a problem that cannot be solved by the European Commission. However, the question also arises as to whether diagnosis of these problems is correct at all. An empirical analysis of social and economic policies in OECD countries reveals that (1) since the most recent wave of globalisation the capacity to act of nation-states has not substantially diminished, and (2) political systems with strong elements of joint decision-making are not worse off in coping with challenges compared to systems corresponding to the 'Westminister' model.

I start with a qualitative analysis of policy-making in the European Commission. Subsequently I will deal with the room for manoeuvre of nation-states.

THE EUROPEAN COMMISSION

Is the European Commission less exposed and less helpless with regard to globalisation? Are the supranational elements of the European political system better able to cope with challenges than nation-states are? Both of these questions are of crucial importance in assessing the potential improvement of European policy-making caused by a shift of national competencies to the level of the European Union.

According to the literature on globalisation (cf. Zürn, n.d.), there are at least four fields of public policy in which the nation-state has lost its capacity to act. The first that should be mentioned is the field of social and economic policy-making. Since almost every factor of production – money, technology, factories and equipment – moves effortlessly across borders, the idea of a national economy has become meaningless (Zürn, n.d.: 234). The internationalisation of capital markets, completed in the second part of the 1970s, has taken away national sovereignty in the sphere of monetary and interest rate policies (Scharpf, 1987: 302). A second field of public policy, military security, has lost its effectiveness with the transitions in the Central and East European countries and the ease with which small states or private organisations – terrorists for example – could get hold of nuclear weapons. The notion of national security has become meaningless. In addition, environmental dangers cannot be fought effectively on a national level. And finally, even national culture has become outmoded by modern communication technologies. Only those cultural products which have a large market are now competitive. US products, which are least tailored to a specific national culture, are assumed to meet this criterion because they are developed to meet the requirements of consumers in very different cultural settings.

Provided these analyses are right, the lost capability to act cannot be regained by a shift of competencies from nation-states to the European Union. The European Union enjoys substantial influence in none of the above mentioned spheres of policy-making: EU Member States have no access to international capital markets which is different from that of other nation-states. There will hardly be much change to create autonomous and efficacious systems of military security pertaining solely to the European Union. A number of ecological dangers, caused, for example, by greenhouse gases, will be determined by economic growth processes outside of Europe and North America (Missbach, 1995). The most competitive cultural products and computer software are mainly produced outside Europe in North America. Hence, in this regard the European Union has no qualitatively better opportunity to cope with global challenges than do European nation-states on their own. However, when one looks from a quantitative perspective at the sheer size of the European Union and its markets, the possibilities for steering and coping arise, which nation-states do not have at their disposal. Without the European Union nation-states would drift like nutshells exposed to mighty waves on the ocean; compared to that, the Union is a deep-sea vessel on the lake of Geneva, immunised against some minor change and in turn creating some waves of its own.

There is a second crucial question: does the European Union have the capacity to act and is it able to respond quickly and efficiently to external challenges? As far as the European Council is concerned, there is consensus in the literature that it cannot do so due to its intergovernmental structure (Moravcsik, 1991). Because constitutionally the Parliament does not have the necessary competencies at its disposal, the European Commission remains the only supranational institution which could take the lead.

This assumption is supported by a number of findings. First, an increasing number of conflictual issues are submitted to the Union and Union policy-making (Edwards and Spence, 1994: 17). As the Commission's potential competitor, the European Council has difficulty arriving at compromises. This weakness could be a strength for the Commission (Héritier et al., 1994: 180). In every important negotiation the Commission is present as a continuous participant (Edwards and Spence, 1994: 12), while national representatives in the Council come and go. In addition the Commission enjoys increasing external reputation (Edwards and Spence, 1994: 12). Finally case studies of EU decision-making demonstrate the paradox of weakness: the fragmentation and intricate framework of the Commission make it strong against those external actors wanting to capture it (Grande, 1994). This would be much easier if the Commission were hierarchically ordered and simply structured.

However, the assumption of an efficacious and autonomous European Commission is not supported by analyses demonstrating that it is fragmented and highly dependent on internal horizontal processes of coordination. In addition the Commission is, in numerous ways, linked with national agencies – either directly or via the Council. This interlocking relationship hinders the Commission in both deciding and implementing policies autonomously. It is compelled to bargain.

BEING COMPELLED TO BARGAIN: INTERNAL DETERMINANTS

Interdependence inside the Commission is caused by three institutional peculiarities: by the collegial system of the Commission; by the relationship between Commissioners and their cabinets and Commissioners and the Directorates General.

Decisions taken by the Commission are based on the collegial principle: the President of the Commission has no special privileges, like a casting vote in case of a tied vote (Metcalfe, 1992: 403–4). Decisions need to have an absolute majority and frequently some members of the Commission are absent. Hence there needs to be broad agreement between Commissioners (Donnelly and Ritchie, 1994: 36–8). This permanent obligation to reach broad majorities prevents strategies of declaring certain issues to be life-or-death decisions of the Commission. This is all the more the case since Commissioners cannot be removed before the end of their term except in extraordinary circumstances, similar to the procedure of impeachment of the President of the United States (Donnolly and Ritchie 1994: 34). Hence Commissioners are under institutional pressure to arrive at a compromise as do Swiss Federal Councillors.[1] This implies that, contrary to governments in competitive ('Westminster') democracies, the political process in the Commission cannot be dominated by a President who wants to establish and implement his or her particular political programme. Rather, the President is a broker trying to coordinate and direct the bargaining process inside Commission.

In addition, the individual Commissioners experience severe restraints on their room for manoeuvre within the Commission. They have their own personal staff at their disposal, their cabinet, but they and their cabinet do not have authority over the Directorates General, as is the case in governments of Western nations. Various Commissioners share responsibilities for a particular Directorate General and there have even been Commissioners who were not assigned to any Directorate (Ludlow, 1991: 92; Fitzmaurice, 1994: 182). Hence there is no clear hierarchical structure in the relationship between Commissioners and the Directorates General. These relations are further complicated and obscured by attempts of cabinet members to counteract the Directorates and trying to direct them (Spence, 1994b). Closely linked to this complex pattern is a diffusion of responsibilities. Although Directorates General are assigned to individual Commissioners, these Commissioners are responsible for politics and policy of the Commission on a collegial and not on a personal basis (Metcalfe, 1992: 404).

While the separate Directorates General are clearly and hierarchically structured, the relations between the various Directorates General are obscure, often shaped by negative coordination and severe differences of power (Spence, 1994b, Metcalfe, 1992: 404)). In particular this is caused by differences in personal resources between Directorates General (Spence, 1994a).

BEING COMPELLED TO BARGAIN: EXTERNAL DETERMINANTS

Interdependence between the Commission and representatives of Member States is the result of a number of institutional mechanisms. They include the distribution of resources, the structures of decision-making and the personal links between nation-states and staff of the Commission.

With regard to distribution of resources, the weakness of the Commission in terms of staff size is of particular importance. While having far-reaching duties, the Commission employs only 18,000 employees (fall 1992). Out of this total there are only 10,000 employees in charge of political and executive tasks (Spence, 1994a: 66; Hay, 1989: 31; Metcalfe, 1992: 404). Therefore, because of its small staff the Commission is dependent at every stage of the policy-making process on the cooperation of national representatives and experts. This explains the strength and potentially high level of influence of lobbying of the European Union.

The decision-making procedure also forestalls autonomous policy-making on the part of the Commission. In the preparatory stage of a policy-making, national interest representatives and experts are of particular importance for policy design. Only one half of all proposals emerge from within the Commission; the others originate from national bodies. In order to increase the probability of the acceptance of a proposal in the Council, communication and concertation with national representatives are necessary. In the decision-making process the secretariat of the Council becomes important. It cooperates with the Commission. Often decisions are taken in the Committee of Permanent Representatives of Member States (COREPER). If COREPER has reached a decision, the Council simply ratifies it without further discussion. In cases where the Council discusses items, COREPER has done the preparatory work. In implementing a decision the Commission is dependent on national institutions and it is also dependent on the committees of national representatives ('Commitology') accompanying the implementation (Spence, 1994b).

An additional layer interwoven between the Commission and Member States is the result of personal dependence of members of the Commission on national governments. Once appointed, Commissioners cannot be removed, but national governments can abstain from nominating a Commissioner for another term if he or she has not adequately taken into account the interests of the nation from which he or she is the delegate. This dependence is most pronounced among cabinet members. Frequently they have got their job through interference by their national governments and circumvention of the normal career pattern – by *parachutage* – or by evasion of the competitive examination – the so-called *Sousmarins* – which is the normal gate to a job inside the Commission. (Spence, 1994a: 75).

Each of these findings demonstrates that the Commission is not an autonomous institution of the European Union and that supranationality and the interest of a common, integrated Europe are not the sole points of reference for its policies. Rather it is restricted to being a 'promotional broker' (Rometsch and Wessels, 1994) with regard to the Council. As an organisation in a closely knit network, the Commission has no autonomous capability of steering the Union (Metcalfe, 1992).

Hence, if globalisation and joint decision-making are the most important threats to the freedom of action of Western nation-states, the European Commission is not very likely to be the efficacious alternative to national governments. In the same way as in nation-states the European Union has to cope with data which cannot be circumvented and which are created outside its sphere of influence. And just as in many nation-states, governing is dependent not on majority and hierarchy but on multilevel bargaining between actors armed with veto capabilities.

Up until now it was assumed that globalisation has really diminished national government capabilities in the course of the last two decades. In addition, it was taken for granted that, compared to competitive ('Westminister') democracies, governments operating on the basis of bargaining are weaker and particularly sluggish in making decisions. However, evidence offered by international comparisons demonstrate that this is not the case.

GOVERNMENTAL CAPABILITIES TO ACT IN INTERNATIONAL COMPARISON

Both starting points of this study are quite plausible. The hypothesis concerning globalisation is founded on clear and impressive changes. For example, the external trade of Western European countries has increased by 150 per cent from the 1950s to the 1980s (IMF, 1994: 89). The number of international governmental organisations has grown dramatically in the last three decades (McGrew, 1992b: 12).

However, these quite plausible assumptions about the squeezed room for manoeuvre of national governments have rarely been put to an empirical test. The few analyses dealing with this question provide no clear proof that this assumption is valid (Garret and Lange, 1991). This could be the result of three blind spots in the globalisation thesis. First, it ignores the fact that Western nation-states have already been for a long time, at least since the end of the Second World War, interdependent, and their political structures, as well as their policies, have been shaped by this inter-dependence. Otto Hintze (1962) was among the first authors stressing this external determination of domestic politics, and Rogowski (1989) and Gourevitch (1986) provided ample evidence of this fact. Recent and important analyses have been done by Strang and Mei Yin Chang (1993) and Finnemore (1993). The increase in quantitative interdependence does not automatically mean shrinking room for manoeuvre of nations although the assumed linear relationship sounds quite plausible.

Second, this thesis often ignores the fact that nation-states are not help-lessly exposed to globalisation. Rather, they have several options from which to choose. Economist Richard Cooper (1986: 9–12) distinguished between five reactions: (1) passive acceptance of external requirements; (2) exploitation by free riding; (3) defence, which frequently appears as protectionism; (4) aggressive control of international markets through national means; and finally (5) constructive reaction, whereby new chal-lenges are seen and used as opportunities for reform. In recent debates, in the social sciences as well as in politics, it is often taken for granted that passive acceptance is the exclusive option.

The third blind spot of the globalisation hypothesis concerns institu-tional inertia and the distribution of political power within a nation. Even if the necessity to change policy type and direction is not under debate due to external restrictions, this does not mean that the respective changes are realised. An increasing number of empirical studies building on March and Olsen (1989) demonstrate path dependence of public policies. This dependence is caused by institutions. These paths cannot be abandoned *ad libitum* even if certain external challenges seem to suggest such a change. Researchers who take into account both the international relations and comparative public policy literature stress this point (Kohler-Koch, 1994: 177). In addition, the effects of differences in the political complexion of parliaments and governments are demonstrated in a number of studies, although some arrive at the conclusion that there is some impact, albeit rather weak (Klingemann, Hofferbert and Budge 1994). This being the case, it is not clear at all that these effects are eliminated by the quantita-tive intensification of transnational social and economic transactions.

The hypothesis linking domestic joint decision-making to inertia in response to external threats is also highly plausible and supported by a number of case studies of regulatory policies (Lehmbruch, Singer, Grande and Döhler, 1988). On the other hand, it has been argued that in cen-tralised political systems relying predominantly on majority decisions, reactions to threatening crises come quicker, but the risks of inadequate or wrong reactions are greater as well (Scharpf, 1991). In addition the decision capability in competitive democracies, the British Westminster model coming close to this ideal type, might be overestimated. Some authors hold that quick decisions are not related to long-term programmes because of the high probability that these programmes will be repealed by the next incoming government. Rather, these quick decisions are confined to policies which have a short-term perspective and are easily implemented. In addition, quick decisions in Westminister democracies may not be implemented at all due to administrative inertia (Abromeit, 1992: 314). A third point is raised against the supposed inferiority of joint decision-making. Once again it refers to the path dependence of public policy. In his most recent study Richard Rose (Rose and Davies, 1994) demonstrates that political programmes can be implemented and changed only in a long-term perspective, in Great Britain as well as in other democracies. Often decisions taken by governments have an observable impact on public policy only after the particular government is out of office for a long time. Contextual factors, a momentary distribution of political power for example, have few impacts in the short run according to Rose and others.

These arguments are compatible with the findings of recent research that decision capabilities in systems with joint decision-making are not inferior to that of Westminister democracies. Lijphart (1994) and Klingemann, Hofferbert and Budge (1994) demonstrate that Westminister democracies are not better with regard to macro-economic steering of the economy, quality of democracy, protection of minorities or 'policy response to electoral promise' (Klingemann, Hofferbert and Budge, 1994: 260). Frequently another advantage of systems of joint decision-making is overlooked. This concerns federal states where in a large number of policy areas – even if there is no formal interlock – competencies at one level are of considerable relevance to the other level. On these grounds they are more dependent on successful coordination between political actors than are centralised political systems. This dependence is much more pronounced in Western Europe than in North America and Australia. Hence one would expect that West European federal states are particularly restricted in their capability to act once a sudden external challenge appears. Making this assumption ignores the reflectivity and the capability to innovate of federal states. Due to the need to argue and convince in bargaining situations in federal states, over-reactions and ideological or not well thought-out policies are less likely than in political systems where few actors can make a decision without being forced to convince others of the soundness of their proposal (Benz, 1989: 192). In addition, in federal states alternative solutions to a problem can be tried in separate states. Once a central policy is needed for the entire country, policy-makers can choose between various solutions which have been put to the test previously and which have already proven their advantages or disadvantages. Regulation of collective labour relations in Australia at the beginning of the twentieth century (Armingeon, 1994a) or Swiss drug or energy policies (Linder, 1994: 59) are good examples of federalist states being flexible.

Following these arguments it is far from clear whether globalisation and joint decision-making have eroded the nation-state's capacity to act. My empirical test is confined to OECD nations and the time span between the beginning of the 1960s and the early 1990s. In this period globalisation takes place and is most pronounced in the years since about 1980 (Zürn, n.d.; McGrew, 1992b; Katzenstein, 1975). Hence it is to be expected that the room for manoeuvre of nation-states is much larger at the start of the research period as compared to its end. In order to test this assumption, statistics related to the strength of relationship between policies, institutions and political power distributions have been calculated for the period between the early 1960s to 1979 separately from the period between 1980 and the early 1990s. The strength of these coefficients should be much less in the last period compared to those for the first period. My data basis consists of quantitative indicators of policies and politics in these 23 OECD countries between 1960 and 1993. A first file was created for a triple cross-sectional comparison for the 1960s, the 1970s and 1980–93.[2] In order to check the results based on this file, an additional file was created. It is a pooled cross-sectional time series from 1967 to 1993, containing the most important variables of the cross-sectional file. As is the case in the first file, data for some variables end in 1990. In addition, in those cases where correlations were calculated using the Lijphart indicator, six countries are excluded due to missing data for that particular indicator.

Policy fields under consideration are current receipts of government, i.e. mainly tax policy, government outlays, social security transfers and public employment. All these policy areas are of major importance for the type and strength of the link between political systems and society. And it is argued that in all these policy areas, OECD countries experienced considerable pressure towards convergence due to globalisation and economic crisis, the latter being a common challenge to review previous policies and the former excluding strategies which give important societal groups, e.g. capital, an incentive to exit the particular nation. Seen from the point of view of globalisation theory, differences in mode and extent of politicisation of economy and society are extremely difficult to realise and are laden with great economic risks. States with an outstanding welfare state, with particularly high tax burdens, extensive public employment and large government outlays are supposed to come under pressure to create a 'lean state' or at least to stop the growth of state intervention. Failure to fulfil that task means that in times of greater transnational economic interdependence, capital outflow, reduced international competitiveness and, hence, low economic growth and high unemployment loom large (Scharpf, 1987; Hall, 1986; Merkel, 1993; Fröhlich, 1991). In accordance with our starting hypothesis, it is to be expected that the impact of genuine political factors decreases in these policy fields and that a convergence will take place towards a common and low level. Moreover, countries with strong interlocking politics should be slower and less perfect in this process of adjustment compared to centralised and competitive democracies.

Political factors underlying the change of welfare states were measured by two indicators. The first concerns the political complexion of government. This has been operationalised according to a formula developed by Manfred G. Schmidt (1982; 1992), which has proved to have some explanatory power in a number of comparative studies of welfare states. His indicators measure on a five-point scale whether a government is composed exclusively of left (non-left) parties (5 or 1), mainly of left parties (4 or 2) or of left and non-left parties to a similar extent (3). Since the expansion of welfare states was not brought about exclusively by the left but also by Catholic centre parties (Esping-Andersen 1990), a second indicator was employed measuring the combined shares of votes for Christian-Democratic and left (Social Democratic and further left) parties. The notion of joint decision-making or interlocking politics ('Politikverflechtung'), consociational democracies ('Konkordanz-Demokratien') or bargaining democracies refers to a different institutional configuration in which decision about policies are predominantly not taken by means of – frequently bare – majorities but by bargaining aimed at broad majorities, compromise and amicable agreement. To operationalise this concept, I followed Arend Lijphart (1984, 1994; Lijphart and Crepaz, 1991). He has developed a combined indicator for various aspects of bargaining democracies. In order to check the results, additional indicators were used which focus exclusively on the structure of party system or extent of unitarism.

Lijphart differentiates between competitive or majoritarian democracies ('Westminister Model') and consensus democracies. The latter are typically characterised by grand coalitions, a weak standing of government *vis-à-vis* parliament and political parties, a multi-party system with multiple underlying cleavages, proportional electoral systems and corporatism.

For all these aspects Lijphart gathered data pertaining to the period 1950–80 and combined the standardised scores to form an index of consensus democracy. This indicator refers to the structural preconditions for bargaining democracies; however, it does not indicate that in these political systems compromise is actually structurally preferred to (bare) majority.

Underlying Lijphart's model of consensus democracy is the assumption that no societal interest organised as a party can have a majority. Hence major political decisions are the result of a compromise between large coalitions of political parties. The larger the number of relevant parties in a given political system, the greater should be the incentive to create political decisions through bargaining. In order to measure the independent explanatory power of this aspect – party fragmentation as a structural incentive to bargaining – an indicator of party fragmentation is employed (Armingeon, 1994b: 73).

Lijphart's indicator is confined to one dimension of his consensus model of democracy. The other, federalism, is not measured. Hence for federalism, or its antipode unitarism, two further indicators have been used. Manfred Schmidt (1993: 141–2) has calculated an indicator for unitarism on the basis of Lijphart's work. It is composed of the elements unicameralism (vs bicameralism), tax centralisation and ease of constitutional change. With regard to the policy areas under study, centralisation of government income and outlays are of particular concern. On these grounds a coefficient was calculated which indicates the central government's share of the budget as a percentage of GNP.[3]

Since the dependent variables cannot be changed substantially in the short run due to institutional-legal restraints, the levels of the respective variables, i.e. government outlays or public employment as a percentage of total employment, are measured in ten-year intervals between 1960 and 1990/93. The major data basis of the dependent variables was the OECD (OECD, *Historical Statistics and Economic Outlook*, various years).

Based on these data and the research design, it can be demonstrated that the hypothesis about the impact of globalisation is hardly supported by empirical evidence. If it were to apply, the differences between national levels, i.e. their heterogeneity, would be less at the end than the beginning of the period under consideration. However, this is not true at all. It is only in the case of current receipts and social security transfers that differences were a bit smaller in 1990 compared to 1980 (Table 6.1). Moreover, the growth rates of the dependent variables should be particularly low, or even negative, in those countries where these variables reached high levels in the early 1980s. Indeed this applies to three of the four selected

Table 6.1 Convergence: heterogeneity of levels (standard deviation)

	1960	1970	1980	1990
Government employment (% total employment)	5.3	5.0	6.1	6.7
Social security transfers (% GDP)	3.3	3.9	5.1	4.8
Total outlays of government (% GDP)	6.1	8.0	10.6	10.5
Current receipts of government (% GDP)	5.6	7.5	9.7	8.9

Source: OECD, *Historical Statistics*, various years.

Table 6.2 Convergence: correlations between level at beginning of decade and changes between beginning and end of decade (1st diff.)

	1960s	1970s	1980s
Government employment (% total employment)	–	–	–
Social security transfers (% GDP)	–	–	0.36
Total outlays of government (% GDP)	0.45*	–	0.40
Current receipts of government (% GDP)	–	–	0.45

– Coefficient of correlation with p > 0.10.[4]
* $p \le 0.05$.

Source: OECD, *Historical Statistics*, various years.

variables, but not to public employment, as demonstrated in the correlation analyses (Table 6.2). Using the notion of a parallel downward shift in level, one could argue that in all the countries the extent of state interventionism has been reduced by the same amount irrespective of the level at the beginning of a decade. However, no systematic empirical evidence is available to support this assumption. No doubt, in all four policy fields growth was slowed down in the 1980s compared to the 1970s, but not necessarily compared to the 1960s. In addition the heterogeneity of change rates in the 1980s does not decrease generally (Table 6.3).[5]

For some European countries, and in the areas of taxes, public employment, and public outlays, the comparisons of 1960–1990 can be extended to nearly the whole twentieth century (data sources are Flora, 1983 and

Table 6.3 Convergence: standard deviation and means of changes
(1st diff., levels at end of decade vs beginning of decade)

Changes	1960s	1970s	1980s
Government employment (% total employment):			
Standard deviation	2.5	2.9	2.1
Mean	3.0	3.3	1.0
Social security transfers (% GDP):			
Standard deviation	2.4	2.7	1.9
Mean	2.6	4.7	1.3
Total outlays of government (% GDP):			
Standard deviation	2.7	5.5	8.3
Mean	6.1	9.9	7.9
Current receipts of government (% GDP):			
Standard deviation	4.0	4.7	4.8
Mean	6.7	6.3	4.8

Source: OECD, *Historical Statistics*, various years.

OECD). In the interwar period the heterogeneities of levels of these public policies were most pronounced. In the 1980s, however, no significant adjustments to a common level can be discerned compared to the three preceding decades. This fits nicely into my revised hypothesis about the impacts of globalisation: the former research on interdependence (Katzenstein, 1975) and most recent studies on globalisation concur that an extremely low extent of transnational interdependence occurred in the interwar period compared to the periods before and after.

Is this lack of strong convergence in public policy-making in the 1980s due to the extent that a political system was a bargaining democracy (or a consociationalism system or a consensus democracy or a system of generalised corporatism)? According to the traditional view, the adjustments caused by an external shock are moderated and less pronounced the more a political system relies on joint decision-making. However, this is not confirmed, as demonstrated by the correlation analyses of change rates of various policies and indicators of joint decision-making (Table 6.4). In slowing down the growth of state interventionism, consensus democracies have not been less successful compared to democracies approaching the

Table 6.4 The impact of institutions: correlation of changes of policies (1^{stt} diff., end of decade vs beginning of decade) with institutional variables

	1960s	1970s	1980s
Government employment (% total employment):			
Variable:			
● Consensus democracy (Lijphart)	–	0.53*	0.50*
● Fractionalisation of party Systems	–	0.60*	0.44
● Unitarism (Schmidt)	–	–	–
● Central government budget in % GNP	–	0.56*	–
Social security transfers (% GDP):			
Variable:			
● Consensus democracy (Lijphart)	–	0.43	–
● Fractionalisation of party Systems	–	–	–
● Unitarism (Schmidt)	–	–	–
● Central government budget in % GNP	–	–	–
Total outlays of government (% GDP):			
Variable:			
● Consensus democracy (Lijphart)	–	–	–
● Fractionalisation of party Systems	–	0.40	–
● Unitarism (Schmidt)	0.48	–	–
● Central government budget in % GNP	0.59*	–	–
Current receipts of government (per cent GDP):			
Variable:			
● Consensus democracy (Lijphart)	–	0.66*	–
● Fractionalisation of party Systems	–	0.57*	0.41
● Unitarism (Schmidt)	0.40	–	–
● Central government budget in % GNP	0.58*	–	–

– Coefficient of correlation with $p > 0.10$.
* $p \leq 0.05$.

Sources: Institutional variables: Lijphart (1984, 1994); Busch (1995); Schmidt (1993, 1994); Armingeon (1994).

ideal type of Westminster democracy. Summarising the results for these policy areas, globalisation and joint decision-making have not curbed the capability to act of Western governments in a significant way compared to the 1960s and 1970s.

On the other hand political power distributions have not remained as important as in earlier decades or have even increased in significance. Rather, the results of cross-national analyses point to a decreasing importance of the political complexion of governments for the course of public policy (Table 6.5).

The data support a view held by Richard Rose (Rose and Davies, 1994) and others. According to this perspective, policies like the ones under consideration cannot be changed in the short term, even if one wants to do that. Tight correlation between levels of public policies at various time points confirm that hypothesis.[6]

Table 6.5   The impact of politics (correlations between changes of policies and political variables)

Changes (*1st diff.*) end of decade vs start of decade	*1960s*	*1970s*	*1980s*
Government employment (% total employment):			
Variable:			
● Share of votes for Catholic and left parties	–	–	–
● Political complexion of government	0.85*	0.49*	0.38
Social security transfers (% GDP):			
Variable:			
● Share of votes for Catholic and left parties	–	0.44*	–
● Political complexion of government	–	–	0.39
Total outlays of government (% GDP):			
Variable:			
● Share of votes for Catholic and left parties	–	–	–
● Political complexion of government	0.70*	–	–
Current receipts of government (% GDP):			
Variable:			
● Share of votes for Catholic and left parties	–	0.49*	–
● Political complexion of government	0.64*	–	–

– Coefficient of correlation with $p > 0.10$.
* $p \leq 0.05$.

Sources: OECD, *Historical Statistics*, various years; Schmidt (1992); Mackie and Rose (1991).

All these findings about a modest impact of globalisation on national governments' room of manoeuvre and about consensus democracies were further confirmed in an analysis of a second file, a pooled time series.

CONCLUSION

The results of this study can be summarised by three points. The first relates to modes of decision-making. There is no systematic evidence for bargaining democracies being worse and slower in adjusting to the challenges of the 1980s in the policy areas compared to political systems approaching the ideal Westminster type. The ability or the willingness to adjust to the model of a 'lean state' did not decrease with the extent to which decisions were shaped by the structural need for bargaining. In the fields under study Westminster democracies were not shown to be more innovative or more able to change the status quo than bargaining democracies (Lehner, 1989: 98). The advantage of these types of political system probably lies less with efficiency than with regard to the ascription of deficits and successes of the various actors. In this regard bargaining democracies have a serious structural problem which was analysed in a paradigmatic study by Lehmbruch (1976) on German federalism.

A second point relates to the supposed divide of public policy at the end of the 1970s. It is assumed that after this time, national politics lost its efficiency due to the globalisation of social and economic relations. With regard to the policies under consideration, this is wrong. Rather, interdependence, apart from international law, has restricted the room for manoeuvre of national politics long before 1970/80. In a long-term comparison of periods of international peace the years between 1918 and 1939 in particular were years in which external restrictions on national policy-making were least felt. Studies based on more qualitative data support that point (Alber, 1987). In criticising these results, one could argue that this study's approach is mistaken; it is not the variation of outputs of policy-making but the decreasing correlation between outputs (e.g. fiscal policy) and outcomes (e.g. unemployment) which is of interest. However, this hypothesis starts from the assumption that there has been a more or less tight correlation between outputs and outcomes which has been destroyed by globalisation. The challenge is to estimate complex models for this relationship before and after 1980, which is outside the focus of this chapter. However, looking at the variation of public policy outcomes in the 1980s it is far from clear – at first glance – that there has been a major decrease.

The third result concerns the European Commission. It is forced to compromise, just as are governments in national bargaining democracies, and it is affected by globalisation rather than steering the transnational cooperation of societal actors. Hence it is not very likely that it will play a dominant and autonomous role in the development of the politics and policies of the European Union. To do that it would need to gain independence from national institutions and the Council, it would need to have more resources at its disposal and its personnel policy would need to become more independent of national influences. Internally it should be modelled on national governments; the collegial system as well as the recruitment of Commissioners and their relations to authority should be changed fundamentally. With regard to its external relations, it should be elected exclusively by the European Parliament, to which it should be responsible (Weidenfeld, 1994). However, the chances are very small that these reorganisations will be decided upon at the Intergovernmental Conference in 1996. Even if such a far-reaching reorientation towards more democratic legitimisation takes place, it is far from clear whether this will result in increased capacity to steer the European Union autonomously. The results of this study cast some doubts on this.

NOTES

1. However, the Swiss constitution does not have the procedure of impeachment.
2. In some cases time series ended in 1989 or 1990 and hence for these variables calculations pertain only to this shortened period.
3. It was calculated using the data in Schmidt (1994: 48) and Scharpf (1987) relating to 1986 or, in the case of Austria, to 1979. Due to the small variance of this value in longitudinal respect (Busch, 1995: 121) there is no need to calculate averages for longer periods.
4. In order not to confuse the reader correlation coefficients are reproduced only in cases amenable to interpretation. As a theseheold we use 90 per cent (.10) significance level; in cases with as asterisk significance level is .05, or 95 per cent.
5. One could argue that policy changes in the 1980s were dependent on the severity of the economic crisis in these times. This assumption is not be borne out by a correlation analysis of the various change rates of the average level of unemployment. Correlation coefficients are low and not significant.
6. Correlation coefficients between policy levels at the beginning of the three decades under consideration vary between 0.69 and 0.95.

7 Forging European Union:
What Role for the European Parliament?
Donatella M. Viola

INTRODUCTION

Post-Cold War society has exposed the inability of states to deal with the economic, political and social challenges looming on the horizon. It has also reopened the debate on the future of the 'oldest continent': the arguments in favour of closer integration have re-emerged within the countries of Europe in order 'to realise the potential gains from the evolution of a multi-polar world and to avoid [its] potential dangers' (Marquand, 1988: 2). However, the difficulty in finding a formula acceptable to all Member States, most notably with regard to Denmark and the UK, due mainly to the diverging interpretations of the nebulous term 'European identity', has delayed and, to a certain extent, even suspended the dynamics of the unification process. At the same time, it has raised several awkward questions: Can the ambitious goal of deepening the European Union (EU) in economic, monetary and political terms be fulfilled without altering its multifaceted social and cultural base and without distorting its institutional balance?

The present chapter is intended to be a contribution to the discussion concerning the future of the European Union, to be dealt with in the forthcoming 1996 Intergovernmental Conference. Its scope extends to 'rethinking' the nature and the actual and potential significance of the role undertaken by the European Parliament (EP) within the process of European integration.

WHAT MODEL FOR THE EUROPEAN PARLIAMENT?

As has been described in the previous chapters, the European Union is an entity *sui generis*, far from the nation-state model. By analogy, it follows that the role of the EP varies from that performed by national parliaments.

But to what extent does it differ from its national counterparts? And to what extent must it retain political and legal characteristics of those counterparts in order to qualify for assessment as a 'proper Parliament'? The search for a parliamentary structure at European level poses the question as to whether '...it [matters] that the European Parliament is something other than a parliament [as it was traditionally conceived]?' (Herman and Lodge, 1978: 66). As Jacobs, Corbett and Shackleton (1992: 7) argue the reason for misunderstanding the EP derives mainly from 'the fact that all Member States have Parliamentary bodies and everybody has some expectation as to what a Parliament should be'. 'Parliaments are seen as performing certain functions and inevitably the EP is viewed against this background.'

A brief glance at Member States' parliaments will assist us to illustrate the difficulty, if not impossibility, of finding an appropriate and consistent model at national level to the European Parliament. For reason of space, however, only three national parliaments have been selected and will be analysed briefly.

The French National Assembly

In reaction to the 'immobilisme' of the 1940s and 1950s, mainly due to a timorous executive *vis-à-vis* the Assembly, the French Constitution of the Fifth Republic aimed at creating 'a parliamentary regime without parliamentary sovereignty' (Ashford, 1982: 60). The extensive use of the motion of censure between 1949 and 1958, leading to frequent government failures, was considered the primary cause of political instability. As a result, the constituent assembly fixed strict limitations to parliamentary right of censure (Blondel, 1974: 167). Supervisory parliamentary powers are limited to specific activities of the executive. The National Assembly can still, theoretically, express its disagreement by passing a motion of censure against the government, though this entails high risks. Any confrontation between the executive and the legislative therefore sees the latter always in the losing side as the President, acting within the powers attributed by Article 12 of the Constitution, may decide to dissolve the National Assembly.

By looking at the French Parliamentary system it can be noticed that, in reality, political responsibility does not extend to the right of dissolving the government. The French Assembly cannot exercise the right of increasing expenditure under the 1958 Constitution (Jacobs, Corbett and Shackleton, 1992: 6) and the proposals and the amendments formulated by

Members of Parliament cannot be accepted when their adoption involves a decrease of public resources or an increase of public expenditure (Art. 40, French Constitution).

In the realm of international politics, the power of control of the National Assembly appears to be very limited, in accordance with the Gaullist idea of the executive's reserved dominium in foreign affairs (Cot, 1980: 14). The President of the Republic has the task of negotiating and ratifying international agreements, without envisaging any participation for the Parliament except with regard to the authorisation to declare war. However, some categories of international agreements such as peace treaties, commercial accords or those that involve a commitment for the finances of the state or a modification of territory still need to be ratified by law. In addition, if either the President or the Prime Minister or the Presidents of the Assemblies raise the question of the constitutional compatibility of an international agreement, the latter may be ratified only after a revision of the Constitution undertaken by the Constitutional Council (Art. 54).

It can therefore be maintained that, with the distribution of powers between the legislative and the executive in France, the former represents the *dernière roue du carrosse*.

The British Parliament

Although based on an unwritten constitution, the British political system boasts one of the most ancient parliamentary traditions (Brownlie, 1980: 1). However, notwithstanding the general principle of parliamentary sovereignty, Westminster today appears dominated by the Cabinet, consisting of the leaders of the party having the majority in the House of Commons. Government formulates policies that Parliament can accept or reject, by taking the risk in this last case of a dissolution. When the Cabinet presents its policies before the House, it assumes that its party will vote in favour. In such circumstances it appears evident that the Cabinet's majority will have its proposals approved regardless of the view of the opposition (Brownlie, 1980: 3–4). The dominance of the Cabinet limits the ability of Parliament to channel policy issues. The executive, namely the sovereign through her ministers, has a prerogative power in the conduct of external relations, including the conclusion of treaties and the declaration of war. Parliament is not even required to ratify foreign policy agreements as this, constitutionally speaking, is performed by the Crown, consisting of the Cabinet and the Civil Service, through Ministers. However, the most politically significant treaties are debated and scrutinised by Parliament (Ware, 1991: 48).

Cabinet accountability does not escape control since ministers are individually and collectively responsible to Parliament in informing the latter as to foreign policy decisions. Parliamentary questions and debates in this field take the form of retrospective examination of the consequences of irrevocable decisions already implemented. By virtue of the so-called 'Ponsonby' rule,[1] introduced under a former Labour government, it is now possible to lay the texts of international agreements before both Houses for 21 days before ratification where this is required (Carstairs and Ware, 1991: 166). In the constitutional tradition of the nineteenth century, 'Parliament was not expected to concern itself with foreign affairs, and indeed this circumstance derived from the assumption that foreign policy was not the concern of public opinion' (Brownlie, 1980: 5). Since the end of the First World War, despite the increasingly strong popular interest, foreign affairs decisions have been carried out by the executive in secrecy.

Although, in theory, the government is accountable to Parliament, in reality, the British system displays more a cabinet than a parliamentary type government (Brownlie, 1980: 3). The House of Commons has, for all practical purposes, delegated its sovereignty to Cabinet government through the party political structure. In addition, an increase in secrecy in foreign policy-making has been acknowledged. As Aron (1949) reminds us, even in the 'motherland' of parliamentarism the executive dominates the legislative: *'On oublie trop sur le continent que, dans la patrie du parlementarisme, l'exécutif a une predominance de fait sur le législatif.'*

The Italian Parliament

The Italian Parliament seems to share some characteristics of its English counterpart. However, with regard to the budget, every year the Chambers must approve each of the headings included in the various judicial units of the budget (Article 81(1) of the Italian Constitution of 1948). Through the approval or rejection of the budget or by increasing or decreasing a certain area of spending, Parliament has the possibility of influencing the course of government's policies. The Italian political direction is agreed between the secretaries of the major political parties, the minister competent in the policy area and the president of the Council of Ministers.

In the context of foreign affairs, the Constitution envisages instances of parliamentary participation and scrutiny in relation to the declaration of war and the conclusion of treaties. Similar to the French Parliament, '[T]he Chambers [may] authorise by law the ratification of international treaties that are of political nature, or that provide for arbitration or judicial settlement, or that involve changes of territory, financial commitments, or any modification of the law' (Art. 80). Parliament has the right to be consulted over most international treaties and with regard to any government decisions to undertake external commitments (Cassese, 1980: 87). Evidence suggests, however, that the executive owns almost un-limited and arbitrary powers in shaping foreign policy.

In accordance with the model of parliamentary democracy, the government has to obtain the confidence of the Chamber of Deputies and the Senate of the Republic. This denotes that Parliament may co-determine foreign policy-making through the approval or disapproval of that part of the Cabinet's programme relating to international politics.

Although, in theory, parliamentary investigation of the Cabinet's foreign policy can be carried out, in practice both Houses have not resorted to this option, preferring instead to use interviews and general questioning addressed individually or in groups by the MPs to the Cabinet in order to obtain information regarding general or specific aspects of foreign affairs (Cassese, 1980: 84).

The above three examples of national parliamentary systems reveal a sort of 'involution' in terms of national parliamentary roles in policy-making, characterised by the loss of their original prerogative of issuing legislative and judicial norms (Masclet, 1992: 83). Parliament essentially intervenes in the foreign policy-making process only when a decision has been already taken by the government, even if this rule differs according to the various constitutional systems. The democratic deficit can therefore be conceived as a reflection of a wider problem common to the above countries and to most Western European democracies: the hegemony of the executive (Masclet, 1994: 79). It seems that these countries suffer today from a 'democratic deficit', a concept which is often associated with the construction of the European Union and with regard to the European Parliament, but has not been so widely expressed with respect to the Member States' constitutional systems and to their respective parliaments. Criticism addressed to the EP is somewhat weakened when it comes from parliaments, when, as in the French case, it does not have the power of initiative and legislative competence on most Community issues, or in the Italian case where parliamentary control over the executive is rather limited (Masclet, 1994: 78) and, in the UK case, where often no parliamentary ratification is required.

The EP embodies in its internal organisation and constitution all nationalities, political groups and languages of the Member States. The EU is distinguishable from the state or federal constitutional system neither does it directly conform to other international organisations as it possesses supranational characteristics. The EU adopts legislation which is binding on the Member States without the need to be approved by national parliaments. On this basis it can be argued that a real democratic legitimacy is still lacking within the EU framework due to the absence of a strong parliamentary institution (Jacobs, Corbett and Shackleton, 1992: 2).

THE EVOLUTION OF THE EUROPEAN PARLIAMENT: THE STRUGGLE FOR POWER

With regard to its ability to participate in the policy-making process, the EP has evolved during its forty years of existence from very modest beginnings. At the inception of the European Economic Community in 1957, the European Assembly only had a consultative role in legislation and its supervisory powers included only the right to sanction the Commission by a vote of no confidence. In 1978, a year before the first EP direct elections, Herman and Lodge (1978: 64–5) underlined the significant absence of a clear division of competence between the legislative and executive branches within the EC institutions.

Some fifteen years later, the EP has enhanced its involvement in some policy areas through various pieces of institutional reform, introduced by the Single European Act of 1986 and the Treaty on European Union of 1992. The EP represents a unique institution with at least some form of involvement in almost all the roles traditionally associated with parliaments such as influencing legislation, defining a budget, supervising the executive and contributing to the political debate (Jacobs, Corbett and Shackleton, 1992: 6). The EP has the right of determining the allocation of expenditure on non-compulsory items. It shares with the Council of Ministers the so-called co-decision powers over various policy areas such as single market, cultural, research and environment measures. It also enjoys the assent power over the conclusion of international agreements and association agreements, the ratification power for the accession of new states, and on citizenship (Dastoli, 1994: 10). The European Parliament can exercise the power of dismissing the Commission collectively: 'If the motion of censure is carried by a two-thirds majority of the votes cast, representing a majority of the members of the Assembly...' (Art. 144, EC). For Herman and Lodge 'the European Parliament performs, or has the potential for performing[...] five remarkable functions' relating to information, communication, education, legitimation and representation (Herman and Lodge, 1978: 21–2). It continues to lack full legislative powers, despite the introduction of the new co-decision legislative procedure brought in under the TEU framework (in accordance with Article 189b, EC). The EP cannot be considered an equal partner to the Council as co-decision is restricted in scope so that in most cases 'the Council remains the only legislator' (Raworth, 1994: 16–33). In order to exert its right of veto after the third reading stage against the Council, Parliament is faced with the tough political challenge of summoning an absolute majority of its constituent members within a six-week period. With regard to its budgetary powers, the EP has the last say only on non-compulsory expenditure, otherwise being subject to the principle of power-sharing or co-decision with the Council. Finally its supervisory powers do not extend to the right of censuring the Council of Ministers either collectively or individually (Nugent 1994: 206).

As Raworth (1994: 25) has pointed out, 'the legitimate defence of the Member States' interests in the legislative process [would be] guaranteed by retaining the Council in its present form and making it a co-legislator.' By reaffirming the superiority of the Council, the TEU has raised the issue of democratic legitimacy within the European Union. Namely, the introduction and expansion of qualified majority voting within the Council, instead of making the legislative system more democratic, has contributed to creating a new democratic deficit within the Union. With the adoption of majority voting national parliaments have lost the chance to hold their own governments to account for decisions taken within the Council, as the decision may have been reached without the consent of all ministers (Marquand, 1988: 12). Regardless of the severity of national parliamentary scrutiny and control over their representative ministers' activities sitting in the Council, nothing can prevent the prospect for the minister himself of being outvoted by his colleagues or even abstaining (Prout, 1993: 9).

Through its 'transnational' political group structure, the EP intends to reflect distinct ideologies with a view to reconciling opposing interests from diverse sections within European society. It might be regarded as a sort of microcosm of the European Union. By taking a holistic approach, the EP has been trying to transcend the plain collection of the national interests of its members. The tension existing within the EP exemplifies the strain between national and European interests in the context of political external relations of the EU. The question arises whether the EP represents a European identity or a collection of national identities when attempting to influence foreign policy.

Looking at the EP's internal organisation it can be noticed that '[t]he distribution of members in political groups cutting across nationality and the less clearly defined boundary between left and right on the ideological spectrum contribute to an environment which is original (Jacobs, Corbett and Shackleton, 1992: 7). In addition, the EP, particularly through recourse to its Committees in specialised policy areas, is capable of diminishing national and political differences present in the political groups with regard to European integration issues (Weiler, 1980: 156). As Attinà has pointed out, if the new competencies conferred on the European Parliament by the TEU represent an important achievement, a 'more democratic and viable Union depends (...) on the evolution of relations between EU/EP parties and the electorate' (Attinà, 1994: 2).

The EP partition into transnational political groups is, however, still far from fully achieved. As Michael Greven (1992: 92) has pointed out 'like almost all other actors on the European level, the parties and their members still act as nationalists' and the European Union remains in many of its aspects intergovernmental. It seems that the two issues, nationalism and intergovernmentalism, are strictly interrelated and that the challenge of transnationalism of political groups within the EP runs parallel with the challenge to create a supranational European Union.

Taking into account what has been discussed above, it can be assumed that the EP cannot be regarded as a 'proper' Parliament in the sense of the nineteenth-century tradition (Masclet, 1992: 83). Notwithstanding the differences with its national counterparts, the EP's value as a parliamentary body should not be diminished (Jacobs, Corbett and Shackleton, 1992: 6). It embraces a unique combination of roles and identities which are clearly visualised within its political groups and its committees. However, in order to understand the nature and the meaning of the European Parliament it is necessary to look at its multiple structure reflecting more than the simple sum of its constituent parts.

The EP is not directly comparable with any national parliament or assembly of an international organisation. By recognising that the EP differs from conventional national parliaments, 'should [it] then strive to take a national parliament as its model or should it try to be something quite different?' (Neunreither, 1994: 301). Neunreither's suggestion of increasing classical parliamentary functions with regard to the European Parliament seems to be rational and feasible; however, the formula envisaged will not save the EU from continuing to suffer a democratic deficit, as this is shared by the national parliaments themselves. From this perspective 'rethinking' the European Parliament also implies exploring new frontiers and a new parliamentary *modus operandi* within the EU.

EUROPEAN INTEGRATION: UNIVERSAL SUFFRAGE AND
EUROPEAN PARLIAMENTARISM

According to Bogdanor (1990) neither the citizens nor the EP have performed a major role in defining the evolution of European integration. The EP's recent involvement in the process of European integration dates from February 1984 when the House adopted a Draft Treaty establishing a European Union, inspired by the Italian MEP, Altiero Spinelli. The Draft Treaty intended to foster democratisation within the EC institutional framework, on the basis of Montesquieu's principle of the separation of powers, while supporting the preservation of the historical and cultural identity of the peoples. In the course of the same year, also as a result of parliamentary pressure, the Heads of Government and of State agreed to define new objectives in the context of integration. An '*ad hoc*' committee was charged with the task of evaluating the possibility of Treaty reform. The content of the Report was less ambitious than the EP Draft Treaty but very similar in its general content. The eventual outcome of these initiatives was the Single European Act (SEA) signed by the Member States in February 1986, later ratified by national parliaments and approved by the European Parliament.

After the coming into force of the SEA in July 1987, the EP tried to extend the application of majority voting in the Council and to promote a cooperation procedure in the EC decision-making process. It started a campaign to promote further reforms to remedy the Community's democratic deficit and, in November 1989, the European Parliament launched an initiative to promote the convening of an Intergovernmental Conference (IGC) on political union, insisting that a new round of Treaty reforms should encompass, in parallel, both economic and monetary union and political union (Neunreither, 1994: 302).

To prepare for the IGC the Parliament assigned the task of drafting a report to one of its vice-presidents, the Labour MEP David Martin, who agreed to carry out such a process in three stages. On 14 March 1990 the first Martin Report was adopted by the House. It reviewed general principles and guidelines of the European Parliament including a list of subjects to be addressed to the IGC. The second Martin Report was adopted by the European Parliament on 11 July 1990 and elaborated upon the EP proposals. The third Martin Report, adopted on 22 November 1990, aimed at giving a more technical and legal terminology to parliamentary resolutions on the eve of the opening of the IGC on Political Union.

As to the crucial question of the enlargement of the Union, the European Parliament and the citizens of the countries involved have been called to confirm the decisions attained at governmental level. On 4 May 1994, the EP voted in favour of the admission of Austria, Finland, Norway and Sweden into the European Union. Notwithstanding its exclusion from the negotiating stage and against its common belief that deepening should precede enlargement, the Parliament approved the entry of the new members. It is interesting to note that in the future the EP's right to decide over the accession of new members could become an important instrument to gain influence over the Council as regards external matters. The accession treaties were also submitted to popular referenda in the applicant states which resulted in Austrian, Finnish and Swedish assent to the EU.[2]

FORGING EUROPEAN IDENTITY: THE EUROPEAN PARLIAMENT'S PROPOSITION

The hypothesis which envisages the settlement of the existing democratic deficit by endowing the national parliaments with more power within the legislative process and, in particular, with regard to the Council seems to be neither 'practical nor desirable' (Raworth, 1994: 16). Within the Member States' parliaments, national interests would most likely prevail over 'European' concerns, discouraging and obscuring the chance to achieve a more supranational, collective perspective. The EP itself has advocated a solution at the European level in its Resolution on the democratic deficit of June 1988. Inability or only delay in providing a suitable answer to the above issue has reopened the issue on the acceptability and adequacy of the intergovernmental structure and the increasing need for a supranational framework. The British MEP Glyn Ford has commented: 'The fundamental qualification for [EU] membership is that the applicant must be a democracy. If the [EU] were to apply to join itself, it would be turned down on the [ground of being insufficiently democratic]' (Ford, 1993: 201).

For Masclet (1994), the discussion over democracy in Europe and the powers of the EP raises other fundamental concepts. In his interpretation of Rousseau's theory, parliamentary sovereignty consists of two main factors, the national identity and the general will, Parliament being the voice for the latter. How is it then possible to conceive such sovereignty at European level within a Union which is still seeking an identity and which is composed of a plurality of countries reflecting distinct and sometime conflictual interests? How is it possible to make the EP a real and effective democratic legislative institution without a representation detached from the idea of nation and of the will prevailing in the various Member States? Even though the institutional and operational dimension of the democratic deficit within the EP and the EU would be resolved, another problem would need to be faced, namely the absence of a sense of belonging among the citizens to the European entity which is the result of a normative process largely derived from treaties, jurisprudence of the European Court of Justice and decisions of an unelected Council (Masclet, 1994: 79).

The recent debate on the construction of Europe has revealed a growing perplexity among people as to the abstraction of the concept of 'Europe' and the remoteness of its institutions. Beyond the constitutional problems, as Dominicé has noted, for the EU, meeting the urgent task of making institutions closer to the peoples by building up a constitutional framework will have to be done by associating national and regional entities in a democratic process (Dominicé, 1992: 87). As Jacobs, Corbett and Shackleton state, 'the European Parliament remains remote and unfamiliar to the majority of the European electorate', due mainly to the absence of press and media information available to people (Jacobs, Corbett and Shackleton, 1992: 2). The media continue to ignore the activities of the EP by preferring to report the Council's policies without devoting much space to the political arguments leading to the formulation of such decisions. In order to become more visible in the eyes of its electorate, and in view of establishing contacts with its citizens, the EP will have to increase its powers with regard to decision-making shared with the Council.

The factors which might contribute to an enhancement of European identity can be found in the application of the universal suffrage and parliamentarianism at the EU level. As Marquand suggests (1988: 12), a possible solution could be to revive and elaborate the idea of federalism. In accordance with the principle of the separation of powers, it is possible to know in advance within the federal structure who is responsible for taking decisions. The first direct parliamentary elections at European level did introduce, though in embryonic form, some political rights for the peoples of Europe, but, as Welsh argues (1993: 2), 'they did not prove strong enough to generate a coherent notion of Community citizenship.'

The role of the European Parliament and its constituent political groups must be seen against this background as a vehicle for respecting differences. In 1984, a draft constitution, based on the Spinelli Report, was adopted by the House. The Draft Treaty incorporated in its text the principle of subsidiarity[3] according to which the European Union should not withdraw powers from its Member States and that its intervention is justified only in specific circumstances. The principle reflects another fundamental tenet of federalism: the idea of fostering unification by safe-guarding, at the same time, diversity. According to the European Parliament, the linkage of the principle of subsidiarity with institutional reforms is an integral part of the process of European integration and of democratisation of its institutional structures (Cass, 1992: 122).

Delors also explained, in his speech before the EP on 10 June 1992, that subsidiarity cannot work without other classical principles of federalism: mutual trust and solidarity. These not only reflect ideological concepts, but they also correspond to the legal principles stated in Article 5 of the EC Treaty. Furthermore, as Emmanuel Décaux suggests, solidarity and loyalty imposes a real legal obligation on the Member States represented also in foreign and security policy (Simon, 1992: 217). The relationship between Parliament and European citizens also reveals the dilemma faced by the latter to choose between 'national loyalties' and acquiescence in the endowment of more powers to a supranational body (Jacobs, Corbett and Shackleton, 1992: 11).

The EP urged reforms as a step towards the realisation of European Union and as a necessary condition for forging European identity. Although a 'European identity has not yet been engrained in peoples' minds' (De Clerq, 1993: 2), Europeans share some common values and common needs such as the rejection of war, the safeguarding of the environment, the respect of human rights, freedom and democracy and respect for the diversity of national cultures. In March 1989, during the debate in plenary on European citizenship, the EP raised the following questions warning against the threat of generating a European ethnocentrism or an extreme form of 'Euro-patriotism' (*OJEC*, No. 2–376, 14 March 1989: 98; 15 March: 180): But what kind of a Europe do we intend to construct? Will it arise as an open Union which aims at safeguarding and encouraging diversity? Or will it develop as a 'Fortress Europe'?

The tenuous relationship between the EP and its electorate, deriving perhaps from poor communication channels, also reflects the overall liaison between the European Union and its citizens. Parliament seems aware of the importance of its role in fostering European integration: for this reason it has been elaborating proposals aimed at improving its internal organisation and to gain more visibility and strength.

FORGING EUROPEAN FOREIGN POLICY: THE ROLE OF THE EUROPEAN PARLIAMENT

Is foreign policy a common parliamentary taboo? In the domain of international politics national parliaments tend to contribute to the formulation more through general political influence rather than effective constitutional legal pressure on the government. The degree of influence obviously varies in the different countries and depends on the relationship between the legislature and the executive.

The brief overview of the French, British and Italian systems together with the attempt at comparing the role of national assemblies and the European Parliament in the context of foreign policy has revealed that 'the old prejudice, according to which foreign policy must be made mainly by the cabinet and in the utmost secrecy, protected from the "intrusions" of representative organs and of public opinion, is still largely in force' (Cassese, 1980: 85). This viewpoint, expressed by Cassese with regard to Italian foreign policy, can be applied generally to most European states as well as to the European Union.

As Monar (1993: 4) argues, unlike national parliaments resigned to play a limited role in foreign policy, the EP, particularly since the 1979 direct elections, has tried to exercise more influence in EU external relations and in foreign policy. In the case of national parliaments the absence of effective participation in foreign affairs can be counterbalanced by the fact that a government which is dependent on a parliamentary majority will normally avoid adopting foreign policy positions which might jeopardise its majority support. Vice versa, in the foreign and security policy structure there are no direct ties between the executive and its parliamentary majority. The EP does not necessarily reflect the political affiliation of the Council and neither does it determine the composition of the latter. Therefore, it has to find other instruments to influence and control common foreign policy. In addition, as Gaja (1980: 191) has emphasised, while the Member States' national parliaments exercise only a limited influence over their governments in shaping foreign policy and their function is to contribute to the establishment of the majority national point of view, the EP's task is to influence directly a policy under a European, not a national perspective. The intervention of the EP becomes increasingly more necessary once decisions are taken by governments at a European level where it is exceedingly difficult for national parliaments to exert any form of effective control.

In addition, the EP's efforts to influence foreign policy have been viewed suspiciously by the other EU institutions as well as by national parliaments and governments who regard it as an attempt to encroach on the powers of the executive (Monar, 1993: 1). In accepting the commonly held assumption that there is a strict link between democratic government and national sovereignty, as well as the proposition that national sovereignty should be exercised in the field of foreign policy, it seems obvious that any shift of power in this domain from the national institutions to

European supranational institutions, such as the Commission and the Council, can appear to be a threat to the sovereignty and to the democratic process of and within the Member States. In this context, the EP could fulfil the 'counter-balancing role of providing the democratic foundation and legitimating body for the process' (Weiler, 1980: 158) of definition of EU foreign policy.

It has been suggested that the current institutional framework exposes a dangerous lacuna in parliamentary control which needs to be taken into consideration and rectified within the 1996 Intergovernmental Conference. While it exerts an increasingly greater influence over the vast majority of political affairs compared to the more 'executive dominated' parliaments of some Member States (Nugent, 1994), 'the EP and not national Parliaments are challenged far beyond the catalogue of their competencies or functions' (Neunreither, 1994: 313).

CONCLUSION

The European Parliament does not conform to any stereotyped model of national or international assemblies. It is also questionable whether the EP should refer to them as archetype models to guide its future development. It seems indeed that, on the basis of the parliaments examined in this chapter, most Western countries suffer, at present, from a democratic deficit.

The dominant ambition of the EP remains in being able to contribute to moulding European Union and 'to influence directly the [evolution of] the making of a common policy – under a European, not a national perspective' (Gaja, 1980: 191). Its role in defying intergovernmentalism and, therefore, the national sovereignty of the state in favour of a more supranational structure and perspective, could be viewed as increasingly necessary as more decisions are made by governments at the European level. The legitimacy of the EU is often identified with the functions of the Parliament so that an increase in the powers of the EP may be essential to allow the completion of an oversight function. This argument is founded on the recognition of deficient legitimacy within the present EU institutional structure and that the shift of functions from a national to a EU level is diluting the powers of national parliaments.

NOTES

1. This procedure was introduced in 1924 by the Foreign Minister Arthur Ponsonby, under Ramsay MacDonald's Labour government.
2. Austria was the first country to go to the polls. With a turnout of 81 per cent of the population, the referendum held on 12 June 1994 registered 66.4 per cent of voters in favour of the accession (*The Week in Europe* 16 June 1994, European Commission, London office). In Finland a referendum took place on 16 October 1994 supporting accession to the European Union (*The Week in Europe*, 20 October 1994). On 13 November Sweden also went to the polls and with a positive outcome of 52.2 per cent of the citizens, it joined the EU (*The Week in Europe*, 17 November 1994). Following the referendum held on 27–28 November, Norway decided by a majority of 52.2 per cent that it did not need full EU membership (*The Week in Europe*, 1 December 1994).
3. Invented by a German Jesuit in 1931 the principle of subsidiarity became the leading inspirational concept of the *Enciclica Quadragesimo Anno*. The principle was later rediscovered by Altiero Spinelli, and applied to the European Community framework by Jacques Delors and Giscard d'Estaing. It was also strongly supported by Margaret Thatcher.

Part Three
Interests and Identities: Cleavages and Commonalities

8 European Values and National Interests

Esther Barbé

From the end of the Cold War, European construction has been in a state of permanent uncertainty, due not only to the structural changes of the international system, but also to a 're-culturalization' of the behaviour of the European countries.[1] Along these lines, Soledad García (1993: 11) states that 'within the European Community, the debates on the Maastricht Treaty uncovered a concern for national identity in the face of the push for "more Europe". Thus, identity became an issue.' This is particularly acute when the subject of the debate concerns the high politics of the state. Indeed, diplomacy and defence have for a long time been taboo issues in the process of European integration.

Whereas some authors emphasise the unifying processes taking place in Europe, others stress the strength of national identities and/or interests as opposed to European ones. The latter focuses on the difficulties entailed in the formal process of integration (Wallace, 1990: 54) which encompasses the attempt to implement a Common Foreign and Security Policy (CFSP).

An Italian diplomat (Januzzi, 1994/95: 15), involved in the European foreign policy-making process, has expressed the view that:

> With respect to the economic sector, the dynamics of market forces will favour greater integration without political will having to intervene in any way, and furthermore, may even go against it. The same is not true of foreign policy in which integration requires specific political wills to converge in opposition to certain customs, traditions and deeply-rooted interests. Although there are many sound reasons in favour of a Common Foreign and Security Policy, the behaviour of even those countries that have been collaborating for decades does not reflect the said 'reasons', but rather continues to be motivated by national sentiments.

The aim of the present chapter is to evaluate precisely up to what point national interests and values or identities have had an influence on the appearance and development of mechanisms characteristic of a European foreign policy.

THE EUROPEAN DEFENCE COMMUNITY: A FALSE STEP

In the process of European integration, diplomacy and defence have been, as mentioned above, two great taboos. Badly healed wounds are not pleasant and the subject of foreign policy and common defence is one of those disagreeable wounds in the already extensive history of European construction. In fact, the inclusion of Title V, Provisions on Common Foreign and Security Policy, in the Treaty on European Union (TEU) can be considered as the opening of a door which had been closed from 1954. In 1954 the French National Assembly failed to ratify the Treaty on the European Defence Community (EDC) signed by the Six two years earlier (Aron and Lerner, 1955).

The failure of the EDC implied, on the one hand, the reorientation of European construction towards the field of economic integration, and on the other, it highlighted the determining factors of any future Community project in the sphere of foreign policy and defence. Indeed, the EDC experience shed light upon two features that have influenced since then and down to our day the success or the failure in the creation of a European foreign policy: the existence of cleavages between Community countries and the prominent role of some of the foreign actors.

In the first place, the 1954 failure showed that there were enormous differences between the Community countries that made the creation of a common foreign and defence policy difficult. These differences can be classified into three big cleavages that divide the Fifteen into opposing groups today (Barbé, 1989). The cleavages, a combination of values and interests of the states, have formed around three subjects: first, the state's view of European construction (the traditional division between federalisers and intergovernmentalists (García, 1993: 98); secondly, the concept of European defence that basically consists of the opposition between Atlanticists and Europeanists (opposed to the centralised nature of NATO in the sphere of security and defence in Europe); thirdly, the world-view that marks the diplomacy of the states and that is conditioned by multiple cleavages: big countries, in diplomatic terms, such as France[2] and the United Kingdom, against small countries; countries of the north, in geopolitical terms, such as the Nordic countries against countries of the south (Baltic versus Mediterranean); countries with a common history that share the experience of the two world wars as against 'ahistoric' countries in twentieth century European terms such as Spain.

In the second place, the creation and development of European foreign policy was conditioned whether negatively or positively by the international context. Within the international context, the outstanding role of the two superpowers deserves mention and, within it, the direct role of the United States which, in the specific case of the EDC, played a conspicuous role as *external federator*, initially in an indirect manner through the pressure it exerted to remilitarise Germany because of the Korean war, and later directly through Washington's lobbying in favour of the EDC.

So far, we have established the two main factors (internal cleavages and an external federator) that have conditioned the birth and evolution of 'European diplomacy'. It is on the basis of these factors that this chapter will broach the three stages in the generation of a European foreign policy. In the first place, the 'prehistory' of the current CFSP (the mechanism of European Political Cooperation (EPC), created in 1970) will be dealt with briefly, indicating the main periods in its evolution until its incorporation in the Single Act 1987. In the second place, the above-mentioned two factors will be applied to the diplomatic activity of the (then) Twelve during the period 1987–90. The latter period is of great significance as it constitutes the transition between the Cold War and the post-Cold War era. Thus, it posed a crucial question to the Twelve: are the mechanisms created during the Cold War adequate for the contemporary international situation? In the third place, the negative response to the above question unleashed a process of reforms that led to the signing of the Maastricht Treaty, which includes the creation of the CFSP.

To what degree do the traditional cleavages between the Fifteen persist in the post-Cold War era? How has the post-Cold War era modified the attitude of the United States with regard to European foreign policy? Has the north–south cleavage gained importance in the new Europe? What effect will the enlargement to Fifteen have on the cleavages? The questions are many and complex. This shows that we are confronted today, just as in the 1950s, with a matter that stirs up the emotions.

EUROPEAN FOREIGN POLICY: FROM PLATEAU TO PLATEAU

The creation, in 1970, of a mechanism to coordinate the foreign policies of the Community countries, European Political Cooperation (EPC), was the result of a *quid pro quo* between federalisers and intergovernmentalists. In fact, the Hague Summit (December 1969) resolved the Community deadlock provoked by the Gaullist policy. Thus, while France withdrew the veto on British admission and accepted advancing towards a new stage in the integration process, the federalisers (the Netherlands and West Germany) accepted the proposal for creating a mechanism of intergovernmental cooperation in the sphere of foreign policy among the countries of the Community. The proposal has consequently created a 'second voice' in the Western bloc and enforced the authority of the EC alongside the leadership of the United States in the diplomatic field.

This mechanism reflected a compromise which meant the acceptance of a diplomatic coordination mechanism by the Community countries. This mechanism, on the basis of the Luxembourg Report, pursued three main objectives: to develop an information network, to harmonise points of view and, *whenever possible and desirable*, to reach agreements on common actions. The analysts defined them as *communauté d'information, communauté de vues and communauté d'action* respectively (de Schoutheete, 1986: 49).

From its creation until its 'legalisation' in 1987, with its inclusion in Title III of the Single Act (Provisions on European Cooperation in the sphere of foreign policy), the EPC underwent remarkable changes (Ifestos, 1987; Nuttall, 1992). Analysts tend to divide this evolution into various stages or plateaux, a form coined by Hill and Wallace (1979: 49), based on the internal developments of the Community itself and developments in the international context.

We can speak of three plateaux between 1970 and 1987 (Regelsberger, 1988: 3–48). The first (1970–74) is the period when the machinery was being initiated, and it was the working procedure that absorbed most of the Member States' energy. At the same time the then Nine had to face two important challenges: on the one hand, the détente between the USA and USSR which impacted on the European scene and, on the other, the oil crisis that brought to light the differences between the Europeans, as well as the timid beginnings of a European policy in the Middle East, the 'Euro-Arab dialogue' (Allen, 1982: 69–82).

The second plateau (1974–79) was a positive period for the diplomacy of the Nine. The machinery became more familiar and the European leaders were less reticent at this stage than at the beginning. In the latter part of the plateau there were indeed some signs of optimism demonstrated by elections to the European Parliament by universal suffrage and the creation of the European Monetary System. As regards the functioning of EPC, the Nine played a significant role in the CSCE, where they assumed the leadership outside the logic of the blocs (von Groll, 1982: 68; Ghebali 1991: 8–13). In the Middle East conflict, the Nine differed from the United States policy, centred on the Camp David process (Ifestos, 1987: 611).

The third plateau (1979–87) was a difficult stretch, both for the Community, which went from Nine to Ten and finally to Twelve, and for international relations in general. The period began with the Soviet invasion of Afghanistan which wrecked a good part of the achievements of the détente policy between the USA and USSR. The tough American policy under President Reagan clashed with the will to maintain the East–West dialogue in Europe. As is normal at times of tension, a conspicuous role was played by the military tool of NATO. Thus it was the deployment of Euromissiles that gained importance during this period, an event which caused discomfort in wide sections of Western Europe.

The difficulties in the international arena were accompanied by a paralysis at Community level occupied by the British budgetary dispute and negotiations with Spain and Portugal. However, it can be stated that the pessimistic atmosphere began to give way, from 1985, to a hopeful situation. In the sphere of the Community, the resolving of the budget dispute, the accession of Spain and Portugal and the signing of the Single Act led the way into a new era. In the Single Act, EPC was included for the first time, together with other policies, in an amendment to the Community Treaties.

However, the Single Act merely represented a codification of the existing mechanism. The intergovernmental cooperation machinery grew increasingly important links with the Community institutions (Commission and Parliament), due, above all, to the application of sanctions in the 1980s. As Nuttall (1985: 260–1) observed, 'the most eye-catching example of the use of Community instruments to pursue EPC policies is the application of sanctions.'

The new demands of the international sphere dating from Gorbachev's arrival at the Kremlin in 1985 required the greater presence of the Twelve and an increasing degree of compromise among the Member States, entering thus into what could be called the maturity of European diplomacy, heralded by the transition from the Cold War to the post-Cold War era.

THE TRANSITION TO THE POST-COLD WAR ERA (1987–90): THE TWELVE AS A DIPLOMATIC UNIT

Between 1987 and the decision to convene an Intergovernmental Conference for Political Union in 1990, European diplomacy underwent a period of tremendous change. There is no doubt that the most important external factor in these changes was the policy articulated by Gorbachev, in which changes in attitude towards both Eastern Europe and the Third World 'Europeanised' international relations, in the sense that diplomatic, economic and cultural relations gained ground over military capacity

(Kelstrup, 1992: 21–40). These processes culminated in the fall of the Berlin Wall.

The Europeanisation of international relations required the European Community to play a more active role in the diplomatic field, especially at a time when the Europeans' confidence in the United States had dropped. The 'mistrust syndrome' towards the United States explains the reactivation of the Western European Union and the creation of new security structures, such as the Franco-German Council on Common Defence in Western Europe (Jopp, Rummel and Schmidt, 1991: 27).

In the late 1980s, the will of the Twelve to create a strong image as a single diplomatic actor encountered, as is to be expected in the Community, the big cleavages that have tended to delay or paralyse the integration processes. Nuttall (1992: 2–4) broached the subject by identifying the existence of three sets of tensions between the then Twelve: organisational, institutional and political.

Organisational tensions tended to separate the countries more actively involved in the EPC from the more cautious states reluctant to lose national ground in favour of an explicitly European presence in international institutions. Thus it was that some countries, such as the United Kingdom or Denmark, always tried to maintain the lowest possible level of representation through the rank of the officials involved. Nevertheless, practice has shown that the Community countries found a positive factor for their national interests in the EPC, above all because the EPC enables smaller or medium-sized countries to enjoy greater prestige and leadership possibilities, and big countries for their part also to obtain benefits (Edwards, 1984). It must not be forgotten that the semestral presidency makes the presidency-in-office the representative of a 'world power', a matter that, on the other hand, also gives rise to some criticism and is linked to the cleavage between big countries and small ones; during the Gulf War, for example, Europe's diplomatic representation was in the hands of Luxembourg.

Some countries have stood out particularly for their desire to enhance the EPC machinery. The case of Spain is one of the most evident. Perhaps the fact of the late incorporation of Spain into the process, 16 years after EPC began functioning, and its admittance after Greece, a dissident country in the EPC framework, may help explain the interests behind Spain's 'activism' in backing the day-to-day activities of the EPC. What is more, Spain's admission to the EPC machinery was considered an important development factor in the process (Regelsberger, 1987: 118–24), in as much as Spain's membership had direct positive consequences. Spain contributed positively to the information apparatus of the Twelve through better relations with Latin America, Spanish activism in the information networks of the Twelve (Saba, 1989), and, above all, gave the EPC agenda a prominent place during its Presidency of the Community in the first six months of 1989 (Barbé, 1990: 109–20).

Spain's membership also had indirect consequences from the moment in which its attitude became a 'model to imitate' for Greece, a country which, from the time it became a member of the Community (1981) until Spain's membership (1986), had carried out a divergent policy, negative for the image of common diplomacy of the Ten. The Greek differences were, to a large degree, associated with the Middle East conflict and East–West relations. The change in the Greek attitude, coming closer to the common position, was significant in the voting of the United Nations' General Assembly (UNGA). The UNGA has been the ideal forum to appreciate the degree of cohesion among the Europeans in international matters. If we look at the votes at the end of the 1980s, the common position of the Europeans in the UNGA was patent in figures that reflect the differences between the Twelve: 'common positions' on all votes at UNGA 43 in 1988 was 76.2% (1987: 75%), omitting consensus resolutions, the level was 47.4% in 1988 (1987: 46.7%)' (Brückner, 1990: 189).

Despite their differences, one of the most outstanding successes of the Twelve in international policy was the creation of an image of diplomatic unity. This is what transformed them into a collective actor in international relations towards the end of the 1980s. The concept of collective actor has two basic components: convergence of interests and a communication structure that facilitates the interchange of shared preferences.[3]

The communication structure of the Twelve, or the *communauté d'information* in EPC terms, was an instrument functioning at full capacity at the end of the 1980s. With regard to the convergence of interests, we will now go into the subject of the cleavages, which have become consolidated with the passage of time as the sum total of national interests and European values.

THE TRANSITION TO THE POST-COLD WAR ERA (1987–90): THE INTERNAL CLEAVAGES OF EUROPEAN DIPLOMACY

The 1989 earthquake that initially provoked the fall of the Berlin Wall led many states to adapt their 'bipolar mentality' to the new circumstances. Thus it was that the more or less consolidated cleavages came undone to a certain degree. It was not until the Intergovernmental Conference (IGC) on Political Union (1991) that one would see up to what point these cleavages, created in a bipolar context, were altered.

Three principal topics enable us to establish the main cleavages between the Member States in the sphere of a common foreign policy: (1) the extra Community dimension of the state; (2) the content of its Europeanism; and (3) its position in the sphere of security.

The extra community dimension of the state is the level of privileged relations it has outside the international subsystem created by the Member States. If the state has important external relations (linked to its colonial past or its being a part of another community framework) or a peculiar diplomatic style, its participation in a collective framework is more difficult. The first big cleavage, based on the capacity of each state to facilitate collective functioning, permits us to discern, throughout the history of the EPC (1970–91), three groups of countries.

The first is made up of those countries that see the EPC as an ideal framework for their foreign policy. Either because of their physical dimensions (Luxembourg, Belgium) or the limitations of their recent history (West Germany), these countries found in the diplomatic coordination mechanism of the Twelve a way of 'enhancing' their policies. The transition to the post-Cold War era introduced very reasonable doubts with regard to Germany continuing in this group. In fact, Germany, for the first time since the creation of the FRG, found it had a framework of 'privileged relations' encompassing Central and Eastern Europe. The pressure exerted by Germany on the other Eleven to recognise Croatia and Slovenia in 1991, including its resolve to provide unilateral recognition, is a good example of the change effected after the end of the Cold War.

The second group is made up of those countries that have privileged extra Community relations, or a peculiar diplomatic style, but whose objectives are not incompatible with the actions of the Twelve; Spain, Portugal and Greece have been incorporated within this group made up of Ireland, Italy, Denmark and the Netherlands. The Greek case is explained by the 'Spanish model', as we have already noted, but also, in addition to internal motives, by the turn of events in Eastern Europe well before the fall of the Berlin Wall. It is clear that Greece liked to have the support of the diplomacy of the Eleven in an unstable Europe.

Italy, Spain and Portugal constitute the Mediterranean bloc. This explains their actions (individual or collective) in the said region. In addition, all three have areas of their own particular interests – Spain in Latin America, Portugal in Africa and Italy in Central Europe. This has sometimes led to specific differences within the EPC framework. This was the case, for example, of Spain when in December 1989 it voted, alone, in favour of a United Nations resolution that condemned the United States' intervention in Panama proposed by the Latin American countries. Portugal, for its part, has on several occasions made relations between the Community and the ASEAN states difficult due to Indonesia's occupation of East Timor. The economic interests of Germany, The Netherlands and, to a lesser degree, of Great Britain in Indonesia have clashed with the Portuguese policy of self-determination and the promotion of human rights in East Timor.

Ireland, Denmark and the Netherlands form the so-called 'moralist'[4] group (Hill, 1983: 187). The position of the latter was noteworthy in the cases in which the former colonial powers applied *realpolitik* to defend their interests when faced with values and principles such as the defence of human rights; South Africa, for example, was a thorny subject (Holland, 1988). Apart from this, it must be mentioned that Ireland stood out as a consequence of its neutrality. The fact that it does not belong to NATO led to all kinds of reservations when it came to including security aspects in the common foreign policy. Denmark, for its part, reserved its position with its priority objective being to concert its foreign policy within the framework of the Nordic Council (Wendt, 1981: 343–94).

The last group is made up of the two great diplomatic powers of the Community, the possessors of nuclear armament and the permanent members of the Security Council of the United Nations: France and the United Kingdom. Their characteristics make them countries that are, by definition, reluctant to dissolve their foreign policies within a collective framework. This explains their radical defence of the intergovernmental option in the sphere of European diplomacy as manifested by Gaullist France in the 1960s and the United Kingdom of Thatcher in the 1980s. However, the end of the Cold War and German unification led to an important change in the French position which went from being anti-Europeanist, in so far as the institutional aspects of the EPC were concerned, to proposing a step forward in the proposal to integrate the CFSP within the proposed Political Union. As in the case of the EDC in the 1950s, the French government placed the Europeanisation of Germany before any other aim. In the 1990s this required placing the Europeanisation of Germany before the traditional French intergovernmental conception of diplomacy and defence.

The second cleavage developed around the institutional options which traditionally opposed intergovernmentalists, the French view and later that of the British, and federalisers. The latter fought hard to link the work of the EPC to the Community institutions and to have Community instruments the only tools capable of making the diplomacy of the Twelve into something more than a simple declaratory diplomacy (Nuttall, 1987: 211–49). This second group of countries has been traditionally led by the Netherlands, West Germany and Italy.

The coming into force of the Single Act in 1987 had already shown that formal institutional matters in the sphere of the EPC constituted a central problem (Nutall, 1987). The Single Act formula that unites the EEC and the EPC in a legal text and the formulation of Title III related to co-operation in the sphere of foreign policy were the result of a difficult compromise between the countries in favour and against, respectively, of establishing closer links between the EC and the EPC. In the group of those not in favour, France and Great Britain played an outstanding role. Another subject that the Single Act introduced was the creation of an EPC Secretariat in Brussels. The Franco-German will to create the said Secretariat clashed with the British position that saw in it the danger of the foundations of another Community building being laid. The pressure applied by the Benelux countries and Italy finally led to the creation of the Secretariat being included in the Single Act, albeit composed of national diplomats and not Community officials. From December 1990, these debates continued in the process of the intergovernmental conferences that led up to the Maastricht Treaty and the CFSP.

The last cleavage between the Twelve was related to security and defence, more specifically the institutional option in the sphere of defence. This exteriorised the cleavages between the Twelve and made an *outsider*, the United States, a participant. This cleavage divided the defenders of NATO as a central institution of European security (Great Britain, the Netherlands and Portugal forming the hard core) from those in favour of a military Europe set up around the Franco-German axis outside NATO. Ireland remained outside both groups, in keeping with its status as a neutral country. The Irish position traditionally made any references by the Twelve to matters of security difficult. The Single Act saved the situation by mentioning the 'political and economic aspects', not military, of security. In this way, the Single Act was in no way different, since earlier EPC texts (London Report, 1981) had included references to the question of security and, concretely, to 'the political aspects of security'.

The differences in the sphere of security and defence re-emerged strongly in the 1991 IGC, the radically different international context of the post-Cold War era. The first proposal, in the sphere of security and defence, was made before the opening of the IGC. France and Germany asserted a joint proposal that the WEU should provide a common defence policy that was required as a component of Political Union.[5] The change in the French conception was apparent, a conception which throughout the

Cold War was based on a radical separation of economic matters (EC) from politico-defensive issues, the latter being inscribed in intergovernmental cooperation frameworks of EPC and the WEU.

These proposals indicated that the Twelve were going through a period of important changes. The biggest shock in this sense came from the Gulf crisis, a moment in which the usefulness and efficiency of the EPC was questioned by many sectors.[6] The civilian power[7] model, defended by the Twelve during the Cold War, entered a period of crisis. Hence the IGC began work in December 1990 with the question as to whether the instruments of civilian power were useful in a post-Cold War world.

THE CFSP: A PROGRAMME OF MINIMUMS IN A NEW EUROPE

The proposal to have a common foreign policy for the Twelve within the framework of Political Union was linked to the changes in Europe in 1990 and, in a very specific way, to German unification. The Gulf crisis strengthened the decision, already adopted, to reform the EPC mechanism. Thus the Twelve went through a stage between December 1990 (the beginning of the IGC) and November 1993 (the coming into effect of the TEU) in which the Community integration process was conditioned by the adoption of political decisions. This was contrary to what had happened in the 1980s, when the techno-economic dynamics imposed the advances of the Community through the Single Market programme (Wallace, 1990: 64). That is to say, the CFSP negotiations were not going to be dealt with in terms of their inevitability, but in terms of a political compromise. Thus the CFSP was the product of the converging preferences of the 'Big Three' Member States, France, Germany and the United Kingdom.

The originators of the proposal, France and Germany, and the behaviour of these two countries throughout the negotiations made them, together with Belgium and Spain (Gil Ibáñez 1992: 99–114; Vanhoonacker, 1992: 37–48), the driving force of the EPC's transformation process into a common foreign policy. In this sense, the Franco-German project revived two central ideas in the Tindemans Report (Commission of the European Communities 1976): qualified majority voting for adopting decisions in the sphere of diplomacy and security and the creation of a common defence within the Community framework.

The Franco-German resolve to advance in the sphere of the CFSP was restrained by British policy to such a degree that the convergence of the preferences of the Big Three reduced the final terms of agreements. Some authors (Ryba, 1995: 15) summarise the differences between the principal actors involved in the negotiations in threefold terms: (1) Is it necessary to globalise foreign policy to incorporate, together with foreign policy itself, the common commercial policy, the cooperation agreements, the development policy? (2) How could a qualitative jump be made, going beyond the EPC system in effect, without, however, placing it on the same level as Community policies? (3) Up to what point can competencies in the field of security and defence be foreseen?

After 12 months of negotiation without reaching a consensus on the CFSP subject, the Maastricht European Council reached a global accord, in which an organisational reform of the EPC machinery was the most striking feature. During the summit, Great Britain led two groups of countries that limited the scope of the reforms. In both cases, long-term issues which touched upon the traditional cleavages were debated, federalisers versus intergovernmentalists in institutional matters, and Europeanists versus Atlanticists in defence matters. A unification of foreign and security policy with economic external relations proposed by the Commission (Commission of the European Communities, 1991) and by the Netherlands (Draft Treaty, 1991) was rejected by a large majority, two of the Big Three, France and the United Kingdom, being opposed to it.

The first group, made up of the United Kingdom, Portugal, Ireland and Denmark, were opposed to introducing qualified majority voting to decide on joint actions to be taken in the sphere of common foreign policy to be previously defined by the European Council. Since introduction by majority vote is a way of legitimising the existence of a common policy of the Twelve the final result came from a Spanish proposal (Barbé, 1992: 364), Spain being in favour of the introduction of majority voting. In effect, the TEU introduced the majority vote mechanism, but subject to the condition that its use was for instances in which a prior decision to move to a joint action had been agreed by unanimity. Thus, formalities apart, the CFSP signified continuity with respect to the EPC in the decision-making sphere.

The second group blocking the reforms related to defence was led by the British and included the Dutch and the Danes. Given the recent Gulf war, the subject was a burning issue. On the basis of a proposal from France and Germany, the Treaty included the term 'common defence policy' and even 'common defence'. Nevertheless, they are mentioned in future terms and are in a compromise text in which the two positions among the Twelve in defence matters are encompassed; the WEU is defined as NATO's European pillar and the WEU is viewed as the defence arm of the European Union. It must not be forgotten that NATO was discussing its own transformation process throughout 1991[8] and this created an area of uncertainty (de Schoutheete, 1994). Hence the ambiguity in the sphere of defence in the Maastricht Treaty left everything open with a view to the 1996 Intergovernmental Conference.

This was perhaps the only possible solution in a set of negotiations that once again confirmed the persistence of the traditional cleavage in matters of defence among the Member States. The subject of common defence inscribed in the Treaty was damaged even further after the Danish renegotiation in 1993 and prior to the second Danish referendum, since Denmark managed an opt-out clause.

The attitude of Denmark prompts a question of vital importance for the future of the CFSP. To what extent has the fourth enlargement to Fifteen countries affected the cleavages among the Member States? Can we talk of greater or less cohesion in the future? With our eyes set on the Europe of the Fifteen and the 1996 IGC, one fundamental fact cannot be forgotten: the scarce results Maastricht had in reforming the diplomatic and military tools of the Twelve were determined by the differences between the Big Three.

THE EUROPE OF FIFTEEN: CFSP AND THE FOURTH ENLARGEMENT

The appearance of EPC was linked to the first enlargement of the Community. The French decision in 1969 to remove the veto on Great Britain's admission to the Community has its counterpart: the creation of a mechanism of diplomatic harmonisation. Therefore, EPC began before the United Kingdom, Denmark and Ireland entered the EC.

The successive enlargements, with the exception of the third including Spain and Portugal, have had an adverse effect on the image of the 'European voice'. With the most recent enlargement from Twelve to Fifteen there is continuation of the pattern of cleavages that was manifested when the accession negotiations were under way.

The Commission itself, in the report on the enlargement prepared for the European Council of Lisbon in June 1992, clearly spelled out the fear that the EFTA enlargement could be dangerous for the development of the European Union, especially CFSP (See Commission of the European Communities, *Bulletin*, 3/1992). Thus, there were several countries, together with the Commission, who wished to obtain binding assurances from the EFTA applicant countries with regard to their commitment to the CFSP. France and Spain were prominent in this direction, their argument being the defence of the deepening process of the Union before its widening.

For the defenders of the deepening process such as Spain, France or Belgium, several issues were significant in the negotiation process. Three main issues come to the fore: the traditional intergovernmental perspective of the applicant countries, well known from the period of the Hague Conference in 1948; the neutrality policy, with the exception of Norway; and finally, the existence of a homogeneous Nordic group with its own profile in international fora.

The institutional cleavage, intergovernmentalists versus federalisers, was present during the negotiations. This must be borne in mind when interpreting the precautions that arose during the European Council of Edinburgh in December 1992 in the sense that the condition imposed on the admission of the EFTA countries was to be based on 'the acceptance in full of the Treaty on European Union'. Another cleavage formed around the subject of defence, which for many years had little value given the scarce weight of Ireland and, concretely, the cleavage between neutral or non-neutral countries.

For many years neutrality was seen as an 'impediment' for admission into the EC; according to Pedersen (1993: 33), 'neutrality was considered incompatible with belonging to an international community with a political objective.' Furthermore, neutrality extends beyond the country's foreign policy and becomes both a sign of of its society's identity and a sensitive issue for public opinion. As Stavridis (1994: 31) has noted, asking the populace to relinquish the condition of neutrality is asking it to forego the 'principal cause of national independence, of security, of economic prosperity and its international role in the world'.

Undoubtedly, those countries, such as Spain, which have from the start stated that the new members should adopt all the *acquis politique* with respect to the CFSP, which would include their membership in the WEU, would like to see a transformation from neutrality. This interpretation of the *acquis politique* was not imposed during negotiations. In matters of security, it can be pointed out that the cleavage did not arise around formal issues, belonging or not to international organisations, but rather around political pragmatism. In this sense, the attitude of Austria, Sweden and Finland in adapting to the requirements of the Political Union during the membership negotiations was totally orthodox, stating their intention to participate actively in the development of the CFSP. This position can be viewed as perfectly coherent with the attitude of the three countries in the context of the great challenges of the post-Cold War, notably the Gulf War and Yugoslavia, and an attitude based on subordinating neutrality to the functioning of a collective system of security (Remacle, 1994: 79–102). Along these lines, the Austrian decision to permit Allied planes on their way to the Gulf to transit in their territory was significant.

The enlargement to Fifteen poses a final question: how far does the North–South cleavage grow in the Union? A response, in economic terms, is clear but in the context of the CFSP it is less certain; can we now talk of a Baltic versus Mediterranean countries cleavage in the future CFSP?

The post-Cold War has altered the known coordinates. The Nordic identity, for example, is now in the grip of a crisis. Although a common space persists based on cultural factors, the same is not true when it comes to identifying the Nordic peoples in international terms and, given their admittance to the EU, the notion that 'the Nordic identity has its roots in being better than Europe' (Waever, 1992: 77). Thus, the fear of the 'Nordic bloc', particularly after the Danish policy of opting out in defence matters, was proven unfounded by the attitude of the Finns and the Swedes during the negotiation process.

None the less, what will happen when it comes to implementing the policies, that is to say when we descend to the terrain of concrete interests? This is where the existence of a North–South cleavage becomes apparent. In the specific matter of the CFSP, the North–South cleavage responds to the logic of the times, that is to say the reappearance in the post-Cold War era of factors of both history and geography noted by Hyde-Price in this volume. In fact, alongside global dimensions of security, for example the environment and migrations, Europe has been experiencing a process of regionalisation of security. This process, determined by historical and geographical factors, has led to the creation of 'privileged international spaces' in the framework of the post-Cold War. Thus, whereas the southern countries, particularly Spain and France, motivated by the risks deriving from destabilisation originating in the Arab world, seek to designate a Mediterranean space for a European Union commitment, in the North, Germany and the Nordic countries have rediscovered the Baltic world. In this way, two different mental maps, organised around the sea as the 'mythical source of identity' (Oberg, 1992: 161), Mediterranean versus Baltic, could serve to indicate the centrifugal forces to which the foreign policy of the Union could be subjected in the years to come.

CONCLUSION

Writing on the CFSP, Giovanni Januzzi (1994/95: 16) has noted:

An efficient foreign policy is the result of lucid thinking, clear ideas and adequate structures and means. But even the most sophisticated mechanism will function badly if it is not backed by a political will, which in

turn implies the existence of either absolute harmony among the actors
or adequate rules to overcome all divergencies.

The present chapter has focused on divergences, analysed in the form of
cleavages. From the Europe of the Six to the current European Union of
the Fifteen, foreign policy has been a subject of debate. In effect, foreign
policy, as well as security and defence, constitute the basic pieces of the
federalist project of the European Union. It is, therefore, paradoxical that
the first coordination mechanism between the diplomacy of the European
Community countries, the EPC, was inspired by an intergovernmental philosophy the *Europe des patries* of de Gaulle.

The cleavage in institutional matters, federalisers versus intergovernmentalists, comprises the first of the three cleavages introduced in this
chapter. The second cleavage is related to security and defence. More
specifically, it can be said that there are two different options in institutional matters among the members of the Union: those who defend the priority of NATO, the Atlanticists, and those who pursue the existence of a
strong organisation of European military security, the Europeanists. In the
third place, we can talk of a more diffuse and multiform cleavage, the
world-view of each Member State. The latter can give rise to diverse
cleavages; for example, in the current Europe of the Fifteen we are obliged
to introduce neutrality as a determining factor of a cleavage in the present
and the future of the CFSP. Other factors, such as the size of the state, big
versus small, or its geographical location, North versus South, are a source
of divergence both when creating mechanisms and implementing policies.

One of the central concerns of this chapter is the permanence, or not, of
traditional cleavages in the post-Cold War world. In other words, how are
cleavages and interests articulated in the post-bipolar world? The
Maastricht Treaty negotiations on the one hand, and the enlargement to
Fifteen on the other, enable us to appreciate new behavioural patterns
alongside the traditional ones. In other words, we can talk of both change
and continuity at the same time. Change can be seen, above all, in those
actions that are immediate responses to the demands of the new international system. In this sense, an evaluation must be made of French policy
in the 1990s in the face of German unification, and the policy of neutral
countries, such as Austria, during the Gulf War.

Continuity is also evident. In this sphere, the diplomatic culture of the
states, particularly when the state has a very structured basis (in the case of
the Big Powers such as the United Kingdom, or the Nordic countries),
plays a very prominent role. In this sense, mention must be made of the
British attitude with respect to two of its 'impelling ideas': on European

security the centrality of NATO, and on European construction inter-governmentalism manifest during the Maastricht Treaty negotiations.

With a view to the 1996 revision, the CFSP appears highly complex. The current ambiguity, reflected in the position of the three recently acceded countries, is a balancing act. The CFSP is, for the time being, the product of a threefold structural tension: firstly, between the new demands of the international system, for example collective security actions in which the neutral countries intervene in a pragmatic manner; secondly, the persistence of classic conceptions of the world linked to values, as notable in the Atlantic conception of the United Kingdom; and thirdly, in the national interests of the Member States and the perception of the risks for national security illustrated, for example, in the case of the Spanish government's Mediterranean policy.

Everything seems to indicate that the CFSP revision in 1996 will only serve to ratify two already well-known tendencies going hand in hand: the continuity of a programme of minimum's, inevitable because of the divergences among the big countries, and the deepening of the *Europe à la carte*, characterised particularly in matters of security and defence, with neutrality, opting out and greater military integration through subregional structures such as the Eurocorps.

NOTES

1. The term 'reculturalisation', wider than that of 'renationalisation', applied to the foreign policies of the European states in recent years, has been adopted. This has been done on the basis of the definition of Faure and Sjöstedt, for whom 'culture is a set of shared and enduring meanings, values and beliefs that characterise national, ethnic, or other groups and orient their behaviour' (Faure and Rubin, 1993: 3).

2. In fact, the failure of the EDC was due, in the final analysis, to French national interests, determined to a large degree in 1954 by the country's colonial policy and the war in Indochina. Along these lines see Ortega Klein (1980).

3. We use the concept of collective actor of Lauman and Marsden in exactly the same way as it is applied to the European Community by Kenis and Schneider (1987). The concept is based on the notion of a collectivity as a plurality of individual actors who act in a concerted manner on the basis of the complementarity of their experiences.

4. The term is open to criticism. Indeed, the attitude of one of the members of the group, the Netherlands, with respect to the East Timor/Indonesia conflict

was characteristically one of a former great metropolis, dictated by its economic interests.

5.   Letter addressed to Andreotti by Kohl and Mitterrand (*Agence Europe*, 10–11 December 1990).

6.   The report elaborated in this sense by a group of experts is revealing. See Denhousse (1991).

7.   Concept coined by F. Duchêne (1972) applies to the Community during the Cold War and refers to its position as an international power, bereft of military coercion mechanisms. This explains the development of alternative policies (economic relations, human rights policies, etc.).

8.   In reality, the Atlantic Council, held in Rome in November 1991, had already included a reference to a 'European defence identity' in the 'New Strategic Concept' of NATO, thereby facilitating later negotiations in Maastricht.

9 The Cultural Semiotics of 'European Identity':
Between National Sentiment and the Transnational Imperative
Ulf Hedetoft

[...] if the sign does not reveal the thing itself, the process of
semiosis produces in the long run a socially shared notion of the thing
that the community is engaged to take as if it were in itself true.

(Umberto Eco)[1]

THE USES AND ABUSES OF A CASE OF IDENTITY ENGINEERING

When Jean Monnet, in 1943, wrote that 'there will be no peace in Europe
if States are reconstructed on the basis of national sovereignty ...
Prosperity and vital social progress will remain elusive until the nations of
Europe form a federation or a "European entity" which will forge them
into a single economic unit' (Monnet, 1988: 20–1), this was basically a
pragmatic vision of European unity, as the emphasis on 'prosperity' and
'economics' indicates.

This pragmatic take is replicated in the 'Schumann Declaration' of
9 May 1950 – the founding document of European integration – where
'United Europe' was conceived not in terms of a grand blueprint, but
rather as a *de facto* solidarity', primarily intended to eliminate the 'age-
old opposition of France and Germany', and only secondarily to take the
'first step in the federation of Europe' (Monnet, 1988: 43–5).[2]

In the scholarly field of European integration, this approach has found
its systematic expression in different variants of neofunctionalist
'spillover' and 'sovereignty-pooling' theories, envisioning a process of
semi-automatic progression from divided to unitary interests on the road to
'an ever closer Union', as the Treaty of Rome chose to phrase it.

147

Nevertheless, it is apparent that the tensions and contradictions on which the imagined road to unity is predicated do contain the makings of discourses and perceptions of a 'European Identity'. Monnet's 'European entity', the 1950 Declaration's mention of 'federation' and the Treaty of Rome's invocation of 'an ever closer Union' all potentially transcend the orthodox relations of interstate cooperation and conflict, prefiguring what the first Delors Commission, on the background of evident signs of 'Eurosclerosis' in the early 1980s, almost programmatically started to pursue: a 'European Identity'.

Concurrently, European integration almost overnight became a matter of concern not just for political scientists, economists and students of law, but also for champions of cultural studies and the history of ideas, and students of communication and intercultural competence as well. European Identity became a catchword, a signifier for the need to go beyond interstate behaviour conceived in neorealist terms. Where scholars had previously, at best, conceived of an 'Identity of Europe' (e.g. Weidenfeld, 1995), i.e. a set of common political, security-oriented and economic interests strong enough to resist centrifugal tendencies, the late-1980s discourses of 'European Identity' carried a hitherto subdued existential ring, echoing connotations of 'national identity'. 'Europe' became a vehicle for a centuries-old intellectual dream of unity-in-diversity (Bance, 1992). For pro-Europeanists, it was a time of optimism, mission and progress.

This enthusiasm – now, post-Maastricht, pervasively replaced by pessimism – cannot conceal, however, that European Identity is a contradictory and volatile notion. The Commission, in its communication to the European Parliament on a 'People's Europe' (Commission of the European Communities, 1988: 245A), in some passages emphasises the homogeneity of 'European Identity', but in others stresses that this identity consists in efforts to preserve the separate identities within Europe; hence, the Commission is set to 'maintain the different national and regional cultural identities and thus [*sic*] the European identity' (*Bulletin*, 1988: 26), to 'respect the national identities of its Member States' (TEU, Title I, Article F), to 'contribute to the flowering of the cultures of the Member States' and hence to 'take cultural aspects into account in its action under other provisions of the Treaty' (TEU, Title IX, Article 128). [3]

It is also worth noting a Eurobarometer poll from 1991 (No. 36, p. 18), where responses to the standard question on 'How frequently does one feel European?'[4] elicited the result that citizens belonging to countries outside the EC (notably Romania and Albania) possessed far more 'European Identity' than any of the peoples inside the Community; where in Romania only 18 per cent answered that they 'never' felt European, in the UK the corresponding figure was 69 per cent (the EC average was 49 per cent).

Perhaps it is this volatility, the fact that 'European Identity' readily lends itself to exploitation by different interests, that has worked as a barrier to more thorough attempts to uncover its meanings and effects.[5] Wedged between idealism and the pursuit of national interests, between symbolistic discourse and popular scepticism, between 'positive' atrophy and 'negative' sense, the concept has too often been either taken for granted or analytically neglected.

This chapter proposes to make some conceptual as well as empirical observations on European Identity in its various constituent patterns and ramifications of meaning, as a topic deserving of attention in its own right, and within the context of a cultural-semiotic reading basically informed by Peircean concepts (Peirce, 1931–58, Vols I–VIII; Peirce, 1991; Eco, 1976; Ahonen, 1993) and by contemporary theories of the discursive construction of social realities (Berger and Luckmann, 1966; Giddens, 1984; Handelman, 1990; Herzfeld, 1992; Lincoln, 1989). Some of the points addressed will be introduced in the form of theses. Others will be given fuller empirical treatment. The methodological framework will be laid out in the following section. In the following sections we will firstly address European Identity 'top down' as constructions and discourses of 'elite' meaning. The fourth section will situate European Identity on a terrain of dislocated and contested patterns of meaning. The next section will investigate European Identity 'bottom up' in terms of the forms it assumes when imagined by European citizens. The final section will present some concluding and synthesising remarks on the concept of European Identity suspended between the analogue of national identity and the transnational imperative of global interdependence.

EUROPEAN IDENTITY: FRAMING THE QUESTION IN SEMIOTIC TERMS

Having seen little of the twentieth century and neither of the two world wars, for obvious reasons Charles S. Peirce (1839–1914) never addressed the notion of European Identity (henceforth: EI). He did, however, occasionally address questions of social identity from a pragmatic-communicative perspective, i.e. the way the social individuation process takes place through a 'semiosic' process of appropriating the world through symbolisation and dialogue (M. Singer, 1984: Chapter 1). This

Ulf Hedetoft

legacy can be traced in a number of contemporary scholars that have drawn important inspiration from Peircean semiotics; Umberto Eco, Milton Singer, Richard Parmentier, Thomas A. Sebeok and many other students of semiotic-cultural processes have, often from the vantage-point of the anthropologist, demonstrated the germaneness of Peircean sign theory for the understanding of identity,[6] though to my knowledge EI has never been made the subject of such investigation.

My purpose is not to conduct a detailed analysis of EI along these lines, but rather to outline in broader terms an alternative way of conceptualising the notion. The basic point is simple: It makes sense to think of EI as one point (the 'Sign'-part) of a Peircean 'triangle of signification', consisting of 'Object', 'Interpretant' and 'Sign' (see Figure 9.1).[7] A brief comment on this triangle is appropriate before proceeding to its explanatory value for EI.

Peirce in a well-known statement defined a Sign as 'something by knowing which you know something more'. Umberto Eco, following the same line of thinking, defines it as 'everything which can be taken as significantly substituting for something else' (1976: 7). Thus defined, the Sign is inherently relational, stands for, substitutes, hints, connotes, etc., even though what it signifies 'does not necessarily have to exist', as Eco emphasises, and even though the relation between the Sign and its 'referent' may be oblique and even contradictory.

This is partly because the linkage between the Sign and its ultimate referent, the Object, is transmitted via the Interpretant, i.e. a unit or frame-

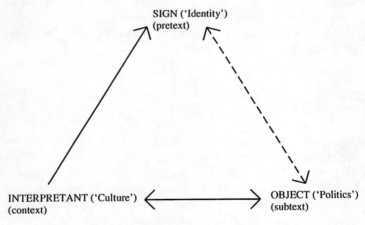

Figure 9.1 The Peircean triangle of signification

work of perception and interpretation (e.g. cultural norms, values of a generalised, 'objective' nature) , that necessarily interposes itself in order to try to make sense of the Sign, to translate it, invest it with meaning. And though the Interpretant is often/always intrinsic to human agents, Eco correctly makes a point of stressing that '(t)he interpretant is not the interpreter [...]. The interpretant is that which guarantees the validity of the sign, even in the absence of the interpreter. [...] the most fruitful hypothesis would seem to be that of conceiving the *interpretant as another representation which is referred to the same 'object'* [*sic*] (1976: 68).

This takes the Interpretant beyond individual whim and total contingency, without presuming any logical or structural constant between these two points of the triangle. In an important sense, the Interpretant is just another sign that works as the prism of interpretation, the 'medium' or 'frame' according to which the Sign is made to refer to the Object. But from another perspective, the Interpretant may transform into Sign (and vice versa), within a process which Eco defines as 'unlimited semiosis' (Eco, 1976: 69), a cultural system of signification and meaning that works as its own cause and effect, is epistemologically self-contained and self-perpetuating, and hence may refer to – respectively create – its 'reality', the Object (be this internal or external to the human mind). Hence, Eco provocatively describes a general semiotics as '*in principle the discipline studying everything which can be used in order to lie*' (Eco, 1976: 7). In other words, the Object is always read in terms and contexts that are both self-defining and intrinsically multiple and deflective: through Signs that refer to Objects through Interpretants (also Signs) that need Interpretants (also Signs) *ad infinitum*. No 'triangle', therefore, is stable, but its structure of meaning will shift with any change of any definition/reference/interpretation of any of its three poles.

Let us now return to EI, which presents us with a clear case of triangular signification. Starting from the perspective of the Object, i.e. the pragmatic referent always implicated in EI discourses as their stable underpinning, it is constituted by 'European political integration'. Integration is the overarching objective underlying efforts to engineer a European Identity – its *sine qua non*. Without this presumption, EI would make little sense. The striven-for 'identity' of Europe is ultimately of a political nature,[8] a question of states, state interaction, institutionally embedded cooperation of a unique type, an always volatile balancing point between intergovernmental, transnational and supranational modalities of integration, of framing the disputed sovereignty question in radically new ways.[9] Thus politics, without always being directly implicated in the discourses and symbolics of EI, makes up its indispensable subtext,[10] as a kind of integration that calls for a mentality of unity (as both condition and effect).

It is because we are here faced with an identity of Europe that looks to go beyond mere intergovernmentalism that constructions of a less politically charged nature are needed, constructions that transcend what is merely instrumental. The identity of Europe always veers towards a more value-oriented European Identity, symbolically and emotively imaginable along lines akin to the structuration of *national* identities, on the one hand because of the political dimension of integration, on the other in an effort to relegate this dimension to a terrain of 'subtext' rather than overt 'text' (not as manipulative efforts, but based on structural necessity). However, in thus construing the political commonalities of 'Europe' as EI – a presumptive community of destiny – EI not merely replaces the Object, i.e. 'politics', but turns into a Sign of that which it stands for, a pretextual area of discourse and signification.

Initially, however, this manifests little more than a negation, a signifying void that needs to be filled, not just in the sense that the Sign craves inventors and interpreters (i.e. 'Euro-politicians' and their intellectual supporters), but more acutely in that it needs some substance beyond the sphere of politics that may lend itself as the Interpretant for this new type of intra-European regime. And for this purpose the political sphere itself, with its mundane and instrumental connotations, will not do. The sphere making sense of EI beyond politics to a larger social stratum as well as to the constructors of the European Union themselves is located elsewhere.

This is where, and why, 'culture' enters by the back door. As Pieterse (1993) correctly observes, a cultural definition of Europe as a 'community of nations [...] largely characterised by the inherited civilisation whose most important sources are: the Judaeo-Christian religion, the Greek-Hellenistic ideas in the fields of government, philosophy, arts and science, and finally, the Roman views concerning law' (McBride, 1988; Bance, 1992) has by now become so pervasive as to be almost 'official' or, as I have elsewhere termed it, a new orthodoxy (Hedetoft, 1995: III, IV and VII). The orthodoxy contains ideal constructions of a (putative) common value basis for all European nation-states, interpretations and inventions of cultural homogeneity, respectively a 'unity-in-diversity' construct across national borders, a blueprint in turn used for the forging of a contemporary symbolic-cultural context serving as a vehicle for the well-known idealisation of European integration: the EU flag; the passport; the Ode to Joy; the circle of stars; discourses of communitarian purpose; interventions into the world of sport (so far only partially successful); the twinning of towns; the exchange of students; the protection of European media culture from

American encroachments (Shore, 1993). At a meeting in 1994 convened by Jacques Delors to discuss EI, *pace* a Danish member of his so-called 'think-tank', participants were reportedly agreed that at least two features characterised a pan-European culture: universalism and relativity/self-criticism. However, more interesting than the precise characteristics singled out is the fact that here, as in almost all other contexts, the Sign (Identity) was obviously discussed vicariously in terms of its Interpretant (Culture) – a practical orchestration of that which is constantly being assumed and thus thematised: 'European Identity'.

By discursively signifying EI in those terms, it is somehow created in the very same process; the discourse becomes reality (however much the Sign may 'lie'), and hopefully accepted in those terms by larger sections of the European popular landscape (however much this may prove to be a pipe-dream). Ultimately, the Interpretant will have shaped the Sign in the minds of people. This is given an extra twist by the Danish think-tank member in the same article: Islamic 'civilising' influences on the history of Europe are proffered as an argument for the widening of Europe to include Islamic values, or at least for the softening of the present Islamic enemy image.

In semiotic terms, attempts such as these to inscribe European integration into an interpretive framework consisting of 'culture' – to use culture as the contextual Interpretant mediating between Object and Sign – are saddled with two basic problems. One is that the Sign, for which the Interpretant is supposed to stand in and which it is meant to refer to, is anaemic, typified by perceptual atrophy. Hence, no matter how effective or substantial the cultural-symbolic constructions may (or may not) be, their eventual success is dependent on being interpreted in relation to what is signified. This is far from certain.

The other is that the political Object for which this Sign–Interpretant nexus is ultimately a representation is equally heterogeneous, characterised by differences in national interpretations of European integration. The Sign–Interpretant linkage is not just dependent on the progress of political unity, but it is ultimately far more than a representation; it is also an important instrument in the creation of political unity, i.e. in the construction of the homogeneous Object which is simultaneously its subtextual underpinning – quite a burden to place on a relatively innocuous sign relation, and one that makes it significantly different from its national analogue.[11]

Thus, the EI problematic may schematically be framed as in Figure 9.1. In the following, this framing conceptualisation will be thrashed out on the three levels previously indicated: as a top-down invention; as it relates to orthodox parameters of Self–Other dualities; and as the notion is imagined and conceived of by representatives of EU populations.

EUROPEAN IDENTITY FROM ABOVE: CONSTRUCTIONS, BOUNDARIES, IMAGININGS

This first level can adequately be addressed along three different dimensions (sketched conceptually below, but each in need of more thorough empirical investigation):

(1) *EI as discursive construction and symbolic engineering.* This is what I would term the vertically exogenous dimension of EI, i.e. embracing a communicative angle having European populations as, hopefully, the eventual recipients and carriers of EI – rarely in the sense of orchestrating EI as a rival identity, but rather as a supplementary identity layer (Schlesinger, 1987; Shore, 1993; A.D. Smith, 1992).

(2) *EI as a construct feeding off imagined differences from 'extra-Europe' as a common Other,* i.e. the 'cultural' underpinning of European identity on the international scene, as the TEU phrases it (Title I, Article B). This is the horizontally exogenous dimension, most often these days couched in terms of a European security identity (Waever et al., 1993) – the modernised European shape given to Karl Deutsch's security community (Deutsch et al.,1957).

(3) *EI as teleological sign,* i.e. as a mode in which future intent and the purposive 'mission' aspect of the EU can be expressed, both 'inwardly' in closed circles of decision-makers, and 'outwardly' for consumption by the media and public opinion.

It has already been indicated that the uniqueness of European Identity as a discursive construction mainly resides in its immanent ontological paradox, and secondarily in that, as a Sign, it is signifier and signified simultaneously, in the process of its construction ideally shaping that which it supposedly articulates through 'talk' on the commonality of cultural values and historical roots. EI expresses, and tries to fill, a vacuum of meaning and mission at the same time: 'The recognition by the European citizen of this [European] identity will be strengthened by initiatives of a symbolic value', as the formerly mentioned document from 1988 states (*Bulletin*, 1988: 8).

However, even more significant than such immanent tensions and expressive absences is the basic grounding of such EI discourse in its simultaneous necessity and contradictory nature. True as it may well be, as frequently argued, that the EU is not a zero-sum game, but that all actors stand to gain more than they lose (e.g. in terms of influence, security or economic benefits), still, as far as power/sovereignty as well as identity are concerned, the opposite option should also be considered (and might not be at odds with the former). As Robert Keohane and Stanley Hoffmann have argued (1989: 44 ff.), the European integration process, as it impinges on sovereignty, power distribution, decision-making procedures and competencies, etc., should perhaps be conceived less in terms of replacing one centre of control with another than as one resulting in a vacuum of control and decision-making and in partial power dispersion: things made impossible or difficult at one end of the 'competency scale' (the nation-state) should not be imagined as being, in turn, smoothly transferred to the other (the EU). This is a 'negative' structure without a clear centre and a lot of uncertainty and conflict as regards decision-making – a structural 'vortex' (Keohane and Hottmann, 1989: 44) where the rules of the game are being continuously redefined and actors are suspended between two poles of the pendulum of power and influence, but also one that constantly hankers for clear rules and a stable centre on the analogy of the orthodox nation-state. Such a negative structure may be precisely the breeding-ground for cost-benefit calculi showing figures (political or economic) in the black rather than the red for most actors, but must also be one with a serious identity problem – and hence one in search of a stable identity core.

In this format, EI manifests, in one process, both positive ambitions and their negative underpinning in the shape of one centralising and uniform speechification of identity – and hence the immanently volatile nature of the (political) Object in the triangle.

Whether conceived of as an identity of Europe in political and security terms, or as European Identity in more existentialist senses, the discourses and forging of EI have substantively been, and are still, based on attempts to subordinate the intra-EU duality between Self and Other to a practical redefinition in terms of 'EU-Europe' as Self, and 'extra-EU' as Other. Thus, Europe as cultural and value-based sameness has pervasively been proffered as an argument for 'identity' along lines of negative demarcation: democratic and freedom-loving Europe against Asiatic despotism to the East, against Islamic fundamentalism to the South, and against American materialism to the West.

As long as the first of these equalled 'actualised socialism' and the Cold War lasted, this notion, backed by the political and security demarcations in Europe, seemed tenable, in spite of the fact that Europe patently comprised more than the EC/EU area of Western Europe, and in spite of the fact that the integration processes in Europe had from the very outset been dependent on the aid and support of the USA, institutionally encrusted in the objectives and structure of NATO. In this light, it makes sense that the heyday of EI discourses and enthusiasm, top-down, coincided with the 'victory phase' of the West during the Cold War: the late 1980s. Defeated, but not yet gone, the East constituted the best possible moral and ideological backdrop for the cultivation of EI, since it negatively reinforced political cohesion, the belief in the superiority of common democratic values, and the incipient expansionism of European unity and identity to include also parts of the East.

Since the major upheavals in the political landscape of Europe in 1989–90, the production of images of EI along such lines of absolute contrastiveness has become seriously weakened. It is now far more difficult to pinpoint the nature of EI in terms of what it is not. The Object's determination of the Interpretant of identity, i.e. 'culture', has become blurred as the Object. Political integration along lines of widening and/or deepening has also become less well-defined and conceptually homogeneous. The Sign becomes emptied of meaning. Apart from the fact that national identities are evidently less willing to let themselves be defined, if only discursively, in a position of subordination to EI, all the three above-mentioned negative parameters have taken on a hue of paradox and fluctuation: the security question in the East has turned into a dilemma in the sense that attempts to push NATO eastwards are coming up against Russian remonstrances, objections that can no longer be countered by drawing an 'iron' line in the sand; in spite of renewed spouts of anti-Islamic imagery, the Bosnian conundrum has contributed towards muddying this politico-cultural-religious line of demarcation as well; and although rifts in the transatlantic link have opened up, the USA is not (for combined reasons of power, geography and history) as useful as a negative backdrop for the creation of unity and identity in Europe as the other two.

This implies that the 'negative' agenda for the construction of EI in any of its ramified meanings has deteriorated as the 1990s have progressed. The usefulness of a contrastive Other for internal cohesion has abated as questions regarding what basically constitutes European homogeneity have been foregrounded, as the geopolitical lines of demarcation have become blurred, as widening (but how far?) is being considered, as common security and defence is hanging in the balance and is being practically questioned by EU waffling in ex-Yugoslavia, and as lines of dissent concerning world trade can be traced internally in the EU. What the Europe of European Identity is, in other words, is becoming increasingly obfuscated (Shore, 1993). The global as well as the regional situation for the EU as an international actor is propitious for neither the discourse nor the practical manifestations of EI, which hence is thrown back on its own 'internal' resources and definitions respectively, and on a reforging of a new regional strategy for acting on the global stage (e.g. common security and defence) in order to recast what will be addressed now, i.e. the teleology of (future) integration.

The third dimension concerns EI as a signifier of dynamic purpose and destiny, a trajectory pointing towards a centripetality of future development, towards an increasing degree of co-extensiveness between different national positions, between culture, politics and popular identifications, and between identity and territory. In this sense, this dimension consists of the symbolic-idealistic baggage on a train in constant motion, a train that is perhaps centrally defined in terms of this very process (and its imagined destination) rather than its (putative) end-results, let alone its constituent components in a structural-synchronic context. In other words, we are here addressing, for example, the functionality of original 1950s images of the EEC as a 'peace movement', of the idealistic purposiveness underlying the 'ever closer Union' (in itself a processual definition), of the visionary content of the late 1980s Single Market Programme (including the role of European culture and identity) – but also of the lack of such teleological imaginings in, for example, the mid 1970s and the early 1980s as part and parcel of diverse crises of Eurosclerosis and the like (perhaps the early 1990s should be included as well).

Way beyond any simplistic explanation of this aspect of EI as mere ideology or justification, a strong case can be made for seeing it as a materially necessary force underlying EC/EU integration – a 'symbolic construction' of a reality in the making; in a significant sense, such unifying visions and missions functionally replace of the weakness and heterogeneity of the political centre, the diversity of national interests, and can be seen as necessary in order to catapult the EU beyond the status of an interstate cooperative regime. This aspect of EI, in other words, relies on the EU being, at least partly, 'more than' intergovernmentalism, as reflected in its supranational institutions.

For the same reasons, it is understandable how and why such EI discourses must originate in and be most strongly cultivated by these very institutions (Commission and Parliament), for such discourses are consistent with the unifying purpose that they represent. In this sense, the teleological component is an important subcategory of the overall construction of EI discourses and symbolism as addressed in the first section above, and as such are targeted at the 'anonymous masses' in Europe.

However, it would seem to be even more significant as an aspect of intra-political communication, i.e. as a coded Sign useful for the sending and receiving of political signals among the political actors on the stage of European integration, that is among the national elites supportive of European unity, though in highly different ways and to varying degrees (Schlesinger, 1987). In this sense, EI talk about the future of Europe is a signifier of different forms of commitment to European integration along the linear trajectory and as such becomes a terrain of political contestation (cf. the next section below).

One thing, therefore, is the defiant and partly divisive import of Margaret Thatcher's well-known Bruges address in 1988, where she directly tackled the question of 'the identity of Europe itself' (Thatcher, 1988: 1) along lines such as: 'We British are as much heirs to the legacy of European culture as any other nation' (Thatcher, 1988: 1); '(t)he European Community is *one* manifestation of that European identity. But it is not the only one' (Thatcher, 1988: 2); and '(c)ertainly we want to see Europe more united and with a greater sense of common purpose. But it must be in a way which preserves the different traditions' (Thatcher, 1988: 4) – in the process travestying the venerable idea she was addressing as 'some sort of identikit European personality' (Thatcher, 1988: 4). It is quite another to discursivise the European Community in existential terms as a '*historische Schicksalsgemeinschaft*' ('a historical community of destiny'), as did Helmut Kohl in 1984, as homage paid to a supranational ideal, though there the Chancellor's basically national orientation and underlying national objectives were also in plain view.[12] And it is yet a third to enthuse about EI in the vein of Jacques Delors, because in the case of the former President of the Commission it was a less than coded way of expressing his desire for a federalist Europe in which EI would equal national identity.[13]

EUROPEAN IDENTITY AS A TERRAIN OF SYMBOLIC CONTESTATION[14]

As a form of discourse originating in the institutional form of EU cooperation, EI, as seen from the perspective of the Member States, takes on another set of meanings and a more instrumental dimension. Basically, it translates into a medium for the distribution of blame and shame, credit and recognition, among the Member States, into a new receptacle for images and evaluations of both the national Self and the national Other, for signalling the extent and depth of one's European commitments (see above), and turns into a mental and discursive modifier of the orthodox linkage between 'Us' and 'Them' as national categories of self-definition. Thus, EI as Sign may be read according to a number of rather disparate Interpretants, in turn referring to – and respectively creating – each their own Objects (in terms of the degree, form and depth of 'integration').

In this way, EI – though not the product of the Member States *eo ipso* – can be instrumentalised from this perspective as an ideological-symbolic competitive parameter, making it a terrain of contestation rather than unity. EI becomes a battleground of discursive interpretation, a prism through which 'Europe' as well as other nations can be evaluated – a new form of stereotyping mechanism. In June 1991, *The European* headlined an article condensing the results of a survey on European orientations in six member states in this way: 'French enthusiasm puts Danes to shame' (*The European,* June 1991), in the process providing an apt example of such uses of 'Europe': if member states can be projected as having a pragmatic, 'minimalistic' or reluctant attitude to integration, this can enter into a new politics of blame and become a new negative stereotype, not only on the part of the genuine enthusiasts at the EU core, but also – more interestingly somehow – by other Member States (or potential Member States wanting to document their eligibility) (Mouritzen, 1993).

What particularly makes this phenomenon interesting is its immanent contradictoriness: *that* in the process of allocating this kind of blame and shame, the presumption (that the sender must be somehow less 'national' and more 'European') is eroded by the very conditions constituting the efficacy of this peculiar Self–Other dialectic, i.e. being a 'better' European only becomes meaningful within the context of that which the discourse denies, namely national orientation (in the above example, 'enthusiasm' for Europe is still 'French'!); and, consequently, *that* messages of this kind are sent in order to project a 'Self' as better than a particular 'Other' – a Self which is, of course, national. Or, inversely, as I have phrased it elsewhere, 'Europe' as a shorthand commendation of one nation is simultaneously the stigma of another. In this way EI becomes absorbed into national identity constructions, but also modifies them in the sense that the discourse and the symbolics itself constitutes a recreation and reinterpretation of nationalism through the introduction of an important new Interpretant – the present-day European equivalent of political correctness in the USA.

Like 'PC', and for much the same reasons, EI is subject to different normative evaluations. It can be constructed as more or less strong, more or less committing, more or less desirable (cf. the Delors-Kohl-Thatcher continuum in the previous section above). What on the part of Germany and (especially) Catholic member states – à la 'French enthusiasm' – has often

been constructed as a moral obligation and an avenue towards the diminu-
tion of nationalism has just as frequently been countered by representatives of Protestant ethics in the North as hypocrisy, superficiality or
downright deception. From the latter perspective, EI as a national quality
encompassing wholehearted commitment is a sham, an intentionally
manipulated simulacrum (frequently subverted with reference to the
failure of Italy, Spain, etc., to comply with EU rules and rulings). And it is
countered by what is seen to be less idealising, more realistic assessments
though still accompanied by commitments to a 'Europe' – sometimes even
a 'European Identity' – of sorts. However, this is a kind of EI which sub-
ordinates any EI to the traditional comforts of the National – as 'interest',
'culture' or 'identity' – and wishes to weaken the connotations of 'supranationality' that refuse to be completely eliminated from notions of
European unity and identity.

   Naturally, this could be approached from the perspective of ideal unity,
in which case EI would seem to be fraying at the edges, contaminated by
national interests and identities. But it is also, and more appropriately,
accessible to discussions from another vantage-point: the construction of
(national) Otherness. Here, EI re-emerges as an intermediary between
national identities and foreign stereotypes, as a factor containing the direct
(often negative) construction of the Other. This intra-EU Other may well
be branded as menacing and suspect, but only indirectly by means of the
morality of EI – as units infringing against the non-nationalistic (though
not necessarily non-national) objectives and mentality of 'Us'. Sign and
Object, signifier and signified grate against each other. EI turns into the
weakened substance of the competing national interests in the EU, interests that ever more clearly are acknowledged as making up its foundation,
but which on the other hand are not allowed to present themselves for
what they are (except occasionally in the tabloids, the sports arena, and the
sphere of private morality).

   As the Maastricht debates demonstrated, EU-Europe is locked into a
frequently painful oscillation between national fact and supranational
ideal. EI is the discursive product thereof, and therefore so volatile. It
emerges as a new form of the mutual recognition among nation-states –
and it is precisely – and only – in this form of recognising the national
Other that even hostile sentiments and objectives are compelled to express
themselves if they want to stay legitimate and above board. Even the allocation of 'shame' is predicated on recognition, in an ideal pursuit of a
common goal. This is the 'cultural' reflection of the institutional interdependence of states that have agreed to modify their competitive anarchy
– to sustain their differences in the guise of a unitary idealism. This – the

severance between different national interests and their political-ideological form of manifestation – is probably the rational underpinning of the claim (not infrequently encountered) that European integration is a threat to national identities: the less a national identity is permitted to vent itself contrastively (in direct comparison with the Other), the more it is thrown back on its own domestic resources – on properties, values and achievements that it can legitimately take credit for as national. The alternative is, as already indicated, to transfer exclusivist sentiments to the extra-EU Other.

EUROPEAN IDENTITY FROM BELOW

It has been mentioned on a couple of occasions above that the ideal – though often not real – target group for the discourses of EI are the European peoples. It makes sense, therefore, to enquire into the ways and forms that EI enters into the value patterns, orientations and modes of affective belonging of representatives of the 'common man'.

This is most frequently done by means of quantitative surveys along the lines of 'Eurobarometer' – which regularly poses questions on 'feelings of Europeanness' and on the percentage relations between 'nationality' and 'Europe'. Recently the issue was covered in 1993 (December, p. 83), concluding that '40% say they see themselves as (*nationality*) only, while 45% feel (*nationality*) and European'. Such figures, however, are not only difficult to interpret (Hedetoft, 1995; Shore, 1993; Smith, 1992; Tarrow, 1994), they are basically ill-suited to getting to grips with a question that calls for more qualitative-interpretive approaches. Figures are not inappropriate as such, but they are likely to fall short when confronted with two kinds of identity (national and European) that must be presumed to rest on widely different ontological bases.

What follows is an attempt to go about analysing EI in a hopefully more satisfactory way – to tease out some typical patterns and correlations of 'identity' by comparing the reactions of three sample populations in Britain, Denmark and Germany to questions (posed in questionnaires as well as interviews) such as 'Do you ever feel European? If affirmative, in which ways and when? What do you feel you have in common with other Europeans?' (Hedetoft, 1995).

In the three groups, the issue of 'European Identity' triggered a number of cross-national similarities as well as some very distinct differences between the national texts. In the *Danish* group, the most prominent feature is the number of respondents answering in the negative to this question, and in very curt verbal forms not found in the other two groups: 'I feel like a Dane only. I suppose we mostly have the skin colour in common with other EC countries' (Dk-2); '…it is not really a European feeling' (Dk-6); 'I never feel European' (Dk-28); 'No!' (Dk-31); 'No' (Dk-43); 'I feel Danish much more frequently than I feel European, because it seems vague' (Dk-44). Others are more doubtful or sceptical: 'Yes, I think so' (Dk-3); 'I feel Danish and as such also European. Geographically I am European' (Dk-7A); 'Yes, as a rule I feel European when for instance I am together with both Europeans and non-Europeans' (34). This last point is echoed by a few others, e.g. Dk-24: 'Yes, when I am together with people from other parts of the world, particularly the 3rd World, but to some extent also with Americans', and also Dk-25 and Dk-33 argue along such lines, situating their feelings within a range of different (hierarchically structured) relativising dualities, from locality to sports events to attending conferences in the Far East. However, the most striking feature is the above-mentioned incidence of references to 'Scandinavianness' or 'North Europeanness': 'I feel considerably more affinity with the other Scandinavian countries, which historically and culturally are more akin to us than Europe, which is an inhomogeneous mass' (Dk-66); 'Yes, as a *Northern European* at any rate' (Dk-26); 'Not exactly as a European, more like a Scandinavian' (Dk-36); 'I don't feel particularly European, more Scandinavian' (Dk-38); '…a common past and history, especially in Scandinavia. For instance, I wouldn't say we have much in common with Albanians' (Dk-44). What is striking here is less the fact that Danes conjure up a Scandinavian 'brotherhood' than that this image clearly steps in and takes over from their Europeanness, acting almost as their international-ist, legitimising escape route.

Thus, almost all the Danes deny having a European identity or hedge it around with ifs and buts, qualifications and limitations. At best it is a fleeting, situationally determined 'negative' feeling. Only one, in fact, starts her answer more robustly by stating that 'I always feel European', but immediately adds '…. as well as always feeling Danish', while contin-uing, 'i.e. it is not something I ever think about at all' (Dk-5). She qualifies her Europeanness, interestingly, by first noting that '(w)hen I can cross frontiers without any identity documents, then I *am* European' and sub-sequently by arguing that '(m)y history back in time is part of the history of the others, and vice versa', thus confirming once again the peculiar argumentative European dialectic between Self and Other; the fact that the past linked people in *antagonistic* ways is now, by a few (and many more in the other two texts), seen as a reason for their *common* identity; cultural diversity is transformed into an argument for common interests and iden-

tity. What, at earlier points in history, was interpreted as the legitimate
justification for conflicts and wars is now – in this variant – offered as the
prime reason for unity. However, in the Danish text this is the odd one out.
Generally the Danes reject, in all substantive senses, the notion that they
'are' European in other than negative and/or ephemeral meanings.

In the *German* data, where one might, perhaps, expect a more
Europeanist inclination, the most striking phenomenon is partly the highly
guarded and circumscribed nature of the respondents' European sentiments and commitment – here the German discursiveness of rational post-
nationalism is conspicuously, and predictably, present – and partly the
frequency and character of the extra-European thought figure. In addition,
it should also be emphasised that a fair number of the German respondents readily concede that they do not feel European, though this is, in
most cases, coupled with some form of relativised statement (e.g. *'(i)ch
fühle mich noch nicht als Europäer, da ich in einer entsprechenden
Situation noch nicht war'* – FRG-23),[15] and is *never* explained – as in the
Danish text – with reference to the respondents' *German* identity.[16] In two
cases, respondents reject the notion of a European identity by interpreting
the postnational argument in humanistic and individualistic terms:

*Ich fühle mich als Mensch. Als solcher versuche ich, menschlich zu sein
und zu denken.*[17] *(FRG-17)*

*Ich fühle mich, wenn ich es genau prüfe, weder als Deutscher noch als
Europäer, sondern als ein Individuum, eingebunden in nähere und
fernere Lebenskreise und eben dadurch geprägt. Ich fühle mich nicht
als Europäer, aber (...) wir [kommen schon] aus einem gemeinsamen
Verstehens- und Verständigungsraum. Wenn Sie so wollen [!], fühle ich
mich dann als Europäer. (Vielleicht auch im hilflosen Umgang mir
einem fernen Eingeborenen).*[18] *(FRG-21).*

This last point echoes the most pervasive feature of the German text, i.e.
the frequency with which Europeanism is situated in negative, relational
'*Ausland*' images. If the six respondents who clearly feel no European
identification at all are subtracted,[19] no less than eight out of the remaining
12 conjure up some image of '*das Ausland*' (the abroad) to explain their
Europeanness, including the two respondents most unequivocally sub-
scribing to a European identity. A few examples:[20]

Eigentlich immer. Insbesondere ausserhalb Europas. (FRG-2)

*Ja. Ich will das an einem Beispiel erläutern: Aufgrund meines
Auftretens und Aussehens hat man mich bereits in jedem Land für einen
Einheimischen gehalten. (FRG-4)*

Am ehesten fühle ich mich als Europäerin, wenn ich mich weit weg von Europa befinde, z.B. in den USA. Dann wachsen auch in meiner Sicht die vielen kleinen [!] Staaten zu einem kleinen [!] Europa zusammen. (FRG-12).

Even a respondent who clearly feels no European identity (FRG-27 – a former GDR citizen) volunteers the subjunctive thought experiment that '*(i)ch denke, ich würde mich bewusst als Europäerin fühlen, wenn ich in Amerika oder Asien wäre*',[21] in the process echoing FRG-12's experientially based statement to the same effect.

The German text thus evinces a clear tendency towards (1) negative or conditional statements concerning European identity, and (2) a negative, extra-European and situational European identification. Many of the respondents in the latter category imagine their identity in 'us–them' dualisms of varying depth and degree, and seem to be drawing imaginary circles round themselves: Europe, particularly Western Europe, does constitute a 'them', but an Otherness which is better and closer than cultures in the next circle, which for some comprises Eastern Europe, for others the USA, and a lot easier to identify with than countries/cultures in the Third World – 'Asian', 'Islamic' or whatever – which are placed in the outer circle and provide a residual of hostile images on the background of which Europe seems like 'home'.

This raises the important question of whether the preponderance of such negations in the German text (and, as we shall see, in the British one as well) is not, in fact, evidence of the conflation of national identity with European identity, or, differently, of the slow replacement of national with European identities. I would dispute such an argument, however. The interesting difference between Self–Other modulations as far as nationalism and Europeanism goes is that in the latter case they are the sole, situationally based determinants of 'European identity' and/or simultaneously grounded in a relatively self-confident *national* sentiment. It is no coincidence that those respondents in the German group who most emphatically embrace the notion of a European identity (FRG-2, -4, and -33) are also those who possessed a 'Germanness' of a fairly confident nature, in great measure liberated from the shackles of the past, and with hardly any qualms about criticising '*das Ausland*'. Conversely, another respondent, FRG-34, strongly linked to the negative German legacy of guilt and expiation, states that she feels '*vorwiegend als Europäer*'.[22]

Somewhat surprisingly perhaps, the *British* text is, in a sense, the one most explicitly European. The embarrassment of contemporary Britishness – 'I feel European (...) in my lack of feeling British, (...) in my desire to be European and to share the cultures of these countries to enrich our-selves' (UK-46) – liaises with the cosmopolitan element of orthodox Anglo-British identity to produce a number of pledges of allegiance to Europe. This is often defined within the same type of negative Self–Other modality as was discussed above in relation to Germany, but the British text also contains a couple of examples of more 'positive' cultural deter-minants of Europeanness, considerably more detailed than the correspond-ing Danish cases. At the other end of the scale, it it interesting that two expatriates in the British group (UK-28 and -31), both living in Denmark, belonged to the respondents who rejected any feeling of Europeanness and aligned themselves with more orthodox British notions of continental Europe: 'No – despite my best efforts. I was born on an island, with its island mentality, and I can see others are "European" but I do not feel it or see it in myself' (UK-31). Also on this count, Britishness as a 'condition of the mind' (UK-19) for those *in* exile, overrides their attachment to their place *of* exile, unlike the configuration evident in the minds of those living in Britain. However, there does seem to be a general tendency in the British group, consonant with these 'expatriate' perceptions, to refer, as did many Germans, to extra- rather than intra-European experiences or imaginings as the kind of basis on which a European sentiment can be/has been erected: 'I still tend to regard Europe as starting on the other side of the Channel, but perhaps feel more European when meeting Americans or Australians' (UK-37); '…especially when talking to Americans or con-templating American foreign policy; also when thinking about Eastern Europe' (UK-51); 'The luxury of waste in Australia or the US is not for us' (UK-54). These snippets represent a dominant anti-American compar-ative perspective – supplemented by a 'Chinese', 'Muslim' or 'African' one – in the British text. Still, it is far removed from transmuting into an identity configuration akin to that of 'national identity'. It is mainly a (negative) 'conviction', born of frustrated Britishness. When I asked another respondent (UK-19), during an interview, 'what is it that makes you feel at home, say, in Brussels or in Paris rather than in Toronto?' (reacting to a statement to this effect), he replied by giving a set of clearly 'negative' reasons:

(T)he differences to begin with. The fact those differences are there, and that they are respected. The fact that there is this enormous varia-tion, […] this huge number of people, with such an enormous number of differences, all living within a relatively small space, shoulder by shoulder, and having for the last forty-odd years succeeded in not fighting any wars with one another of any serious order.

Elsewhere, however, this respondent made it plain that he did not wish to see this form of intercultural recognition and tolerance develop into a national identity proper: The differences are the very reasons why it is possible to live on that continent which we call Europe, and why it will remain vibrant, because the cultural differences are there. [...] I think the national differences will persist, and I think the national differences should be encouraged to persist....' Thus, Europe may be a place for *cultural identification*, but no place for *national identity*. Interestingly, the concept of difference plays a somewhat chameleon role for this respondent and in large parts of both the remaining British and the entire German texts as well. The differences, more or less pronounced, to America, Asia, Africa, the Muslim world, etc. indicate that these respondents are *not* 'American' etc., *but*, on the contrary, European. The differences, more or less pronounced, *within* Europe partly constitute a reason for their Europeanness, therefore, but also a reason why there is no equivalence between this identification with Europe and their national identities, however negatively expressed/perceived these latter may be. Finally, differences within their *nations* are differences of Selfhood – with the exception of the East/West German divide. Crudely put, therefore, differences between Europe and extra-Europe are culturally cosmological (and hence the only domain in which the textual discourse on 'European Identity' occasionally approximates existentialist signification); differences within Europe are those of cultural metonymy (contiguity); and intra-national differences hover between the mode of the cultural simile (e.g. Scotland and England: 'they are *like us*') and the icon of identity (i.e. they are *our likeness*). Each level thus bears the inscription of a different kind and complexity of difference, distributed along the scale from negative to positive determination, from culture (cognitive Interpretant) to identity (essentialist Sign).

CONCLUSION

The progression from top-down constructions via symbolic contestation to bottom-up liminalities has been a trajectory characterised by ever-growing paradox and indeterminacy. Between the confidence of EI discourse and the vacuity of subjective identification with Europe lies a terrain inhabited by noble pretexts and mundane subtexts, a contextual Interpretant of culture that must constantly bear the brunt of whatever the inventors and imaginers of EI elect to make it signify – depending on the particular ethos of the period and the constellations and configurations of political interests.

I have argued that the indeterminacy and contested qualities of EI are the displaced reflection of this notion's precarious position between its analogue – *national* identity/sentiment – and what is best formulated as the transnational political-economic imperative – which the EU is a reflection of, but also a response to. It is this crunch that basically determines the need for constructing European integration in terms other than mere pragmatic, interstate cooperation, and also the difficulties inherent in realising the concept in any comprehensive, let alone socially and affectively 'lived' sense.

In semiotic terms, the disparities – sometimes discrepancies – between Sign and Object, pretext and subtext, are too wide to be mended for good. Not because different levels of identity cannot coexist as total determiners of individuation (this is the optimistic argument often posited), but because both national and European identity lay claim to, i.e. are predicated on, a core political presumption, though the Interpretant – more or less effectively – wraps it in the apparel of 'culture' pure and simple.[23] Nevertheless, EI is nothing without the political dimension – and this Object is too heterogeneous to be internalised as 'identity'. Hence, though it pretends to be little more than a supplemental layer relative to national identity, its political core as well as its centripetal presumption *de facto* translate into something more serious: a potential competitor, a role for which it is both ill-suited and ill-equipped.

It follows that EI is an extraordinarily dependent variable: dependent on the given predicament and degree of political integration. Jacques Delors' development from optimistic enthusiasm to 'active pessimism' also marks the decline of EI notions (and uses) between the late 1980s and the early 1990s. The question is whether EI is little more than a form of 1980s hype that went out with the Cold War, no longer needed or useful after the adhesive tape of integration optimism vanished.

No doubt the post-Cold War scenario is less than propitious towards the production and dissemination of EI notions: the resurgence of national particularism bears witness to this, as does the declining incidence of EI discourse from the EU centre. This does not have to signify the fall of EI and the objectives underlying it, however. Other possibilities exist. It may represent a short-lived phase of pessimism following dramatic changes in the European political landscape. It may herald a change of EU strategy following the subsidiarity drive after 1992. It may indicate tactical caution while preparing for the 1996 Intergovernmental Conference. And it may reflect a more subtextual confidence that both the forging of a common foreign and security policy and the practical advances made in the areas of culture, communication, education, research, environment, etc. will eventually be conducive towards creating the kind of unity desired – with or without discourses of 'European Identity'. Or, for that matter, any of the above in different combinations, depending on national vantage-point. EI is, of necessity and in any phase of integrationist development, a contradictory and liminal construct. For that reason, it must logically oscillate between the extremes of 'unity' and 'diversity', 'enthusiasm' and 'defeatism'. If I am right about the objectivity of the transnational imperative, however, it will only go away if political Europe no longer chooses to respond to, i.e. partially to counteract, this imperative through unified action towards an 'ever closer Union'. This does not seem likely; at least it is a point that has not yet been reached. Until such time, EI and the unique correlations it both contains and works back on will stay on our agenda, and hence need to be more squarely and comprehensively addressed through a combination of political, semiotic and anthropological studies.

NOTES

1. Eco (1990/94: 41). References are to the Midland Book edition, 1994.
2. *Jean Monnet, A Grand Design for Europe*, Periodical 5/88, European Documentation Series, Luxembourg, pp. 43–5. Referred to as Monnet (1988).
3. *A People's Europe: Communication from the Commission to the European Parliament*, COM/88, final edition. Luxembourg: Bulletin of the EC, Supplement 2/88. Henceforth referred to as Bulletin (1988). (Quotes are my translations from the Danish edition of this document.)
4. A question that should not be confused with those enquiring into support for European integration; 'support' and 'identity' are miles apart – about as far as rational-choice orientations and emotive allegiance. For an analysis of the 'support' issue, see Eichenberg and Dalton (1993).
5. Garcia (1993); Goddard, Llobera and Shore (1994); Hedetoft (1994b, 1995); Macdonald (1993); Shore (1993); A.D. Smith (1992).
6. See Eco (1984, 1990/94); Parmentier (1994); Sebeok (1991); Singer (1984).
7. On the meaning of 'Interpretant' and other key concepts, see the detailed discussion in Eco (1979: Chapter 7), where the author points out that apart from being an intellectual or emotional quality, the Interpretant of a Sign may also be 'energetic', i.e. constitute (change of) behaviour, and so be directly immersed in dynamic experience. Looking ahead to the discussion of EI, this would be pertinent in the sense that the common 'cultural' Interpretant is, on the part of the creators of discourse, envisaged as a stimulus giving rise to interpretations of EI in socio-national contexts.
8. Though underlying (and sometimes undercutting) politics is a not-to-be-ignored economic rationale.

9. On nation-states and sovereignty in Europe, see, for example, Hedetoft (1994); James (1986); Keohane (1993); Walker and Mendlovitz (1990); Waever (1995) – as well as Lisbeth Aggestam's chapter in this volume.
10. On the distinction between subtext, context and pretext (my concepts, not Peirce's) – corresponding to Object, Interpretant and Sign in the analysis of national imagery – see my discussion in Hedetoft (1995 Part I, Chapter III).
11. Where national identity is the existential manifestation of instrumentalist *Gesellschaft*, European Identity in the EU is the symbolic shell enveloping the non-existence of a European common consciousness and society, and simultaneously a means towards its hoped-for materialisation.
12. Kohl (1984). See my analysis of the 'German' interaction between national and supranational orientations in Hedetoft (1995: Part I, Chapter VII).
13. In one of his last statements before stepping down, 'Europe according to Delors', he never used the term 'European Identity', but – referring to himself as an 'active pessimist' – addressed the need to develop more powerful institutions, democratic legitimacy, a well-defined security agenda and a stronger sense of unity and mission in the world. Faced with the prospect of fragmentation, he even condoned closer unification in terms of allowing 'the members who are ready and willing to consider extended political and economic integration to unify into a federally constituted community of states', and leaving the rest to take part in no more than a 'common market'. This scenario effectively precludes speaking of a common *identity*. (The document is referred to in its Danish form as reproduced in *Information*, 9 December 1994, as translated by Birgit Ibsen from a German original in *Frankfurter Hefte/Neue Gesellschaft*). A comprehensive assessment of Delors' significance for European integration can be found in Ross (1994).
14. I have explored the issues of this section in another context in Hedetoft (1995: Part I, Chapter III).
15. 'I don't as yet feel European, since I haven't so far been in a corresponding situation.'
16. This does not imply that the existence and strength of German identity is not the factor actually underlying some of these responses, but the fact that none of the Germans has the self-confidence to articulate this represents an important difference from the Danish text. Only FRG-25 comes close to a pattern found in Denmark by curtly answering 'Nein!'
17. 'I feel as a human. As such, I try to be human and to think in a human way.'
18. 'On contemplating the question more precisely, I feel neither German nor European, but as an individual, enmeshed in closer or more distant life circles and influenced by this. I do not feel European, but (...) we [do come] from a common space of comprehension and understanding. If you wish [!], I feel European in that sense. (Perhaps also in my helpless way of relating to some distant natives.)'
19. In view of the fact that such a large portion of the German group are sceptical of a European identity or rebut it outright, and of the fact that the group consists of a fair number of well-educated and well-informed people, it is not unreasonable to assume that feelings of Europeanness in the German population at large cannot run very deep. This is in line with for example *Eurobarometer,* No. 36 (1991), which, in Figure 1.10, quotes 51 per cent of

their German respondents as 'never feeling European' and less than 10 percent as feeling European 'often'.

20. 'Basically always. Particularly outside Europe.' 'Yes. I would like to illustrate that by means of an example: On account of my behaviour and appearance people in every country have already regarded me as a native.' 'I feel most European when I am away from Europe, e.g. in the USA. In those cases, from my perspective, the many small [!] states grow together into one small [!] Europe.'

21. 'I imagine I would feel consciously European if I were in America or Asia.'

22. 'Primarily European.'

23. This has not, so far, progressed to the point of presenting itself as 'nature', as is often the case with national identity.

10 Conclusion
Alice Landau and Richard G. Whitman

The project of rethinking the European Union in the late 1990s consists of two dimensions. Firstly, there is the wider debate on the future development of the Union centred around a number of issues. These encompass three interlinked dimensions: the possibility of implementing the provisions and aspirations detailed in the Treaty on European Union; the ability of the Union to accommodate those countries who aspire to become members of the Union; and the agenda and remit for the 1996 Intergovernmental Conference. Secondly, there is the debate to which this volume is intended to directly contribute. The latter debate is how the contemporary and future dynamics of the European Union might best be conceptualised and studied. The premise that underlies this project is that organised eclecticism provides the best way forward for the latter debate.

This volume has not attempted to comprehensively map the contours of the contemporary study of the European Union. The study of the European Union could be said to have reached a certain level of maturity in that the 'state of the art' cannot be contained within a single volume. The literature is now awash with a variety of specialisms and particular foci encompassing leadership, institutional and inter-institutional relationships, the political economy of the EU, policy areas, foreign policy and area studies specialists. A *study des patries* appears to be the governing condition. In this context there is the absence of a common research agenda and common theoretical standpoints to unite the explanation or understanding of the European Union. Furthermore, the question can be raised as to whether there is any utility in seeking such a common explanatory framework.

In recognising this condition the approach that we have adopted in this volume is an attempt to at least chart some of the frontiers of the study of the European Union. The ordering device we have used is not one of a common methodology but the concepts of institutions, interests and identities. Each author has been free to interpret and to utilise these concepts in their own manner.

Working from a common cluster of concepts each author has selected different subject-matter for their own enquiry. However, a number of

171

common features are apparent in these disparate approaches. Firstly, there is the absence of clear-cut geopolitical or theoretical boundaries. That is, the geopolitical context that our authors render as significant for comprehending the contemporary dynamics of the Union ranges from global to domestic phenomena. The boundaries of the theoretical contexts within which to study the Union are also disparate, ranging from neofunctionalism to semiosis. On the basis of the work of authors in this volume we draw a number of conclusions on the contemporary and future study of the Union.

FALSE DICHOTOMIES

There has long been a praxis between the frameworks which have sought to capture European integration and the process of realising European integration itself. The wider debate about the status and future direction of European integration has been intrinsically linked to the frameworks for the study of the Union. Perhaps this is best illustrated in the relationship between Monnet's *savant progressivité* and Haas's *spillover*. Debates have been cast in terms of dichotomies between intergovernmentalism and supranationalism, widening and deepening, unity and difference.

In rethinking the European Union we must start from the observation that the study of the European Union cannot be based upon false dichotomies, primarily the debate between intergovernmentalism and supranationalism. From the outset of European integration there was the rationale that there would be the creation of autonomous supranational agents, constraining the role of the states. Above the Member States, supranational institutions would not only guarantee the process of integration, but would also be a demonstration of its success. This project of integration was certainly assisted by the environment within which it took place: the Cold War in Europe. The imperatives of the Cold War required a subsuming of profound differences between the Member States, and alongside there was the development and progressive enlargement of the EC as an increasingly important arena for state-to-state relations in Western Europe.

In the ideal-type of the process of European integration the engine of integration would function with the Commission being the agenda-setter, the engineer fuelling the project of integration with new ideas. From its outset the project was complicated by the creation of the Council of Ministers accepting or rejecting proposals and thereby introducing a complex pattern of bargaining and trade-offs between benefits and burdens. Alongside this emergent system of multilevel governance the body that was to become the European Parliament struggled for both a role and a recognition of its own legitimacy.

The Maastricht Treaty formally codified the supranational and the intergovernmental dimensions of European construction into a common structure for the first time. On one hand, there was the opening of the final act of the Treaty of Rome, with a timetable for Economic and Monetary Union. Alongside there was the formal establishment of a Political Union, citizenship of the Union and an attendant Common Foreign and Security Policy.

The attempt by the Union to frame a wider and more coherent political role has made it more visible in the international system. However, the instruments in its possession do not automatically guarantee the appropriate responses to the changing environment. When the situation in the former Yugoslavia demanded a common stance, the EU demonstrated a timidity that was in contrast to the far-reaching goals it had set for itself. There continues to be an ambivalence about pursuing a common or harmonised stance in international affairs.

New concepts have been progressively created in the debate on European integration to cope with new realities. It is in the creation of these new concepts that we find the second false debate on the EU: that between widening and deepening. Widening and deepening were reconcilable when widening was part of a longer-term process and the Cold War limited the list of possible candidates for membership. Each successive enlargement has had a consequential affect upon both the scope for political coalition-building and the effectiveness of EU institutions. It is pertinent to ask whether the Union will be able to continue to deepen the level of integration when successive enlargements continue to add new economic and political interests to the already heterogeneous EU. Whatever institutional arrangements are made there is no certainty that these will deepen integration by strengthening the powers and competencies of the EU institutions. The European Union has reached a stage in its development when debate is needed on the appropriateness and the adequacy of the present political structures and levels of government. Institutional effectiveness, scope and the divisions of responsibility in the EU are issues that have to be contemplated. So far, the European Union has not provided a strong sense of collective identity. With a potential membership of twenty upwards from the early part of the next century, the challenge of promoting a collective consciousness is likely to increase.

The third false dichotomy is between unity and the differences in the EU. Variable geometry was intrinsic to the integration process from its beginning. The European construction can really be characterised as the multilateralisation of national interests, which accommodate domestic preferences and increase the collective influence of the Member States. If the Member States can find trade-offs that compensate the loss of autonomy that derives from membership then they balance their costs and benefits. However, as was witnessed in the Maastricht ratification debate, there is not necessarily a congruence of opinion between the political elites and the general public over the value of the bargains that have been cast.

Domestic politics have been an element of the Community process from the very beginning. Each Member State views the EU through the lens of its own policy preferences, and adheres to a project because the EU aggregates their preferences. As the EC/EU operates across a range of sectors, there has been the opportunity to construct both bargains and to obtain trade-offs. The EU is essentially an accommodative instrument. Governments have avoided granting open-ended authority to the supranational institutions which would infringe Member State sovereignty.

Rethinking the EU also requires a focus upon the weakness of the Union. First of all, the Union lacks an effective supranational political organisation which could legally and morally represent all the peoples within the EU.

There are presently 15 governments that legitimately represent their people, but no European authority which can directly represent either the population of the Union or all the Member States with the degree of legitimacy that accrues to the governments of the constituent states. Secondly, the EU lacks a proper defence system. The Member States are mainly organised either individually or under the aegis of NATO. However, some kind of a European defence identity will probably grow from the increasing defence cooperation that is taking place between the EU Member States, although it will hardly be in competition with NATO, but rather in some kind of association with it.

FUTURE CONDITIONALITIES

In the medium term the European Union is likely to be beset by a number of challenges that will both occupy the policy-makers and the citizenry of the Union and impact upon attempts to study the Union. The first challenge is the widening of the membership of the Union. The digestion of the recent enlargement extending the Union to Austria, Finland and Sweden and the commitment through pre-accession strategies to enlarge the Union to encompass the Central and Eastern European states, Malta and Cyprus presents the first challenge. The second challenge is the attempt to realise the objectives set down in the Treaty on European Union. The most notable of these objectives are the project and timetable for Economic and Monetary Union and the aspiration to create a Common Foreign and Security Policy. The third challenge is the commencement of the Intergovernmental Conference scheduled for 1996, preparation for which is already underway through the work of the Group of Reflection meeting from early 1995.

Enlargement

In the beginning of 1995 the EU increased its membership to 15 Member States. Measured in terms of capabilities the enlargement increased the geographical extent, populace and economy of the Union. The enlargement went beyond institutional tinkering to accommodate three new members and brought three new sources of influence and three new sets of interests into the Union. Furthermore, the enlargement brought three new states into the Union who had previously stepped aside from the European integration project. Austria, Sweden and Finland had each defined their place in the landscape of international relations in terms of neutrality, although each state had interpreted and imbued this concept with a distinct meaning. If Barbé's thesis outlined in this volume is accepted, the impact that these new members may have is in reinforcing existent cleavages among the Member States.

In terms of classifying states within the landscape of contemporary international relations in Western Europe it now an easier exercise to define the non-Member States rather than the Member States of the European Union. The aberrant states are those that have remained outside the Union – Iceland, Norway and Switzerland. Non-membership of the Union rather than a standpoint of neutrality adopted by some states during the Cold War becomes part of the typology by which nation-states in Europe can now be ordered. Increasingly it is the depth or the extent of intra-Union differences between the Member States that are of first rather than a second order in understanding the contemporary interstate dynamics of Europe.

The lengthening queue of aspirants to join the European Union raises intra-EU questions as to how the existing institutional and policy arrangements can cope with a substantive widening of the Union. Hence, for the next decade enlargement is the terrain over which theological battles will be fought as to the appropriate principles that should guide the Union. A more temporal concern will be the nature of the bargains that will be struck to accommodate an expanded membership. Although the Union could be said to be occupied with the project implied in its name the motivations of the aspirant members are not to be found in the words of the Schumann declaration. Rather, the attraction offered by being a part of a club that has an image of material prosperity and as the best guarantor of security in its widest sense is of more immediate attraction. In short, aspirations for a common European home has given way to the desire for residence in the European Union condominium.

The consequence of a succession of enlargements also extends beyond Europe. The successive enlargements increase the relative international significance of the Union. It is not necessary to buy the logic of geo-economics or head-to-head competition to reflect upon the enhanced standing of an enlarging Union as measured through figures for volumes of international trade or as a coalition within international organisations.

Realising the TEU Objectives

The Treaty on European Union codified a set of aspirations for the Union. Through the creation of the three-pillar structure and a set of opt-outs and opt-ins there is the formal recognition that the classic supranational project had long given way to a variable geometry of involvement.

A reading of the European integration process prior to the TEU could characterise an integration project constrained by the aberrant or *un-communitaire* behaviour of leaders such as de Gaulle or Thatcher. The popular reluctance and challenges to integration by its citizenry, manifested through opposition demonstrated during the Maastricht ratification process and the election of anti-integrationist candidates to the European Parliament in 1994, demonstrated that conceptions of a wholly elite-governed process were no longer appropriate. The imperatives of the timetable for EMU and the maintenance of persistently high levels of unemployment, despite the promotion of economic prosperity as a part of the Union *raison d'être*, would appear to mitigate against attempts to generate universal support for the Union through economic means.

The 1996 IGC

The attempt to take forward both the aims and objectives detailed in the TEU together with the planned enlargement of the Union looks set to occupy the deliberations of the 1996 Intergovernmental Conference that was envisaged in the TEU.

The IGC is already *de facto* under way with the work of the Group of Reflection. The issues that could be said to be shaping up as Union issues of discussion are institutional arrangements and the functioning and codification of the existent policy areas and inter-institutional arrangements, the relationship of citizens to the Union, the external actions of the Union including the Common Foreign and Security Policy and questions of defence.

The backdrop to these events is provided by a series of interrelated intra- and extra-EU developments that have flowed through the contributions to this volume: firstly, the manifestation of globalisation that problematises distinctions between the domestic and the international and creates a condition to which the Union is forced to accommodate; secondly, the changing landscape of international relations in Europe and beyond and to which the Union is a contributing agent; thirdly, both the role and the appropriate remit that the Member States, both individually and collectively, conceive for the Union across the territories of the Union, within the wider Europe and in the international system.

The project of rethinking the European Union in the late 1990s is one of accommodating an ongoing process. The attempt to capture the many facets and the complexity of the Union has itself generated a disparate body of literature. The wealth of academic literature that is currently being generated in the study of the European Union should be viewed as a demonstration of the vitality of the subject area. Indeed, just as the European Union seeks to come to terms with the complexity of the changed geopolitical landscape of the late twentieth century those engaged in rethinking the study of the Union are faced with the absence of clear-cut intellectual structures.

Bibliography

Abromeit, H. (1992) Staatstätigkeit und Immobilismus: nur ein Schweizer Phänomen? In H. Abromeit and W.W. Pommerehne (eds), *Staatstätigkeit in der Schweiz*. Bern/Stuttgart: Haupt Verlag, pp. 305–25.

Aggarwal, V. (1994) Comparing regional cooperation efforts in the Asia Pacific and North America. In A. Mack and J. Ravenhill (eds), *Pacific Cooperation: Building Economic and Security Regimes in the Asia Pacific Region*. Sydney: Allen & Unwin.

Ahonen, P. (ed.) (1993) *Tracing the Semiotic Boundaries of Politics*. Berlin: Mouton de Gruyter.

Alber, J. (1987) *Vom Armenhaus zum Wohlfahrtsstaat. Analysen zur Entwicklung der Sozialversicherung in Westeuropa*. Frankfurt am Main/New York: Campus.

Alker, H. and Biersteker, T. (1984) The dialectics of world order: notes for a future archaeologist of international savoir-faire. *International Studies Quarterly*, 28(2), 121–42.

Allen, D. (1982) Political cooperation and Euro-Arab dialogue. In D. Allen, R. Rummel and W. Wessels (eds), *European Political Cooperation*. London: Butterworth.

Allen, D. and Smith, M. (1990) Western Europe's presence in the contemporary international arena. *Review of International Studies*, 16, 19–37.

Andersen, S.S., and Eliassen, K.A. (1993) The EC as a new political system. In S.S. Andersen and K.A. Eliassen (eds), *Making Policy in Europe, The Europeification of National Policy-Making*. London: Sage.

Andreotti, G. (1990) L'Italia e il suo semestre di presidenza della Comunità europea. *Affari Esteri*, Anno XXII, 81, 385–96.

Apunen, O. (1993) 'Eurodiscipline' wanted? International relations as a research orientation and academic discipline in Europe. In F.R. Pfetsch (ed.), *International Relations and Pan-Europe: Theoretical Approaches and Empirical Findings*. Hamburg: Lit Verlag.

Armingeon, K. (1994a) *Staat und Arbeitsbeziehungen. Ein internationaler Vergleich*. Opladen: Westdeutscher Verlag.

Armingeon, K. (1994b) Ante el final de la socialdemocracia? Los partidos socialdemocratas en el poder: evolución desde una perspectiva comparada, 1945–1990. In W. Merkel (ed.), *Entre la modernidad y el postmaterialismo. La socialdemocracia europea a finales del siglo XX*. Madrid: Alianza Editorial.

Aron, R. (1949) Les articles du Figaro, 26 Janvier, quoted by Masclet, J.-C. (1994) *Où en est l'Europe politique?* La Documentation française, Note 2, 79.

Aron, R. and Lerner, D. (eds) (1955) *La querelle de la CED, Essais d'analyse sociologique*. Paris: A. Colin.

Ashford, D.E. (1982) *Policy and Politics in France: Living with Uncertainty*. Philadelphia: Temple University Press.

Attinà, F. (1994) *On Political Representation in the European Union: Party Politics, Electoral System and Territorial Representation.* Paper presented at the 22nd ECPR Sessions of Workshop on Democratic Representation and the Legitimacy of Government in the EC. Madrid: 17–22 April.

Axelrod, R. (1984) *The Evolution of Cooperation.* New York: Basic Books.

Baldwin, D.A. (1993) *Neorealism and Neoliberalism.* New York: Columbia University Press.

Bance, A. (1992) The idea of Europe: from Erasmus to ERASMUS. *Journal of European Studies,* **22**(1), 1–19.

Barbé, E. (1989) La Cooperación Política Europea, *Revista de Instituciones Europeas,* **16**(1), 95–100.

Barbé, E. (1990) El año español de la Cooperación Política Europea. *Anuario Internacional CIDOB 1989.* Barcelona, CIDOB, 109–120.

Barbé, E. (1992) Spanien. In W. Weidenfeld and W. Wessels (eds), *Jahrbuch der Europäischen Integration 1991/92.* Bonn: Institut für Europäische Politik.

Barnett, M. (1990) High politics is low politics: the domestic and systemic sources of Israeli security policy, 1967–1977. *World Politics,* **42**, 529–63.

Beck, N. et al. (1993) Government partisanship, labor organization, and macroeconomic performace: a corrigendum. *American Political Science Review,* **87**, 945–8.

Benz, A. (1989) Regierbarkeit im kooperativen Bundesstaat. Eine Bilanz der Föderalismusforschung. In S. Bandemer and G. Wewer (eds), *Regierungsstystem und Regierungslehre.* Opladen: Leske und Budrich.

Berger, P.L. and Luckmann, T. (1966) *The Social Construction of Reality. A Treatise in the Sociology of Knowledge.* New York: Doubleday.

Berglas, E. (1986) Defense and economy. In Y. Ben-Porath (ed.), *The Israeli Economy.* Cambridge, MA: Harvard University Press.

Bieber, R. (1990) Democratic control of foreign policy. *European Journal of International Law,* **1**(1/2), 148–73.

Blackbourn, D. and Eley, G. (1984) *The Peculiarities of German History: Bourgeois Society and Politics in Nineteenth Century Germany.* Oxford: Oxford University Press.

Blondel, J. (1974) *The Government of France,* 2nd edn. London: Methuen.

Bogdanor, V. (1990) *Democratising the Community.* Discussion Paper No. 2, London: Federal Trust.

Boulding, K.E. (1956a) *The Image: Knowledge in Life and Society.* Ann Arbor: University of Michigan Press.

Boulding, K.E. (1956b) General systems theory – the skeleton of science. *Management Science,* **2**(3), 197–208.

Brewin, C. (1987) The European Community: a union of states without unity of government. *Journal of Common Market Studies,* **26**(1), 1–23.

Brown, C. (1993) Sorry comfort? The case against 'international theory'. In F. Pfetsch (ed.) International Relations and Pan Europe: Theoretical Approaches and Emprical Findings. Munster: Lit Verlag.

Brown, C. international theory and international society: the viability of the middle way, *Review of International Studies,* **21**, 183–96.

Brown, R. (1992) Introduction: towards a new synthesis of international relations. In M. Bowker and R. Brown (eds), *From Cold War to Collapse: Theory and World Politics in the 1980s.* Cambridge: Cambridge University Press.

180 *Bibliography*

Brownlie, I. (1980) Parliamentary control over foreign policy in the United Kingdom. In A. Cassese (ed.), *Parliamentary Control over Foreign Policy*. Alphen aan den Rijn, The Netherlands/Germantown, MD: Sijthoff & Noordhoff.

Brückner, P. (1990) The European Community and the United Nations. *European Journal of International Law*, 1(1/2), 189.

Bull, H. (1977) *The Anarchical Society: A Study of Order in World Politics*. London: Macmillan.

Bull, H. (1982) Civilian power Europe: a contradiction in terms. *Journal of Common Market Studies*, 21, 149–70.

Bull, H. and Watson, A. (eds) (1984) *The Expansion of International Society*. Oxford: Oxford University Press.

Bulmer, S. (1983) Domestic politics and European Community policy-making. *Journal of Common Market Studies*, 21(4), 349–63.

Bulmer, S. (1985) The European Council's First Decade: Between Interdependence and Domestic Politics. *Common Market Studies* 24(2), 92–4.

Bulmer, S. (1991) Analysing European political cooperation: the case for a two-tier analysis. Chapter 4 in M. Holland (1991).

Bulmer, S. and Scott, A. (1994) Economic and political integration a decade on. In S. Bulmer and A. Scott (eds), *Economic and Political Integration in Europe, Internal Dynamics and Global Context*. Oxford: Blackwell.

Busch, A. (1995) *Preisstabilitätspolitik. Politik und Inflationsraten im Internationalen Vergleich*. Opladen: Leske und Budrich.

Calhoun, C. (1991) The Problem of identity in collective action. In J. Huber (ed.), *Macro-Micro Linkages in Sociology*. Beverly Hills, CA: Sage.

Calleo, D. (1978) *The German Problem Reconsidered: Germany and the World Order*. Cambridge, CUP.

Carlsnaes, W. (1994a) Compatibility and the agent-structure issue. In W. Carlsnaes and S. Smith (eds), *European Foreign Policy. The EC and Changing Perspectives in Europe*. London: Sage.

Carlsnaes, W. (1994b) In lieu of a conclusion: compatibility and the agency-structure issue in foreign policy analysis. In W. Carlsnaes and S. Smith (eds), *European Foreign Policy. The EC and Changing Perspectives in Europe*. London: Sage.

Carlsnaes, W. and Smith, S. (eds) (1994) *European Foreign Policy.The EC and Changing Perspectives in Europe*. London: Sage.

Carr, E.H. (1946) *The Twenty Years' Crisis 1919–1939*, 2nd edn. London: Macmillan.

Carstairs, C. and Ware, R. (eds) (1991) *Parliament and International Relations*. Milton Keynes/Philadelphia: Open University Press.

Cass, D.Z. (1992) The word that saves Maastricht? The principle of subsidiarity and the division of powers within the European Community. *Common Market Law Review*, 29, 1107–36.

Cassese, A. (1980) Foreign affairs and the Italian constitution. In A. Cassese (ed.), *Parliamentary Control over Foreign Policy*. Alphen aan den Rijn, The Netherlands/Germantown, MD: Sijthoff & Noordhoff.

Cassese, A. (ed.) (1980) *Parliamentary Control over Foreign Policy*. Alphen aan den Rijn, The Netherlands/Germantown, MD: Sijthoff & Noordhoff.

Christensen, T. (1993) Conclusion: system stability and the security of the most vulnerable ssignificant actor. In J. Snyder and R. Jervis (eds), *Coping with Complexity in the International System*. Oxford: Westview Press.

Clark, I. (1989) Making sense of sovereignty. *Review of International Studies*, **14**(4), 303–7.

Clarke, A. (1992) François Mitterrand and the idea of Europe. In B. Nelson, D. Roberts and W. Veil (eds), *The Idea of Europe: Problems of National and Transnational Identity*. New York/Oxford: Berg.

Clarke, M. (1989) The foreign policy system: a framework for analysis. In M. Clarke and B. White (eds), *Understanding Foreign Policy: The Foreign Policy Systems Approach*. Aldershot: Edward Elgar.

Clarke, M. (1992) *British External Policy-making in the 1990s*. London: Macmillan for RIIA.

Clarke, M. and White, B. (eds) (1989) *Understanding Foreign Policy: The Foreign Policy Systems Approach*. Aldershot: Edward Elgar.

Cohen, R. (1994) Pacific unions: a reappraisal of theory that democracies do not go to war with each other. *Review of International Studies*, **20**(3), 207–24.

Coker, C. (1992) Post-modernity and the end of the Cold War: has war been disinvented? *Review of International Studies*, **18**(3), 189–98.

Commission of the European Communities (1976) Euopean Union: Report by Mr Leo Tindemans, Prime Minister of Belgium, to the European Council. *Bulletin of the European Communities*, Supplement 1/76.

Commission of the European Communities (1987) *Treaties Establishing the European Communities (ECSC, EEC, EAEC) – Single European Act – Other Basic Instruments* (abridged edn). Luxembourg: Office for Official Publications of the European Communities.

Commission of the European Communities (1988) A people's Europe: Communication from the COM (88) 331 final. *Bulletin of the European Communities*, Supplement No. 2.

Commission of the European Communities (1991) Contribution by the Commission on the development of a common external policy. *Bulletin of the European Communities*, Supplement No. 2, 89–96.

Coombes, D. (1975) Introductory study to papers on national Parliaments. In Directorate-General for Research and Documentation of the European Parliament (ed.), *Symposium on European Integration and the Future of the Parliaments in Europe*. European Parliament, pp. 23–6 at p. 23. Quoted in Lodge, J. (1978) The functions powers and 'decline' of parliaments. In V. Herman and J. Lodge (eds), *The European Parliament and the European Community*. London: Macmillan.

Cooper, R.N. (1986) *Economic Policy in an Interdependent World*. Cambridge, MA: MIT Press.

Corbett, R. (1993) Governance and institutional developments. In N. Nugent (ed.), The European Community 1992, Annual Review. *Journal of Common Market Studies*, **31**, 27–50.

Cot, J.P. (1980) Parliament and foreign policy in France. In A. Cassese (ed.), *Parliamentary Control over Foreign Policy*. Alphen aan den Rijn, The Netherlands/Germantown, MD: Sijthoff & Noordhoff.

Council of the European Communities and Commission of the European Communities (1992) *Treaty on European Union*. Luxembourg: Office for Official Publications of the European Communities.

Cox, R. (1981) Social forces, states and world orders: beyond international relations theory. *Millennium*, **10**(2), 126–55.

Cox, R. (1993) Structural issues of global governance: implications for Europe. In S. Gill (ed.), *Gramsci, Historical Materialism and International Relations*. Cambridge: Cambridge University Press.

Crockatt, R. (1993) Theories of stability and the end of the Cold War. In M. Bowker and R. Brown (eds), *From Cold War to Collapse: Theory and World Politics in the 1980s*. Cambridge: Cambridge University Press.

Dastoli, P.-V. (1994) *L'elezione del parlamento europeo e il suo ruolo nelle istituzioni comunitarie*, Europa, 1, Bologna, Il Mulino, 43, 5–12.

de Clerq (1993) *Reflection on Information and Communication Policy of the European Community*. Report by the Group of Experts chaired by Mr Willy de Clerq, Member of the European Parliament, March 1993.

Deheusse, R., Regelsberger, E., Weiler, J.H.H. and Wessels, W. (eds) *European Political Cooperation Documentation Bulletins* (various edns). Luxembourg: Office for Official Publications of the European Communities.

de Schoutheete, P. (1986) *La Coopération politique Européenne*, 2nd edn. Brussels: Labor.

de Schoutheete, P. (1994) *The negotiations concerning Chapter V of the Treaty of Maastricht*. Paper (unpublished) presented at the seminar on Regional and Global Responsibilities of the European Union in the 1990s. The Potential and Limits of the CFSP. Brussels: 27–29 January.

de Vree, J. (1972) *Political Integration: The Formation of Theory and Its Problems*. Paris: New Babylon.

Denhousse, R. (1991) *Une politique étrangère pour l'Europe. Rapport du groupe de travail sur la réforme de la coopération politique européenne*. EUI Working Papers, No. 8, European Policy Unit.

Deportes, A. (1979) *Europe Between the Superpowers*. New Haven, CT: Yale University Press.

Deutsch, K.W., Burrell, S.A., Kahn, R.A. et al. (1957) *Political Community in the North Atlantic Area*. Princeton, NJ: Princeton University Press.

Dominicé, Ch. (1992) In Labouz, M.F. (ed.) *Les accords de Maastricht et la Constitution de l'Union européenne*, Centre de droit international de Nanterre. Paris: Montchrestien.

Donnelly, M. and Ritchie, E. (1994) The College of Commissioners and their Cabinets. In G. Edwards, and D. Spence (eds), *The European Commission*. London: Longman.

Dougherty, J.E. and Pfaltzgraff, R. (1971) *Contending Theories of International Relations*. New York: J.B. Lippincott.

[Draft Treaty, 1991] Draft Treaty towards European Union from the Dutch Presidency, *Agence Europe* Documents, No. 1733.

Duchêne, F. (1972) Europe's role in world peace. In R. Mayne (ed.), *Europe Tomorrow, Sixteen Europeans Look Ahead*. London: Fontana.

Duchêne, F. (1973) The European Community and the uncertainties of interdependence. In M. Kohnstamm and W. Hager (eds), *A Nation Writ Large? Foreign-Policy Problems before the European Community*. London: Macmillan.

Dyer, H.C., and Mangasarian, L. (1989) *The Study of International Relations: The State of the Art*. London: Macmillan.

Easton, D. (1953) *The Political System*. New York: Knopf.

Easton, D. (1965) *A Systems Analysis of Political Life*. New York: John Wiley & Sons.

Eco, U. (1976) *A Theory of Semiotics*. Bloomington, IN: Indiana State University Press.

Eco, U. (1979) *The Role of the Reader. Explorations in the Semiotics of Texts.* Bloomington, IN: Indiana State University Press.

Eco, U. (1984) *Semiotics and the Philosophy of Language*. Bloomington, IN: Indiana State University Press.

Eco, U. (1990/94) *The Limits of Interpretation*. Bloomington, IN: State Indiana University Press.

Edwards, G. (1984) Europe and the Falkland Islands. *Journal of Common Market Studies*, **22**(4), 295–313.

Edwards, G. and Regelberger, E. (eds) (1990) *Europe's Global Links: The European Community and Inter-Regional Cooperation*. London: Pinter.

Edwards, G. and Spence, D. (1994) The European Commission. London: Longman.

Eichenberg, R.C. and Dalton, R.J. (1993) European and the European Community: The Dynamics of Public Support for European integration. *International Organization*, **47**(4), 507–34.

Emery, F. (ed.) (1981) *Systems Thinking: 2*. Harmondsworth: Penguin.

Esping-Andersen, G. (1990) *The Three Worlds of Welfare Capitalism*. Princeton, NJ: Princeton University Press.

Etzioni, A. (1965) *Political Unification*. New York: Holt, Rinehart & Winston.

Faure, G.O., and Rubin, J.Z. (eds) (1993) *Culture and Negotiation*. Thousand Oaks, CA: Sage.

Fielding, L. (1991) *Europe as a Global Partner: The External Relations of the European Community*. London: UACES Occasional Paper No 7.

Finnemore, M. (1993) International organizations as teachers of norms: the United Nations Educational, Scientific, and Cultural Organization and science policy. *International Organization*, **47**, 565–97.

Fitzmaurice, J. (1994) The European Commission. In A. Duff, J. Pinder and R. Price (eds), *Maastricht and Beyond. Building the European Union*. London: Routledge.

Flora, P. (1983) *State, Economy, and Society in Western Europe 1815–1975*. Frankfurt am Main/London/Chicago: Campus/Macmillan/St. James Press.

Ford, G. (1993) The European Parliament and democracy. In *The Evolution of a European: Socialism, Science and Europe*. Spokesman for European Labour Forum, Nottingham: 201–6

Franke, J.A. and MacArthur, A.T. (1988) Political versus currency premia in international real interest differentials. A study of forward rates for 24 countries. *European Economic Review*, **32**, 1083–121.

Frankel, J. (1988) *International Relations in a Changing World*. Oxford: Oxford University Press.

Friedrich, C.J. (1963) *Man and His Government – An Empirical Theory of Politics*. New York: McGraw Hill.

Friman, R. (1993) Side-payments versus security cards: domestic bargaining tactics in international economic negotiations. *International Organization*, **47**, 387–410.

Fröhlich, H. (1991) Der internationale Kapitalverkehr. Quantitative Bedeutung und ökonomische Funktion. *Der Bürger im Staat*, **41**, 116–20.

Fukuyama, F. (1989) The end of history. *The National Interest*, No. 16 (Summer), 3–18.

Gaddis, J.L. (1992/93) International relations theory and the end of the Cold War. *International Security*, **17**(3), 51–8.

Gaja, G. (1980) European Parliament and foreign affairs: political co-operation among the Nine. In A. Cassese (ed.), *Parliamentary Control over Foreign Policy*. Alphen aan den Rijn, The Netherlands/Germantown, MD: Sijthoff & Noordhoff.

Galtung, J. (1973) *The European Community: A Superpower in the Making*. London: George Allen & Unwin.

García, S. (1993) Europe's fragmented identities and the frontiers of citizenship. In S. García (ed.), *European Identity and the Search for Legitimacy*. London: Pinter.

García, S. (ed.) (1993) *European Identity and the Search for Legitimacy*. London: Pinter.

Garrett, G. and Lange, P. (1991) Political responses to interdependence: what's 'left' for the left? *International Organization*, **45**, 539–64.

Gazzo, E. (1992) Europe's memory. Agence *Europe*, No. 6223 (n.s.), 4 May 1992.

Ghebali, Y. (1991) Le role de la CE dans le processus de la CSCE. *Revue du Marché Commun* 343, 8–13.

George, S. (1991) European Political Cooperation: a world systems perspective. In: M. Holland (ed.), *The Future of European Political Cooperation*. London: Macmillan.

George, S. (1992) *Politics and Policy in the European Community*, 2nd edn. Oxford: Oxford University Press.

George, S. (1992) The European Community in the New Europe. In C. Crouch and D. Marquand (eds), *Towards a Greater Europe? A Continent Without an Iron Curtain*. Oxford: Blackwell.

Giddens, A. (1984) *The Constitution of Society*. Berkeley, CA: University of California Press.

Giddens, A. (1985) *A Contemporary Critique of Historical Materialism Vol. 2. The Nation-State and Violence*. Oxford: Basil Blackwell.

Giddens, A. (1990) *The Consequences of Modernity*. Cambridge: Polity Press.

Gil Ibáñez, A.A. (1992) Spain. In F. Laursen and S. Vanhoonacker (eds), *The Intergovernmental Conference on Political Union, Institutional Reforms, New Policies and International Identity of the European Community*. Maastricht: European Institute of Public Administration.

Gill, S. (ed.) (1993) *Gramsci, Historical Materialism and International Relations*. Cambridge: Cambridge University Press.

Gilpin, R. (1981) *War and Change in World Politics*. Cambridge: Cambridge University Press.

Ginsberg, R. (1989) *The Foreign Policy Actions of the European Community, the Politics of Scale*. Boulder, CO/London: Lynne Rienner/Adamantine Press.

Goddard, V.A., Llobera, J.R. and Shore, C. (eds) (1994) *The Anthropology of Europe. Identities and Boundaries in Conflict*. Oxford: Berg.

Goldmann, K. (1994) *International Relations: The Promotion of Peace, the Investigation of Institutions, or the Deconstruction of Discourses?* Paper presented at the International Political Science Association. Berlin: 21–24 August, OSA.

Goldmann, K. (1994) *Post-Cold War Europe: Internationalist Vision and the Institution of National Independence*. Working Paper. Stockholm: Department of Political Science, University of Stockholm.

Gourevitch, P. (1986) *Politics in Hard Times. Comparative Responses to International Economic Crises.* Ithaca, NY/London: Cornell University Press.

Grande, E. (1994) *Forschungspolitik und die Einflusslogik europäischer Politikverflechtung, Köln/Potsdam.* Papier für den DVPW-Arbeitskreis Europäische Integration. Potsdam: 25–28. August.

Gray, J. (1993) From communism to civil society: the re-emergence of history and the decline of the Western model. *Social Philosophy and Policy,* **10**(2), 26–50.

Greven, M.Th. (1992) Political parties between national identity and Eurofication. In B. Nelson, D. Roberts and W. Veit (eds), *The Idea of Europe.* New York, Oxford: Berg.

Griffith, R. (1995) *The Dynamics and Stages of European Construction, 1945–1995.* Paris: Discussion paper for the seminar on the Regional Integration Process.

Groom, J.(1993) *The European Community: Building Up, Building Down, and Building Across.* Contribution to the Manresa Conference on People's Rights and European Structures. Barcelona: Centre Unesco de Catalunya.

Haas, E. (1969) Collective security and the future of the international system. In E.C. Balck and R.A. Falk (eds) *The Future of the International Legal Order: a general introduction,* Princeton: Princeton University Press.

Haas, E.B. (1958) *The Uniting of Europe – Political, Social and Economical Forces, 1950–1957.* London: Stevens, 1964.

Hall, P. (1986) *Governing the Economy. The Politics of State Intervention in Britain and France.* New York/Oxford: Oxford University Press.

Halliday, F. (1983) *The Making of the Second Cold War.* London: Verso.

Handelman, D. (1990) *Models and Mirrors: Towards an Anthropology of Public Events.* Cambridge: Cambridge University Press.

Hanreider, W. (1978) Dissolving international politics: reflections on the nation-state. *American Political Science Review,* **72**(4), 1276–87.

Hanson, M. (1993) Democratisation and norm creation in Europe. *European Security after the Cold War, Part I.* Adelphi Paper 284. London: Brassey's for the IISS.

Hassner, P. (1993) Beyond nationalism and internationalism: ethnicity and world order. *Survival,* **35**(2), 49–63.

Hay, P. (1966) *Federalism and Supranational Organizations.* Urbana: University of Illinois Press.

Hay, R. (1989) *La Commission européenne et l'administration de la Communauté.* Luxembourg: Office des publications officielles des Communautés européennes.

Hedetoft, U. (1994a) The state of sovereignty in Europe. In S. Zetterholm (ed.), *National Cultures and European Integration.* Oxford: Berg.

Hedetoft, U. (1994b) National identities and European integration 'from below': bringing people back in. *Journal of European Integration,* **1**. Previously published as Working Paper No. 54 (1994) in *Working Paper Series of the Center for European Studies,* Harvard University.

Hedetoft, U. (1995) *Signs of Nations. Studies in the Political Semiotics of Self and Other in Contemporary European Nationalism.* Aldershot: Dartmouth.

Held, D. (1993) *Political Theory and the Modern State.* Oxford: Blackwell.

Held, D. and McGrew, A. (1993) Globalization and the liberal democratic state. *Government and Opposition,* **28**, 2.

Héritier, A., Mingers, S., Knill, C. and Becka, M. (1994) *Die Veränderung von Staatlichkeit in Europa. Ein regulativer Wettbewerb: Deutschland,*

Grossbritannien und Frankreich in der Europäischen Union. Opladen: Leske und Budrich.

Herman, V. and Lodge, J. (1978) *The European Parliament and the European Community.* London: Macmillan.

Herrberg, A. (1994) *A Search for a New Conceptual Framework for the Study of European Foreign and Security Policy. Systems Determinants towards European Security: An Observation of the NATO Ultimatum towards Sarajevo.* Paper presented at the annual conference of the European Consortium for Political Research. Madrid: 17–22 April.

Herzfeld, M. (1992) *The Social Production of Indifference.* Chicago: University of Chicago Press.

Hill, C. (ed.) (1983) *National Foreign Policies and European Political Cooperation.* London: Allen & Unwin for RIIA.

Hill, C. (1992) The foreign policy of the European Community, dream or reality? In R. Macridis (ed.), *Foreign Policy in World Politics.* Englewood Cliffs, NJ: Prentice-Hall.

Hill, C. (1993) The capability–expectations gap, or conceptualizing Europe's international role. *Journal of Common Market Studies,* **31**(3), 305–27.

Hill, C. and Wallace, W. (1979) Diplomatic Trends in the European Community. *International Affairs,* **1**, 47–66.

Hintze, O. (1962) Staatsverfassung und Heeresverfassung. In O. Hintze, *Staat und Verfassung.* Göttingen: Vandenhoeck und Ruprecht.

Hobsbawm, E. (1994) *Age of Extremes. The Short Twentieth Century, 1914–1991.* London: Michael Joseph.

Hoffmann, S. (1966) Obstinate or obsolete? The fate of the nation-state and the case of Western Europe. *Daedalus,* **95**, 862–915.

Hoffmann, S. (1982) Reflections on the nation-state in Western Europe today. *Journal of Common Market Studies,* **21**, 21–37.

Holland, M. (1988) *The European Community and South Africa: European Political Cooperation under Strain.* London: Macmillan.

Holland, M. (1991) European political co-operation and member state diplomatic missions. In Third countries – findings from a case-study of South Africa. *Diplomacy and Statecraft,* **2**, 236–53.

Holland, M. (1993) *European Community Integration.* London: Pinter.

Holland, M. (ed.) (1991) *The Future of European Political Cooperation: Essays on Theory and Practice.* London: Macmillan.

Hollis, M. and Smith S. (1990) *Explaining and Understanding in International Relations.* Oxford: Clarendon Press.

Holsti, K.J. (1983) *International Politics: A Framework of Analysis.* Englewood Cliffs, NJ: Prentice-Hall.

Holsti, K.J. (1991) *Peace and War: Armed Conflicts and International Order 1648–1989.* Cambridge: Cambridge University Press.

Huntington, S. (1973) Transnational organizations in world politics. *World Politics,* **25**, 333–68.

Hyde-Price, A. (1991) *European Security Beyond the Cold War: Four Scenarios for the Year 2010.* London: Sage.

Hyde-Price, A. (1993) The system level: the changing topology of Europe. In G. Wyn Rees (ed.), *International Politics in Europe: The New Agenda.* London: Routledge.

Ifestos, P. (1987) *European Political Cooperation*. Aldershot: Avebury.
International Monetary Fund (1994) *World Economic Outlook*. Washington, DC: IMF.
Jacobs, F. and Corbett, R. with Shackleton, M. (1992) *The European Parliament*. 2nd edn. London: Longman.
James, A. (1986) *Sovereign Statehood: The Basis of International Society*. London: Allen & Unwin.
Jannuzzi, G. (1994/95). La contribución de la política exterior y de seguridad común de la Unión Europea. *Revista de la OTAN*, **6**(1), 13–16.
Jennings, I. (1959) *The Law and the Constitution*, 5th edn. Quoted by I. Brownlie (1980) Parliamentary control over foreign policy in the United Kingdom. In A. Cassese (ed.), *Parliamentary Control over Foreign Policy*, Alphen aan den Rijn, The Netherland/Germantown, MD: Sijthoff & Noordhoff.
Jervis, R. (1978) Cooperation under the security agenda. *World Politics*, **30**, 2.
Jervis, R. (1993) Systems and interaction effects. In J. Snyder and R. Jervis (eds), *Coping with Complexity in the International System*. Oxford: Westview Press.
Jervis, R. and Snyder J. (eds) (1991) *Dominoes and Bandwagons*. New York: Oxford University Press.
Joffe, J. (1984) Europe's American Pacifier. *Foreign Policy*, **54**, 64–82.
Jopp, H., Rummel, R. and Schmidt, P. (1991) *Integration and Security in Western Europe: Inside the European Pillar*. Boulder, CO: Westview Press.
Jorgensen, K.E. (1993) EC external relations as a theoretical challenge: theories, concepts and trends. In F. Pfetsch (ed.), *Pan Europe and International Relations. Theoretical Approaches and Empirical Findings*. Munster: Lit Verlag.
Jorgensen, K.E. (1994) Beyond European leviathans. Differentiating layers of international transformation. In N. Sorensen (ed.), *Cultural Diversity and European Integration since 1700*. Odense: Odense University Press.
Judge, D., Earnshaw, D. and Cowan, N. (1994) Ripples or waves: the European Parliament in the European Community policy process. *Journal of European Public Policy*, **1**(1), 27–52.
Kant, I. (1992) *Perpetual Peace. A Philosophical Essay, 1795*. Bristol: Thoemmes Press.
Kaplan, M.A. (1957) *System and Process in International Politics*. New York: Wiley.
Kaplan, M.A. (ed.) (1968) *New Approaches to International Relations*. New York: St. Martin's Press.
Karvonen, L. and Sundelius, B. (1990) Interdependence and foreign policy in Sweden and Finland. *International Studies Quarterly*, **34**, 211–27.
Katzenstein, P.J. (1975) International interdependence: some long-term trends and recent changes. *International Organization*, **29**, 1021–34.
Kegley, C.W. (1994) How did the Cold War die? Principles of an autopsy. *International Studies Review*, **38**, 11–41.
Kegley, C.W. and Wittkopf, E.R. (1991) *American Foreign Policy: Pattern and Process*, 4th edn. New York: St. Martin's Press.
Kelstrup, M. (1992) The process of Europeanization: on the theoretical interpretation of present changes in the European regional political system. *Conflict and Cooperation*, **1**, 21–40.
Kelstrup, M. (1993) Small states and European political integration, in *Reflections on Theories and Strategies*. I Tiilikainen og Petersen.

Kelstrup, M. (1994) *On International Relations Theory, Political Theory and Political Integration in Europe.* Berlin: Paper presented at the XVIth World Congress of the International Political Science Association.

Kenis, P. and Schneider, V. (1987) The EC as an international corporate actor: two case studies in economic diplomacy. *European Journal of Political Research,* **XV**(4) 437–57.

Keohane, R.O. and Hoffmann, S. (1990) Conclusions: Community politics and institutional change. In W. Wallace (ed.) (1990) *The Dynamics of European Integration.* London: Pinter, for RIIA.

Keohane, R.O. (1989) *International Institutions and State Power: Essays in International Relations Theory.* Boulder, CO: Westview Press.

Keohane, R.O. (1993) Sovereignty, interdependence and international institutions. In L.B. Miller and M.J. Smith (eds), *Ideas and Ideals. Essays in Honor of Stanley Hoffmann.* Boulder, CO: Westview Press.

Keohane, R.O. (ed.) (1986) *Neorealism and its Critics.* New York: Columbia University Press.

Keohane, R.O. (1984) *After Hegemony: Cooperation and Discord in the World Political Economy.* Princeton, NJ: Princeton University Press.

Keohane, R.O. and Hoffmann, S. (1989) *European Community Politics and Institutional Change.* Center for European Studies, Harvard University: Working Paper No. 25.

Keohane, R.O., and Hoffmann, S. (1991) Institutional change in Europe in the 1980s. In R. Keohane and S. Hoffmann (eds), *The European Community: Decisionmaking and Institutional Change.* Boulder, CO: Westview Press.

Keohane, R.O. and Hoffmann, S. (eds) (1991) *The New European Community. Decisionmaking and Institutional Change.* Boulder, CO: Westview Press.

Keohane, R.O. and Nye, J.S. (1974) Transgovernmental relations and international organizations. *World Politics,* **27**(1), 39–62.

Keohane, R.O., Nye, J.S. and Hoffmann, S. (1993) *After the Cold War. International Institutions and State Strategies in Europe, 1989–1991.* Cambridge, MA: Harvard University Press.

Kirchener, E.J. (1992) *Decisionmaking in the European Community: The Council Presidency and European Integration.* Manchester: Manchester University Press.

Klingemann, H., Hofferbert, R.I. and Budge, I. (1994) *Parties, Policies, and Democracy.* Boulder, CO: Westview Press.

Klöti, U. (1991) *Small States in an Interdependent World.* Paper presented at the World Congress of the International Political Science Association. Buenos Aires: July 21–25.

Knudsen, O. (1994) Context and action in the collapse of the Cold War European system. In W. Carlsnaes and A. Smith (eds), *European Foreign Policy. The EC and Changing Perspectives in Europe.* London: Sage.

Kohl, H. (1984) *Helmut Kohl: Europas Einheit Stärken.* Bonn: CDU.

Kohler-Koch, B. (1994) Changing patterns of interest: intermediation in the European Union. *Government and Opposition,* **29**, 2166–80.

Konrad, G. (1984) *Antipolitics.* London: Quartet Books.

Kotarbinski, S. (1966) *Gnosiology – the Scientific Approach to the Theory of Knowledge.* Oxford: Pergamon Press.

Krasner, S. (1983) Structural causes and regime consequences: regimes as intervening variables. In S. Krasner (ed.), *International Regimes*. Ithaca, NY: Cornell University Press.

Krasner, S. (ed.) (1983) *International Regimes*. Ithaca, NY: Cornell University Press.

Kugler, P. (1994) *International Real Interest Rate Adjustment: An Empirical Note*. Vienna: Ms.

Kugler, P. and Neusser, K. (1993) International real interest rate equalization. a multivariate times-series spproach. *Journal of Applied Econometrics*, **8**.

Kuhn, T.S. (1962) *The Structure of Scientific Revolutions*. Chicago: University of Chicago Press.

Labouz, M.F. (sous la direction de) (1992) *Les Accords de Maastricht et la Constitution de l'Union européenne*. Centre de droit international de Nanterre, Montchrestien.

Landau, A. (1995) *The External Dimension and the Geopolitical Determinants of European Construction*. pp. 85–108 in: *European Union Southern Africa Development Community*. Regional Integration Process. Bordeaux, IEP/CEAN.

Laursen, F. (1991) The EC in the world context, civilian power or superpower? *Futures*, September, 747–59.

Lehmbruch, G. (1976) *Parteienwettbeerb im Bundesstaat*. Stuttgart: Kohlhammer.

Lehmbruch, G., Singer, O., Grande, E., Döhler, M. (1988) Institutionelle bedingungen Ordnungs politischen Strategie Wechsels im internationalen Vergleich. In M.G. Schmidt, *Staatstadtigkert International und historisch vergleichende Analysen*. (PVS-Sonderheft 19) Opladen: Westdeutscher Verlag, 251–83.

Lehner, F. (1989) *Vergleichende Regierungslehre*. Opladen: Leske und Budrich.

Lijphart, A. (1984) *Democracies*. New Haven/London: Yale University Press.

Lijphart, A. (1994) Democracies: forms, performance, and constitutional engineering. *European Journal of Political Research*, **25**, 1–17.

Lijphart, A. and Crepaz, M. (1991) Corporatism and consensus democracy in eighteen countries. *British Journal of Political Science*, **21**, 235–46.

Lincoln, B. (1989) *Discourse and the Construction of Society*. Oxford: Oxford University Press.

Lindberg, L. and Scheingold, S. (1970) *Europe's Would-be Polity: Patterns of Change in the European Community*. Englewood Cliffs, NJ: Prentice-Hall.

Linder, W. (1994) *Swiss Democracy. Possible Solutions to Conflict in Multicultural Societies*. London: Macmillan.

Little, R. and Smith, M. (1991) *Perspectives on World Politics*, 2nd edn. London: Routledge.

Lodge, J. (1978) The functions, powers and 'decline' of parliaments'. In V. Herman and J. Lodge (eds), *The European Parliament and the European Community*. London: Macmillan.

Lodge, J. (1993) From civilian power to speaking with a common voice: the transition to a CFSP. In J. Lodge (ed.), *The European Community and the Challenge of the Future*, 2nd edn. London: Pinter.

Lodge, J. (ed.) (1993) *The European Community and the Challenge of the Future*, 2nd edn. London: Pinter.

Lodge, J. (ed.) (1989) *The European Community and the Challenge of the Future*. London: Pinter.

[London Report, 1981] Report on European Political Cooperation. *Bulletin of the European Communities*, 3/81 (Supplement). Luxembourg: Office for Official Publications of the EC.

Ludlow, P. (1991) The European Commission. In R.O. Keohane and S. Hoffmann (eds), *The New European Community. Decisionmaking and Institutional Choice*. Boulder, CO: Westview Press.

McBride, E. (1988) Western civilisation: from Plato to NATO. *The Activist*, **21**.

McClelland, C.A. (1970) The function of theory in international relations. *Journal of Conflict Resolution*, **4**(3), 303–36.

Macdonald, S. (ed.) (1993) *Inside European Identities*. Oxford: Berg.

McGrew, A. (1992a) Global politics in a transitional era. In A. McGrew and P. Lewis (eds), *Global Politics, Globalization and the Nation-State*. Cambridge: Polity Press.

McGrew, A. (1992b) Conceptualizing global politics. In A. McGrew and P. Lewis (eds), *Global Politics, Globalization and the Nation-State*. Cambridge: Polity Press.

McGrew, A. and Lewis, P. (eds) (1992) *Global Politics, Globalization and the Nation-State*. Cambridge: Polity Press.

Mackie, T. and Rose, R. (1991) *The International Almanac of Electoral History*, 3rd edn. London: Macmillan.

Macridis, R.C. (ed.) (1992) *Foreign Policy in World Politics*. Englewoods Cliffs, NJ: Prentice-Hall.

March, J. and Olsen, J.P. (1984) *Rediscovering Institutions*. New York: Free Press.

Marquand, D. (1988) *East/West Relations: Hope and Fears*. Paper addressed to the 1988 Liberal Summer School. London: ELDR Parliamentary Group.

Masclet, J.-C. (1994) *Où en est l'Europe politique?* La Documentation française.

Masclet, J.-C. (1992) in M.F. Labouz (sous la direction de), *Les Accords de Maastricht et la Constitution de l'Union européenne*. Centre de droit international de Nanterre, Montchrestien.

Masty, W. (1988) Europe in US–USSR relations: a topical legacy. *Problems of Communism*, **37**, 1.

Mearsheimer, J.J. (1990) Back to the future: instability in Europe after the Cold War. *International Security*, **15**(1).

Merkel, W. (1993) *Ende der Sozialdemokratie? Machtressourcen und Regierungspolitik im Westeuropäischen Vergleich*. Frankfurt am Main/New York: Campus.

Mesarovic, M.D. (1962) On self organizational systems. In C. Marshall, G. Yovits, G. Jacobi and G. Goldstein (eds), *Self-Organising Systems*. Washington: Spartan Books.

Mesjasz, C. (1993) International stability: a theoretical framework. In F.R. Pfetsch (ed.), *International Relations and Pan Europe. Theoretical Approaches and Empirical Findings*. Munster: Lit Verlag.

Metcalfe, L. (1992) Après 1992: La Commission pourra-t-elle gérer l'Europe? In *Revue française d'administration publique*, **63**, 410–12.

Miall, H. (1993) *Shaping the New Europe*. London: Pinter for RIIA.

Miall, H. (ed.) (1994) *Redefining Europe, New Patterns of Conflict and Cooperation*. London: Pinter.

Michalski, A. and Wallace, H. (1992) *The European Community: The Challenge of Enlargement*. London: Royal Institute of International Affairs.

Miller, L.H. (1994) *Global Order: Values and Power in International Politics*, 3rd edn. Boulder, CO: Westview Press.

Milward, A.S. (1992) *The European Rescue of the Nation-State*. London: Routledge.

Milward, A.S. (1993) *The Reconstruction of Western Europe 1945–1951*. London: Routledge.

Milward, A.S. et al. (eds) (1992) *The Frontier of National Sovereignty. History and Theory 1945–1992*. London and New York: Routledge.

Missbach, A. (1995) Das Treibhausproblem als Nord-Süd-Thema. *Neue Zürcher Zeitung*, 22 März.

Mitterrand, F. (1987) Address presented to the Royal Institute of International Affairs, London. Reproduced in part in *The World Today*, March 1987, p. 43. Quoted by A. Clarke (1992) François Mitterrand and the idea of Europe. In B. Nelson, D. Roberts and W. Veil (eds), *The Idea of Europe: Problems of National and Transnational Identity*. New York/Oxford: Berg.

Mitterrand, F. (1989) Televised New Year message, 31 December 1989. Text in *Le Monde*, 2 January 1990, p. 5. Quoted by A. Clarke (1992) François Mitterrand and the idea of Europe. In B. Nelson, D. Roberts and W. Veil (eds), *The Idea of Europe: Problems of National and Transnational Identity*. New York/Oxford: Berg.

Modelski, G. (1978) The long cycle of global politics and the nation-state. *Comparative Studies in Society and History*, **20**, 214–35.

Monar, J. (1993) *The European Parliament as an Actor in the Sphere of EPC/CFSP*. Paper given at the Conference on The Community, the Member States and Foreign Policy: Coming Together or Drifting Apart? European Policy Unit, European University Institute, Badia Fiesolana, Florence, 1–3 July.

Monnet, J. (1976) *Mémoires*. Paris: Fayard.

Monnet, J. (1988) *Jean Monnet, A Grand Design for Europe*. Periodical 5/88, European Documentation Series. Luxembourg: The European Commission.

Moravcsik, A. (1991) Negotiating the Single European Act. In R.O. Keohane and S. Hoffmann (eds), *The New European Community. Decisionmaking and Institutional Choice*, Boulder, CO: Westview Press.

Moravcsik, A. (1993) Preferences and power in the European Community: a liberal intergovernmentalist approach. *Journal of Common Market Studies*, **31**(4), 471–524.

Morgan, R.P. (1973) *High Politics, Low Politics: Toward a Foreign Policy for Western Europe*. London: Sage.

Morgenthau, H. (1973) *Politics Among Nations: The Struggle for Power and Peace*, 5th edn. New York: Knopf.

Mouritzen, H. (1993) The two Musterknaben and the naughty boy: Sweden, Finland and Denmark in the process of European integration. *Cooperation & Conflict*, **28**, 4373–402.

Nagel, E. (1961) *The Structure of Science – Problems in the Logic of Scientific Explanation*. New York: Harcourt, Brace and World.

Nelson, B., Roberts, D. and Veil, W. (eds) (1992) *The Idea of Europe: Problems of National and Transnational Identity*. New York, Oxford: Berg.

192 *Bibliography*

Neunreither, K. (1994) The democratic deficit of the European Union: towards closer cooperation between the European Parliament and the national parliaments. *Government and Opposition*, **29**(3), 299–314.

Nicoll, W. and Salmon, T. (1994) *Understanding the New European Communities*. London: Phillip Allan.

Nørgaard, O., Pedersen, T. and Petersen, N. (1993) *The European Community in World Politics*. London: Pinter.

Nugent, N. (1994) *The Government and Politics of the Union*. London: Macmillan.

Nuttall, S.J. (1985(European Political Cooperation and the Single European Act, *Yearbook of European Law*, **5**, 203–31.

Nuttall, S.J. (1987) Interaction between European Political Cooperation and the European Community. *Yearbook of European Law*, **7**, 211–49.

Nuttall, S.J. (1992) *European Political Co-operation*. London: Clarendon Press.

Nye, R.J. and Hoffmann, S. (1993) *After the Cold War. International Institutions and State Strategies in Europe 1989–1991*. Cambridge, MA: Harvard University Press.

Nye, J.S. and Keohane, R. (eds) (1972) *Transnational Relations and World Politics*. Cambridge, MA: Harvard University Press.

Oberg, J.P. (1992) *Nordic Security in the 1990s. Options in the Changing Europe*. London: Pinter.

Olsen, J.P. (1992) Analysing institutional dynamics. *Staatswissenschaften und Staatspraxis*, Heft 2, 247–71.

Olson, W.C. and Groom, A.J.R. (1991) *International Relations Then and Now: Origins and Trends in Interpretation*. London: HarperCollins.

Ohmae Kenichi (1993) The rise of the region state. *Foreign Affairs*, Spring, 78–87.

Ortega Klein, A. (1980) El manto de Penélope: Francia y la Comunidad Europea de Defensa. *Revista de Instituciones Europeas*, **2**, 451–72.

Østerrud, Ø. (1994) *Antinomies of Supra-National State-Building: Centralization, Sovereignty and Democracy in the EU*. Working Paper, Oslo: Department of Political Science, University of Oslo.

Papcke, S. (1992) Who needs European identity and what could it be? In B. Nelson, D. Roberts and W. Veil (eds), *The Idea of Europe: Problems of National and Transnational Identity*. New York/Oxford: Berg.

Parmentier, R. (1994) *Signs in Society*. Bloomington: Indiana State University Press.

Pedersen, T. (1993) The Common Foreign and Security Policy and the challenge of enlargement. In O. Nørgaard, T. Pedersen and N. Petersen (eds), *The European Community in World Politics*. London: Pinter.

Peirce, C. (1931–58) *Collected Papers, Vols I–VIII*. Cambridge, MA: Harvard University Press.

Peirce, C. (1991) *Peirce on Signs: Writings on Semiotics*. Chapel Hill, NC: University of North Carolina Press.

Pfetsch, F.R. (1993) *International Relations and Pan-Europe: Theoretical Approaches and Empirical Findings*. Munster: Lit Verlag.

Pfetsch, F. (1994) Tensions in sovereignty: foreign policies of EC Members compared. In W. Carlsnaes and S. Smith (eds), *European Foreign Policy. The EC and Changing Perspectives in Europe*. London: Sage.

Pfetsch, F. (1995) *The Development of European Institutions*. European Union–Southern African Development Community. Bordeaux: IEP/CEAN. Regional Integration Process.

Pieterse, J.N. (1993) Fictions of Europe. In A. Gray and J. McGuigan (eds), *Studying Culture: An Introductory Reader*. London: Edward Arnold.

Pijpers, A.E. (1990) *The Vicissitudes of European Political Cooperation: Towards a Realist Interpretation of the EC's Collective Diplomacy*. Leiden: Doctoral thesis.

Pijpers, A.E. (1991) European political cooperation and the realist paradigm. In M. Holland (ed.) *The Future of European Political Cooperation: Essays on theory and practice*. London: Macmillan.

Presley, C.F. (1960) Laws and theories in the physical sciences. In A. Danto and S. Morgenbesser (eds), *Philosophy of Science*. Cleveland/New York: World Press.

Prout, C. (1993) The William Elland Memorial Lecture. London.

Putnam, R. (1988) Diplomacy and domestic politics: the logic of two-level games. *International Organization*, **42**(3), 427–60.

Rapoport, A. (1961) Various meanings of 'theory'. In J.N. Rosenau (ed.), *International Politics and Foreign Policy – a reader in research and theory*. New York: Free Press.

Rapoport, A. (1964) *Strategy and Conscience*. New York: Harper & Row.

Raworth, P. (1994) A timid step forwards: Maastricht and the democratisation of the European Community. *European Law Review*, **19**, (1) February, 16–33.

Redmond, J. (ed.) (1992) *The External Relations of the European Community: The International Response to 1992*. London: Macmillan.

Regelsberger, E. (1987) Spain and the European Political Cooperation – no enfant terrible. *The International Spectator*, **24**(2), 118–24.

Regelsberger, E. (1988) EPC in the 1980s: reaching another plateau? In A. Pijpers, E. Regelsberger and W. Wessels, *European Political Cooperation in the 1980s: A Common Foreign Policy for Western Europe?* Dordrecht: Martinus Nijhoff.

Reichenbach, H. (1949) *Experience and Prediction – An Analysis of the Foundations and the Structure of Knowledge*. Chicago: University of Chicago Press.

Reinicke, W.H. (1993) *Building a New Europe: The Challenge of System Transformation and Systemic Reform*. Washington: The Brookings Institution.

Remacle, E. (1994) La Dimension 'Sécurité-défense' de l'élargissement de l'Union européenne. In M. Telo (ed.), *L'Union européenne et les defis de l'élargissement*. Brussels: ULB.

Risse-Kappen, T. (1994) The future of European security. In W. Carlsnaes and S. Smith (eds), *European Foreign Policy. The EC and Changing Perspectives in Europe*. London: Sage.

Rogowski, R. (1989) *Commerce and Coalitions. How Trade Affects Domestic Alignments*. Princeton, NJ: Princeton University Press.

Rometsch, D. and Wessels, W. (1994) The Commission and the Council of Ministers. In G. Edwards and D. Spence, (eds), *The European Commission*. London: Longman.

Rosamond, B. (1995) Mapping the European condition: the theory of integration and the integration of theory. *European Journal of International Relations*, **3**, 391–408.

Rose, R. and Davies, P. (1994) *Inheritance in Public Policy. Change without Choice in Britain*. New Haven, CN/London: Yale University Press.

Rosenau, J.N. (1971) *The Scientific Study of Foreign Policy*. New York: Free Press.

Rosenau, J.N. (1981) *The Study of Political Adaption*. London: Pinter.

Rosenau, J.N. (1990) *Turbulence in World Politics. A Theory of Change and Continuity.* Hertfordshire: Harvester Press.

Rosenau, J.N. and Czempiel, E. (eds) (1992) *Governance Without Government. Order and Change in World Politics.* Cambridge: Cambridge University Press.

Ross, G. (1994) *Jacques Delors and European Integration.* Cambridge: Polity Press.

Ruggie, J.G. (1982) International regimes, transaction and change: embedded liberalism in the post-war economic order. *International Organization*, **36**, 2, 379–416.

Ruggie, J.G. (1989) International structure and international transformation: space, time and method. In J.N. Rosenau and J. Czempiel (eds), *Global Changes and Theoretical Challenges.* Lexington, MA: Lexington Books.

Ruggie, J.G. (1993) Territoriality and beyond: problematizing modernity in international relations. *International Organization*, **46**(1), 139–74.

Rummel, R. (1990) Preparing West Europe for the 1990s. In R. Rummel (ed.), *The Evolution of an International Actor, Western Europe's New Assertiveness.* Boulder, CO: Westview Press.

Ryba, B.C. (1995) La politique étrangère et de sécurité commune (PESC). Mode d'emploi debilan d'une année d'application (Fin 1993/94). *Revue du Marché Commun et de l'Union Européenne*, **384**, 14–35.

Saba, K. (1989) The Spanish foreign policy decision making. *The International Spectator*, **26**(4), 24–33.

Saeter, M. (1993) *Det Europeiske Felleskap: Institusjoner og Politik.* Oslo: Universitetsforlaget.

Salmon, T. (1992) Testing times for European political cooperation: The Gulf and Yugoslavia, 1990–1992. *International Affairs*, **68**, 2, 233–53.

Sandholtz, W. (1993) Choosing Union: Monetary Politics and Maastricht. *International Organization*, **47**, 1–39.

Scharpf, F.W. (1987) *Sozialdemokratische Krisenpolitik in Europa.* Frankfurt am Main/New York: Campus.

Scharpf, F.W. (1991) Die Handlungsfähigkeit des Staates am Ende des zwanzigsten Jahrhunderts. *Politische Vierteljahresschrift*, **32**, 621–34.

Scharpf, F.W. (1992) Einführung: Zur Theorie von Verhandlungssystemen. In A. Benz, F.W. Scharpf and R. Zintl (eds), *Horizontale Politikverflechtung. Zur Theorie von Verhandlungssystemen.* Frankfurt am Main/New York: Campus.

Scharpf, F.W. (1994a) Die Politikverflechtungsfalle. In F.W. Scharpf, *Optionen des Föderalismus in Deutschland und Europa.* Frankfurt am Main/New York: Campus.

Scharpf, F.W. (1994b) Föderalismus im globalen Kapitalismus. In F.W. Scharpf, *Optionen des Föderalismus in Deutschland und Europa.* Frankfurt am Main/New York: Campus.

Schlesinger, P. (1987) On national identity: some conceptions and misconceptions criticised. *Social Science Information*, **26**(2), 219–64.

Schmidt, M.G. (1982) *Wohlfahrtsstaatliche Politik unter bürgerlichen und sozialdemokratischen Regierungen.* Frankfurt am Main/New York: Campus.

Schmidt, M.G. (1992) Regierungen: Parteipolitische Zusammensetzung. In M.G. Schmidt (ed.), *Lexikon der Politik. Band 3. Die westlichen Ländern.* München/Zürich: Beck.

Schmidt, M.G. (1992) Staatsverschuldung. In M.G. Schmidt (ed.), *Lexikon der Politik. Band 3. Die westlichen Ländern.* München/Zürich: Beck.
Schmidt, M.G. (1993) *Demokratietheorie.* Hagen: Fernuniversität Gesamthochschule-Hagen.
Schmidt, M.G. (1994) *Politikverflechtung zwischen Bund, Ländern und Gemeinden.* Hagen: Fernuniversität-Gesamthochschule-Hagen.
Scott, A.M. (1967) *The Functioning of the International Political System.* London: Collier-Macmillan.
Sebeok, T.A. (1991) *A Sign Is Just A Sign.* Bloomington, IN: Indiana State University Press.
Shore, C. (1993) Inventing the 'People's Europe': critical approaches to European community cultural policy. *Man* Vol. 28, No. 4, 779–800.
Simon, D. (1992) Conclusions générales. In Labouz, M.F. (sous la direction de) *Les Accords de Maastricht et al Constitution de l'Union européenne.* Centre de droit international de Nanterre. Paris: Montchrestien.
Simon, H. (1981) *The Science of the Artificial.* Cambridge, MA: MIT Press.
Singer, J.D. (1961) The level-of-analysis problem in international relations. In K. Knorr and S. Verba (eds), *The International System.* Princeton, NJ: Princeton University Press.
Singer, J.D. (1969) The level-of-analysis problem in international relations. In: J. Rosenau (ed.), *International Politics and Foreign Policy.* New York: Free Press.
Singer, M. (1984) *Man's Glassy Essence. Explorations in Semiotic Anthropology.* Bloomington, IN: Indiana State University Press.
Sjöstedt, G. (1977) *The External Role of the European Community.* Farnborough: Saxon House.
Smith, A.D. (1992) National identity and the ideas of European unity. *International Affairs*, **68**, 155–76.
Smith, S. (1988) Theories of foreign policy: an historical overview. *Review of International Studies*, **12**, 13–29.
Smith, S. (1994) Foreign policy theory and the New Europe. In W. Carlsnaes and S. Smith (eds), *European Foreign Policy: The EC and Changing Perspectives in Europe.* London: Sage.
Snidal, D. (1987) The myths of hegemonic stability theory: a critique. *International Organization*, **39**(4), 559–614.
Snyder, J. (1990) Averting anarchy in the New Europe. *International Security*, **14**(4), 5–41.
Snyder, J. and Jervis, R. (1993) *Coping with Complexity in the International System.* Oxford: Westview Press.
Spence, D. (1994a) Staff and personnel policy in the Commission. In G. Edwards and D. Spence (eds), *The European Commission.* London: Longman.
Spence, D. (1994b) Structure, functions and procedures in the Commission. In G. Edwards and D. Spence (eds), *The European Commission.* London: Longman.
Spiro, H. (1966) *World Politics: The Global System.* Homewood, Ill.: Dorsey Press.
Stavridis, S. (1994) *The Impact of Enlargement in 1995 on Europe's Single Voice in World Affairs.* Paper presented in the workshop on EC Enlargement and Foreign Policy Change in Europe: Implications for the EC, the Twelve and the EFTA States in the ECPR Joint Sessions of Workshops. Madrid: 17–22 April.

Stein, A.A. (1983) Coordination and collaboration: regimes in an anarchic world. In S. Krasner (ed.), *International Regimes*. Ithaca, NY: Cornell University Press.

Stein, A.A. (1990) *Why Nations Cooperate. Circumstance and Choice in International Relations*. Ithaca, NY/London: Cornell University Press.

Strang, D. and Mei Yin Chang, P. (1993) The International Labor Organization and the welfare state: institutional effects on national welfare spending, 1960–80. *International Organization*, **47**, 235–62.

Strange, S. (1988) *States and Markets*. London: Pinter.

Sullivan, M.P. (1976) *International Relations: Theories and Evidence*. Englewood Cliffs, NJ: Prentice-Hall.

Tarrow, S. (1994) *Rebirth or Stagnation? European Studies After 1989*. New York: Social Science Research Council.

Taylor, A.J.P. (1967) *Europe, Grandeur and Decline*. London: Pelican.

Taylor, P. (1982) The European Communities as an actor in international society. *Journal of European Integration*, **6**(1), 7–41.

Taylor, P. (1990) A conceptual typology of international organisations. In A.J.R. Groom and P. Taylor (eds), *Frameworks for International Cooperation*. London: Pinter.

Taylor, T. (1994) West European security and defense cooperation: Maastricht and beyond. *International Affairs*, **70**(1), 1–16.

Tejera, V. (1988) *Semiotics from Peirce to Barthes*. Leiden: E.J. Brill.

Terraine, J. (1993) *Impacts of War: 1914 and 1918*. London: Leo Cooper.

Thatcher, M. (1988) Britain and Europe. *Text of the Prime Minister's Speech at Bruges on 20th September 1988*. London: Conservative Political Centre.

Treaty on European Union (TEU) (1992) Luxembourg, Office for Official Publications of the European Communities, 1759/60.

Tsakaloyannis, P. (1989) The EC: from civilian power to military integration. In J. Lodge (ed.), *The European Community and the Challenge of the Future*. London: Pinter.

Van Ham, P. (1994) Can institutions hold Europe together? In H. Miall (ed.), *Redefining Europe, New Patterns of Conflict and Cooperation*. London: Pinter.

Vanhoonacker, S. (1992) Belgium. In F. Laursen and S. Vanhoonacker (eds), *The Intergovernmental Conference on Political Union, Institutional Reforms, New Policies and International Identity of the European Community*. Maastricht: European Institute of Public Administration.

Viotti, P.R. and Kauppi, M.V. (1987) *International Relations Theory: Realism, Pluralism, Globalism*. New York: Macmillan.

von Groll, G. (1982) The Nine at the Conference on Security and Cooperation in Europe. In D. Allen, R. Rummel, W. Wessels (eds), *European Political Cooperation*. London: Butterworth.

Waever, O. (1992) Nordic nostalgia: Northern Europe after the Cold War. *International Affairs*, **68**(1), 77–102.

Waever, O. (1995) Identity, integration and security. Solving the sovereignty puzzle in EU Studies. *Journal of International Affairs*, **48**(2), Winter, 389–431.

Waever, O., Buzan, B., Kelstrup, M. and Lemaitre, P. (eds) (1993) *Identity, Migration, and the New Security Agenda in Europe*. London: Pinter.

Walker, R.B.J. and Mendlovitz S.H. (eds) (1990) *Contending Sovereignties. Redefining Political Community*. Boulder, CO: Lynne Rienner.

Wallace, H. (1989) The best is the enemy of the 'could': bargaining in the European Community. In K. Thompson, P. Pierani and E. Croci-Angelini (eds), *Agricultural Trade Liberalisation and the European Community*. Oxford: Clarendon Press.

Wallace, H. (1994) *Collective Leadership, Confederal Bargaining and the Limits of Political Identity*. Brussels: ECSA Conference.

Wallace, W. (1982) National inputs into European Political Cooperation. In D. Allen, R. Rummel and W. Wessels, *European Political Cooperation: Towards a Foreign Policy for Western Europe*. London: Butterworth.

Wallace, W. (1986) What price independence? Sovereignty and interdependence in British Politics. *International Affairs*, **62**(3), 367–69.

Wallace, W. (1990) *The Transformation of Western Europe*. London: Pinter.

Wallace, W. (1983) Less than a federation, more than a regime: the Community as a political system. In H. Wallace, W. Wallace and C. Webb (eds), *Policy Making in the European Community*. London: John Wiley & Sons.

Wallace, W. (1994) Rescue or retreat? The nation state in Western Europe, 1945–93. *Political Studies*, **42**. Special issue, 52–76.

Wallace, W. (ed.) (1990) *The Dynamics of European Integration*. London: Pinter for RIIA.

Wallerstein, I. (1974) The rise and future demise of the world capitalist system: concepts for comparative analysis. *Comparative Studies in Society and History*, **16**(4), 387–415.

Waltz, K.N. (1979) *Theory of International Politics*. London/New York/Reading, MA: McGraw-Hill/Random House/Addison-Wesley.

Ware, R. (1991) Parliament and treaties. In C. Carstairs and R. Ware (eds), *Parliament and International Relations*. Milton Keynes/Philadelphia: Open University Press.

Webb, C. (1983) Theoretical perspectives and problems. In H. Wallace, W. Wallace and C. Webb (eds), *Policy-Making in the European Community*. London: John Wiley & Sons.

Weidenfeld, W. (ed.) (1994) *Europa '96. Reformprogramm für die Europäische Union*. Gütersloh: Verlag Bertelsmann Stiftung.

Weidenfeld, W. (ed.) (1995) *Die Identität Europas*. Bonn: Bundeszentrale für politische Bildung.

Weiler, J. (1980) The European Parliament and foreign affairs: external relations of the European Community. In A. Cassese (ed.), *Parliamentary Control over Foreign Policy*, Alphen aan den Rijn, The Netherlands/Germantown, MD: Sijthoff & Noordhoff.

Welsh, J. (1993) *A Peoples' Europe? European Citizenship and European Identity*. EUI Working Paper ECS No. 93/2, European Culture Research Centre, European University Institute, Badia Fiesolana, Florence.

Wendt, A. (1992) Anarchy is what states make of it: the social construction in power politics. *International Organiszation*, **46**, 395–421.

Wendt, A. (1994) Collective identity formation and the international state. *American Political Science Review*, **88**, 2384–96.

Wendt, F. (1981) *Cooperation in the Nordic Countries. Achievements and Obstacles*. Estocolmo: Almqvist & Wiksell Int.

Wessels, W. (1991) The EC Council: the community's decisionmaking center. In R.O. Keohane and S. Hoffmann, *The New European Community. Decisionmaking and Institutional Change*. Boulder, CO: Westview Press.

Wiberg, H. (1993) The dissolution of Yugoslavia: a study of interaction. In F. Pfetsch (ed.), *International Relations and Pan Europe. Theoretical Approaches and Empirical Findings.* Munster: Lit Verlag.

Wight, M. (1966) Why is there no international theory? In H. Butterfield and M. Wight (eds), *Diplomatic Investigations.* London: George Allen & Unwin.

Williams, S. (1990) Sovereignty and accountability in the European Community. *Political Quarterly,* **61**(3), 299–317.

Wyn Rees, G. (ed.) (1993) *International Politics in Europe: The New Agenda.* London: Routledge.

Young, O. (1992) The effectiveness of international institutions: hard cases and critical variables. In J.N. Rosenau and E. Czempiel (eds), *Governance Without Government. Order and Change in World Politics.* Cambridge: Cambridge University Press.

Zelikow, P. (1992) The New Concert of Europe. *Survival,* **34**(2), 12–30.

Zürn, M. (n.d) *What has Changed in Europe? The Challenge of Globalization and Individualization.* Bremen: Ms.

Index

Afghanistan, Soviet invasion   159
Africa   32, 165
African Caribbean and Pacific countries
    (ACP)   63
Albania   148
Aron, R.   114
Association of South East Asian Nations
    (ASEAN)   68, 137
Australia   101
Austria   142, 144, 174

Balance of power   2, 59
    and Europe   19, 20
    European   26
Balkans   16, 29
Belgium   136, 141
Benelux   138
Berlin Wall, fall of   16, 5, 134, 135,
    136
Bipolarity, decline of   16, 25
Bogdanor, V.   119
Britain *see also* United Kingdom   2, 101
    Ponsonby rule   114
    and identity   161
    Cabinet   113
    Civil Service   113
    House of Commons   113
Brown, C.   24
Bruges speech   158
Budge, I.   101
Bull, H.   19, 23, 34, 59
Bulmer, S.   61
Bundesbank   6
Bush, G.   16

Calleo, D.   19
Camp David process   132
Carlsson, I.   77
Capability–expectations gap   67
CDU/CSU   53
Central and Eastern European countries
    15, 16, 20, 25, 32, 49, 52, 95
    and European security system   33
    association agreements   68
CFSP   *see* Common Foreign and Security
    Policy
Charter of Paris   16
Chechnya   49
Christmas revolution   16

CIS   *see* Commonwealth of Independent
    States
CMEA   *see* Council for Mutual Economic
    Assistance
Cohen, R.   29
Cold War   5, 8, 15, 17, 21, 25, 54
    see   NATO
    and the division of Europe   20
    and the Transatlantic Community
        23
    end of   15, 25, 26, 27, 33, 36
Commission   3, 7, 8, 9, 37, 38, 47, 49, 50,
    68, 82, 84–85, 91, 94, 96, 148, 157
    Commissioners   96–97
    roles   84
    Directorates General   96, 97
    roles   84
    staff   98
    and supranationality   84
Commitology   98
Common European House   16
Common Foreign and Security Policy
    (CFSP)   6, 7, 9, 36, 39, 50, 53, 55,
    68, 70, 89, 90, 91, 129, 130, 131, 140,
    142, 143, 144, 145, 173, 177
Committee of the Permanent
    Representatives (COREPER)   86,
    98
Commonwealth of Independent States
    (CIS)   49
Concert of Europe   19, 30
Conference on Security and Cooperation in
    Europe (CSCE)   16, 132
Congress of Vienna   19
Consociational democracies   103
Cooper, R.   100
Corbett, R.   112, 121
COREPER   *see* Committee of the
    Permanent Representatives
Corporatism   106
Council for Mutual Economic Assistance
    (CMEA)   21
Council of Europe   24
Council of Ministers   3, 4, 7, 68, 80, 84,
    91, 94, 96, 172
    role 85–6
Court of Justice *see* European Court of
    Justice
Critical theory;   58

CSCE *see* Conference on Security and Cooperation in Europe
Cyprus 175
Czechoslovakia 16

De Gaulle, C. 144
Décaux, E. 122
Decision-making process
bargaining 103
consensus 103
intergovernmentalism 55, 70, 79–80;
qualified majority voting 4, 82, 83, 117
national veto 75
sovereignty 84
supranational 2, 81
Delors, J. 84, 122, 153, 158, 159, 167
Democratic deficit 117, 121
Denmark 111, 134, 137
referendum 141, 167
and identity 161
Detente 133
Deutsch, K. 23, 31, 154
Dominicé, C. 121
Duchêne, F. 65

Eastern Europe 6, 10, 16, 63
East Timor 137
Eco, U. 147, 150
Economic and Monetary Union (EMU) 173, 175
EDF *see* European Development Fund
EFTA *see* European Free Trade Association
EMS *see* European Monetary System
EMU *see* Economic and Monetary Union
Enlargement 52, 75, 85, 175
and deepening 34
to Central and Eastern Europe 9
to EFTA countries 141
EPC *see* European Political Cooperation
Euro-Arab dialogue 132
Eurobarometer 148, 161
Euromissiles 133
European Coal and Steel Community 16, 22
European Construction, concentric circles 16
European Council 3, 87–8, 94, 96
Edinburgh 142
Lisbon 141
Maastricht 140
Rhodes 67
European Court of Justice 3, 82, 84, 85, 90, 91

European Defence Community 6, 22, 130–1
European Development Fund (EDF) 68
European Free Trade Association (EFTA) 63, 142
European integration 76
and complex interdependence 24, 31
formal 3, 22, 24, 30, 77
informal 22, 24, 30, 77
process 1, 155
European Monetary System (EMS) 132
European Parliament 3, 4, 7, 49, 70, 85, 94, 96, 110, 148, 157, 173
direct elections 123
and the budget 116, 117
European Political Cooperation (EPC) 36, 55, 59, 61, 70, 71, 87, 88, 89, 131, 134, 135, 136, 139, 140, 141, 144
and sanctions 133
secretartiat 138
and South Africa 137
'Europe of Versailles' 20
European Union
actor capability 1, 37
actorness 1
civilian power 8, 65, 139
cleavages 2
external competences 7, 54
international actor 80, 157
international role 54
as superpower 65

Federalism 1, 60, 121, 122
cooperative 82, 86
Feminism 58
Finland 142, 174
Finnemore, M. 100
Ford, G. 120
France 2, 139, 143, 147
Fifth Republic 112
National Assembly 22, 112, 113, 130
Revolution 15
Franco-German axis 138
Franco-German Council on Common Defence 134
Frankel, J. 27
Fukuyama, F. 15, 32

G-24 53
Gaja, G. 123
Galtung, J. 65–6
Garcia, S. 129
GATT, negotiations 78

Germany   2, 12, 20, 24, 136, 137, 147
   and identity   161
   and the German Problem   19, 26, 29
   and the United States   20
   federalism   109
   unification   16
Globalisation   5, 9, 27, 62, 94, 99
   and nation states   95
Gorbachev, M.   16, 133
   and the common European house   16
Gourevitch, P.   100
Gray, J.   26, 27, 28
Great War (1914–18)   15, 20, 21
Greece   33, 134, 135, 136
Greven, M.   118
Group of Reflection   175, 177
Gulf War   36, 134, 140, 142, 144

Haas, E.   172
Hague Conference   142
Hague Summit   87, 131
Hassner, P.   33
Herman, V.   116
High Politics   62, 80
Hill, C.   67
Hintze, O.   100
Historical sociology   58
Hobsbawm, E.   15
Hofferbert, R.I.   101
Hoffmann, S.   155
Hollis, M.   39
Holsti, K.   18
Holy Roman Empire   17, 18

Iceland   175
Identities   7, 8
   European   40, 45–6, 50, 149
   national   40
IMF   *see* International Monetary Fund
Independence   77
Institutions   7, 8, 76
Interests   7
   national   3
Intergovernmental Conference (IGC)   81,
      110, 111, 119, 138
   on Political Union   133, 136, 139
   1996   141, 175
Intergovernmentalism   6
International Herald Tribune   6
International Monetary Fund (IMF)   9, 99
International organisations   75
International relations theory 57, 58
   foreign policy analysis   64
   hegemonic stability   60

interdependence   61, 77
   neo-liberal institutionalism   60
   neo-realism   26, 60
   new medievalism   34
   pluralism   58, 59, 61–2, 63, 64
   realism   19, 58, 59, 63, 64
   regime theory   2–3, 60, 61
   structualism   58, 62–3, 64
   transnationalism   61
   world systems   63
International system   47, 50
   balance of power   19, 29
   bipolar configuration   5, 15, 16
   multipolar configuration   26
Ireland   137
Italy   20, 39, 138
   Chamber of Deputies   115
   Parliament   114
   Senate of the Republic   115

Jacobs, F.   112, 121
Januzzi, G.   143
Jorgensen, K.   66, 67

Kant, I.   24
Keohane, R.   32, 155
Klingemann, H.   101
Kohl, H.   158, 159
Korean war   131

Lamers, K.   53
Latin America   135, 136, 137
League of Nations   20, 30
Lehmbruch, G.   109
Lijphart, A.   101, 102, 103, 104
Lodge. J.   116
Lomé Convention   63, 68
London Report   138
Low politics   62, 80
Luxembourg   134, 136
Luxembourg compromise   2
Luxembourg Report   67, 132

March, J.   100
Martin, D.   119
Maastricht Treaty   *see* Treaty on
      European Union
Malta   174
Marquand, D.   121
Masclet, J.C.   120
Medieval order   17
Mediterranean countries   143
Mearsheimer, John   26, 27, 28
Mei Yin Chang, P.   100

Metatheory   58
Middle East   63, 68
   conflict   132
Monar, J.   123
Monnet, J.   1, 2, 22, 147, 148, 172

NATO *see* North Atlantic Treaty
   Organisation
Neofunctionalism   1, 2
Netherlands   137, 138, 140, 145
Neunreiter, K.   118
Nordic Council   137
Nordic countries   130, 142, 143, 144
North Atlantic Treaty Organisation
      (NATO)   8, 21, 22, 23, 24, 25, 26,
      91, 130, 133, 138, 140, 144, 145, 146,
      156, 174
   and enlargement   32–33
   and the EU   26
   North Atlantic Co-operation Council   31
   Partnerships for Peace programme   31
Norway   142, 175
Nuttall, S.   134

OECD   *see* Organisation forEconomic
   Cooperation and Development
Olsen, J.P.   100
Organisation for Economic Cooperation
   and Development (OECD)   93, 94,
   102, 104, 106
Organisation for Security and Cooperation
   in Europe (OSCE)   30, 78
OSCE   *see* Organisation for Security and
   Cooperation in Europe

Parliament
   bicameralism   104
   unicameralism   104
Parmentier, R.   150
Pedersen, T.   142
Peirce, C. S.   149
   and semiotics   150
PHARE (Poland and Hungary Assistance
   for Economic Restructuring
   Programme)   49, 53
Pluralistic Security Community   17, 21,
   23, 24, 29, 30, 33
Poland   16
Political Parties
   Catholic   103
   Christian Democratic   103
Portugal   33, 133, 136, 137, 141
Postmodernism   54, 58
Postpositivism   58

Poststructuralism   54
Prisoner's dilemma   50

Raworth, P.   117
Reagan, R.   133
Realpolitik   2, 23
Reformation   17
Renaissance   17
Rogowski, R.   100
Romania   16, 148, 149
Rose, R.   101, 108
Rosenau, J.   77
Russia   20
   and NATO   9
   and near abroad   16
   and the Balkans   16
   elections   68

Schauble,   53
Schmidt, M.   103, 104
Schuman, R., declaration   46, 147, 148,
   176
Second World War   20, 21
   and post-war order   20
   end of   100
SEA   *see* Single European Act
Sebeok, T. A.   150
Shackleton, M.   112, 121
Singer, M.   150
Single European Act (SEA)   10, 75, 80,
   86, 89, 116, 131, 132, 133, 138, 182
Single Market   10, 139, 157
Sjöstedt, G.   66, 67
Smith, S.   39, 64
Sovereignty   6, 82
   pooling of   47, 60, 83
South Africa 137
Soviet Union   25
Spain   33, 133, 134, 136, 141, 143
Spinelli, A.   119
Spinelli report   121
Strang, D   100
Subsidiarity   121, 125
Summits of Heads of State and
   Government   *see* European Council
   and Hague Summit
Supranationalism   2, 6, 27, 40, 76, 82, 93,
   94, 124
Sweden   142, 174
Switzerland   175
   Federal Council   145
   Federal Councillors   97
Systems analysis   69
Systems framework   42, 69

Systems theory   9, 42–3
Systems thinking   69

Tacis (Technical Assistance for the
   Commonwealth of Independent
   States)   49, 68
Taylor, A.J.P.   19
TEU   *see* Treaty on European Union
Thatcher, M.   158, 159
Thirty Years War   17
Tietmayer, H.   6
Tindemans Report   139
Transatlantic Security Community   23, 24
   and Eastern Europe   32
Treaties of Rome   55, 173
Treaty of Versailles   20
Treaty of Westphalia   17, 18, 33
Treaty on European Union   6, 28, 50, 54,
   55, 75, 80, 85, 86, 90, 116, 118, 129,
   139, 144, 145, 173, 176
   Article A   56
   Article B   56
   Article F   148
   Title I   56
   Title V   55, 68, 89, 130
   Title IX   148
   ratification   of 28, 54
Treaty of Paris   55
Treaty of Rome   22, 54, 86, 90, 147,
   148
Turkey, and the EU   33

United Kingdom (UK)   33, 139, 144

United Nations   137
   General Assembly   135
   Security Council   137
United States   2, 5, 8, 28, 132, 134, 138
   and the EU   10
   as pacifier   25
   benign hegemon   32
   external federator   131
   and the Marshall Plan   25

Velvet Revolution   16

Wallace, W.   61
Wallerstein, I.   63
Waltz, K.   59
Warsaw Pact   21
Welsh, J.   121
Wessels, W.   82
Western European Union (WEU)   8, 24,
   31, 90–91, 138, 139, 140, 142
West Germany   63, 136, 138
Westminster democracies   93, 99
Westphalian states system   17, 18, 23
WEU   *see* Western European Union
Wilson, W.   20
World Bank   9
World Trade Organisation (WTO)   10, 11
WTO   *see* World Trade Organisation

Yalta summit   20
Yugoslavia   36, 142, 173

Zürn, M.   93

Heterick Memorial Library
Ohio Northern University

	DUE	RETURNED		DUE	RETURNED
1.			13.		
2.			14.		
3.			15.		
4.			16.		
5.			17.		
6.			18.		
7.			19.		
8.			20.		
9.			21.		
10.			22.		
11.			23.		
12.			24.